IN SAFE HANDS

Alistair Aird

IN SAFE HANDS

Rangers' Goalkeeping Greats

Foreword by

Michael Beale

pitch

First published by Pitch Publishing, 2023

Pitch Publishing
9 Donnington Park,
85 Birdham Road,
Chichester,
West Sussex,
PO20 7AJ
www.pitchpublishing.co.uk
info@pitchpublishing.co.uk

A CIP catalogue record is available for this book from the British Library.

ISBN 978 1 80150 458 4

Typesetting and origination by Pitch Publishing

Printed and bound in India by Thomson Press

Contents

Foreword By Michael Beale

I AM honoured and privileged to be the manager of Rangers Football Club. The club is an institution, and over the course of our 151-year history, we have been served by some of the greatest goalkeepers ever to play the beautiful game. The likes of Matthew Dickie, Herbert Lock, Willie Robb, Tom Hamilton and Jerry Dawson played with distinction before World War II, and following in their footsteps were Bobby Brown, George Niven, Billy Ritchie and Peter McCloy. And over the past 40 years, the gloves have been worn by among others, Chris Woods, Andy Goram, Stefan Klos, and our current custodian, Allan McGregor. Each of them has played a key role in the multiple successes Rangers has enjoyed, and they have excelled at shutting out opposition forwards.

The position of goalkeeper isn't a glamorous one. When your team wins, the platitudes almost always go to the forward-thinking players, the ones who either play the killer pass or apply the finishing touch to score the goal that secures the victory. In a press conference after a game, it's very rare that someone will refer to the goalkeeper. But if you analyse all the successful football sides in the history of the game, each of them has called upon a reliable, dependable goalkeeper. And while history may not remember all of the saves they make, each one of them is just as important as the goals that are scored at the other end of the pitch.

The role of a goalkeeper has evolved over the years, and some of the attributes a manager like me looks for are perhaps different from what many of my predecessors were after. But while I may consider ability to play out from the back and seek a goalkeeper who is comfortable with the ball at their feet, I am also aware that there are core elements to the goalkeeping role at Rangers that will never change.

Being the Rangers goalkeeper requires focus and concentration. The club has a rich history of playing attacking football, and I have a similar philosophy. I like my team to be dynamic, play on the front foot and press high. A tactical approach like that means my goalkeeper will be inactive for the most part. But he will be called upon at some point to intervene, and when that happens, I want him to be ready.

In my two spells at Rangers, I have been very lucky to work with goalkeepers who have those attributes. Allan McGregor, who has made over 500 competitive appearances for the club, is a prime example. He is one of the most dedicated professionals I have worked with. Allan, who learned from some of the best in Andy Goram and Stefan Klos, is one of the first in every morning. He leads by example, and Jon McLaughlin, Robby McCrorie and the other goalkeepers at the club follow Allan's lead. The success he has enjoyed and the longevity of his career with Rangers can be attributed to the fact that Allan has those core elements that a successful Rangers goalkeeper needs in abundance.

But Allan is just one of many who have kept goal for Rangers over the years, and this book looks at the careers and achievements of those goalkeepers all the way back to the day the club was born in 1872. Their stories are all different, but each of them has played their part in creating the history of this wonderful football club that I am fortunate to manage.

Michael Beale
Manager, Rangers FC
April 2023

Introduction

Who wants to be the Goalie?

I WAS sitting scrolling through my Facebook feed one afternoon when I came across this post from *Junior Grassroots Football UK*. Attributed to a Kev Brown, it said:

> #Shoutout for all GOALKEEPERS
>
> A goalkeeper has to be the best player on the pitch! Weird statement to make, until you realise what you expect of them.
>
> Every goal kick has to reach a team-mate, every kick out of their hands has to reach a team-mate whether that's 5 yards or 50!
>
> They can't afford to have a bad touch; they can't be tackled and heaven forbid they make a mistake or concede a goal.
>
> They have to be brave, loud, strong and they are the first person people look at when teams lose.
>
> I can't think of any other position on the pitch where they have that much pressure!
>
> Yet they give 100 per cent every time and still come back to each training session and each game.
>
> Take a bow keepers you're the most important player any manager has.

The post really struck a chord with me. Back in the days when you played football with your mates on a red ash park or on a rutted green field rather than on a games console, it was very rare to get anyone to volunteer to be the goalkeeper. Most wanted to be the swashbuckling striker, scoring goals at the sharp end, while others were keen when you were on the lookout for a winger or centre-mid to execute a cross or play a killer pass. But when it came to someone to go between the sticks or the jumpers, it was rare for anyone to thrust their hand up and offer their services.

The position of goalkeeper has never been one associated with glamour, yet it is arguably the most specialised position in the team. And although formations and playing positions have evolved over the years, such that you now see teams playing without a striker for example, the only mandatory position that must be filled in a football XI is that of goalkeeper. If the goalkeeper who starts a game is injured or ordered off, someone has to take over.

Although the first Laws of the Game did not specify the requirement for a goalkeeper, the game evolved and, by 1871, the FA had forbidden handling the ball unless you were designated the role of goalkeeper. The rule stated:

> No player shall carry or knock on the ball; and handling the ball, under any pretence whatever, shall be prohibited, except in the case of the goalkeeper, who shall be allowed to use his hands for the protection of his goal.

Subsequent amendments were made – for example, in 1883, a goalkeeper was only allowed to take two steps when carrying the ball, while in 1997 a rule was introduced such that the goalkeeper was only permitted to hold the ball for a maximum of six seconds – and the expectation of goalkeeper in the modern game is significantly different to what it was even 30 years ago when the back pass law was introduced.

The back pass law was brought in to stop teams slowing games down by passing the ball back to their goalkeeper. Games would usually be regularly punctuated by defenders passing the ball back to their goalkeeper who would pick the ball up and slow the game down. But when the law was passed, a team would be penalised if this happened:

> An indirect free kick will be awarded if a goalkeeper, inside their penalty area, touches the ball with the hand/arm, unless the goalkeeper has clearly kicked or attempted to kick the ball to release it into play after it has been deliberately kicked to the goalkeeper by a team-mate or they received it directly from a throw-in taken by a team-mate.

In addition to speeding the game up and reducing time-wasting, the rule also changed the skillset managers were looking for when seeking to recruit a goalkeeper. In addition to looking for a player with good concentration and reflexes, one who was a good shot stopper and who could command their penalty area, managers now wanted a goalkeeper who was adept with the ball at their feet too. And over the three decades since the back pass rule came in, that latter skill has become more of a prerequisite for teams that have a strategy of playing out from the back.

The goalkeeper has thus become more of a key component in tactical planning, and maybe that has made the position a bit more desirable than it once used to be. However, despite its lack of allure historically, someone has always fulfilled the role, and since their inception in 1872, Rangers Football Club has been blessed with a plethora of great goalkeepers.

This book will look into the career of not just the great goalkeepers to have played for Rangers, but also the good, bad and indifferent. From the first recorded Rangers goalkeeper, a chap called D. Smith, to Allan McGregor, there's certainly been an eclectic mix of talent. Each and every one of them have the same goal; to stop Rangers conceding goals, but some have been more successful purveyors of the art of goalkeeping than others.

I would like to thank Jane Camillin at Pitch Publishing for her patience, support and understanding, and Duncan Olner for his superb work with the cover design. I would also like to thank the wonderful font of statistical knowledge on Rangers that is Chic Sharp who helped verify some of the statistical work that is presented at the end of the book. And thanks must be extended to Tom Purdie and Lindsay Herron for the provision of some excellent photos for the plate section.

And to the goalkeepers, former players and club chairmen I spoke to, thank you. A humble supporter has once again been blessed to spend time with so many of the people he idolises. Your personal reflections have considerably enhanced what is already an incredible story.

Alistair Aird
April 2023

Chapter 1

The Days of the Founding Fathers

FINDING EVIDENCE of starting line-ups for some of the early matches played by Rangers is like looking for the proverbial needle in a haystack. For example, according to the excellent compendium, *Rangers – The Complete Record*, ten players are recognised as having played in the club's first-ever match against Callander in May 1872, but it is unclear if any of those named kept goal in that match.

What is clear, though, is that when Rangers played Clyde – a different variant to the one that Rangers would regularly cross swords with over the years – at Flesher's Haugh on Glasgow Green on 20 September 1873, a D. Smith was the goalkeeper. Unlike today, when the goalkeeper is named first in the line-up, Smith was listed last with the word 'goal' in brackets after his name. Each of the four founding fathers – Moses McNeil, Peter McNeil, Peter Campbell and William McBeath – played in what was a comprehensive victory, with McBeath's performance being 'greatly admired' as he 'cleverly made six goals'.

Smith is also listed in the line-up when a team called Argyle, featuring the McNeil brothers, Tom Vallance, McBeath and Campbell, drew with Clyde a couple of months earlier, but this fixture appears to be one of only a handful of matches Smith played for Rangers. He is also in the line-ups for matches against

Gramby in January 1874 and Kelvinside in September 1874, but the next recognised goalkeeper after Smith seems to be a chap called John Yuille.

He was between the posts for a 0-0 draw against Star (later Vale of Leven) on 19 September 1874, and is credited with having played in each of the 15 matches listed in McElroy and Ferrier's *Rangers – The Complete Record* for season 1874/75. Remarkably, he conceded only two goals in those fixtures.

And Yuille has a place in the annals of Rangers Football Club. On 10 October 1874, Rangers competed in the Scottish Cup for the first time, taking on Oxford at Queen's Park's Recreation Ground. Rangers won 2-0, and Yuille kept goal thus earning the distinction of being the first goalkeeper to play in a Scottish Cup tie for Rangers.

Yuille would feature eight times the following season too. He conceded four goals in a 4-0 defeat against Vale of Leven, and he was also involved in the controversial Scottish Cup defeat against Third Lanarkshire Rifle Volunteers.

Peter Campbell's goal looked to have won the tie for Rangers, but Third Lanark lodged an appeal on the grounds that Rangers had kicked off at the start of the first half and the second half. The appeal was upheld, and Rangers lost the replayed match 2-1.

Cue protestations from Rangers – the Thirds goalkeeper had apparently donned 'plain clothes' so couldn't be set apart from the crowd that gathered behind his goal, while John Hunter, who had scored Third Lanark's opening goal, had used his hands to do so – but they were rejected. Thirds made it to the final where they lost to Queen's Park.

Seven days after the defeat against Third Lanark, John Yuille looks to have played for Rangers for the final time – the Light Blues lost 2-0 against Queen's Park – and for the seasons that followed the goalkeeping position was in a state of flux.

James Watt played the majority of games in season 1876/77, including the Scottish Cup Final trilogy against Vale of Leven. And Watt was also in goal when Rangers were thrashed 4-0 by Queen's Park in the final of the Glasgow Merchants' Charity Cup.

The following season, David Hill started the first game of the season against Beith in goal but made the rest of his appearances as an outfield player. Hill was one of NINE players who played in goal during that campaign by Rangers (there may have been more than that too, since some of the line-ups from games played have not been traced). Watt was one of them, but his Rangers career effectively ended when he conceded five goals against Vale of Leven in a Scottish Cup fourth-round replay. Rangers had been rampant in the early rounds, knocking in 34 goals in their opening three matches, but came a cropper in a replayed fourth-round tie, losing five goals without reply.

Watt became club president in 1876 and served the club as honorary treasurer too. Along with captain Tom Vallance, Watt played an instrumental role in the protestations that were presented to the SFA in the wake of the 1897 Scottish Cup Final. More on that later.

Watt, who was a partner in Dimmack and Watt, the iron and steel merchants, died on 22 March 1898. He was suffering from heart disease. He is buried in Craigton Cemetery.

Combining playing outfield and in goal was not uncommon in that era. Indeed, two of the founding fathers, Peter Campbell and Moses McNeil, did so. Campbell played in goal during a 2-0 defeat against Caledonian on 9 April 1879, while McNeil did likewise in a 1-1 draw against First Lanark RV on 7 December 1878. And Alick Vallance, brother of Tom, was another who took his turn in goal too, playing there three times in season 1878/79.

George Gillespie played in goal more than most, though. He initially played as a left-back, a position he occupied in Rangers' first-ever Scottish Cup Final appearance in 1877. He started the following season on the left-hand side of defence too, but when James Watt was absent for the Scottish Cup tie at home to Alexandra Athletic, Gillespie took over in goal. Rangers won 8-0, Peter Campbell and Moses McNeil both scoring hat-tricks.

Thereafter, Gillespie emerged as arguably the best Scottish goalkeeper at that time. In the Scottish Cup campaign of 1878/79, Gillespie was the number one. He played in six of the seven ties – all but one as goalkeeper – including the final against Vale of Leven that ended 1-1.

Rangers refused to replay. Leading 1-0 courtesy of a goal from Willie Struthers, they looked to have gone further ahead when Struthers headed in a cross from Willie Dunlop. The goal was chalked off, the officials insisting that Struthers was in an offside position. Three minutes from time, Vale of Leven equalised to force a replay. Gillespie seems to have been culpable in the concession of the goal, misjudging the shot from Ferguson, thinking it was going wide.

Perhaps in a portent of things to come, the SFA considered a protest from Rangers regarding the legitimacy of their second goal but upheld the result. A date of 26 April was set for the replay, but while the Vale of Leven players turned up at Hampden, Gillespie and his team-mates were enjoying a day at the races! Vale of Leven were awarded the trophy.

George Gillespie was still keeping goal in 1883, although in the intervening period he had played at right-back, left-back, left-half, inside-right and outside-left too. He even notched up some goals, scoring in a 10-0 win over Arbroath in October 1879, netting in an 8-0 win over Caledonian in February 1881 and he was also on the scoresheet when Hibernians were beaten 9-3 towards the end of April 1881.

George was also capped for Scotland. He won the first of seven caps against Wales at the original Hampden Park on 27 March

1880, the same day Rangers were thumping Drumpellier 11-0. He kept goal again when Scotland travelled to London to face England a year later, playing his part in a rousing 6-1 victory. He won two further caps as a Rangers player, matches against Wales in Wrexham and England at Hampden, both of which ended in 5-1 wins for Scotland.

Gillespie played in goal for Rangers for the last time on 24 November 1883. Rangers lost 5-2 at home to Queen's Park. He moved to Queen's Park a few months later and was in goal when the Spiders won the Scottish Cup in 1886 and 1890. Less than ten years later, in February 1900, George passed away, aged 42.

It was a chap called Willie Chalmers who took over from Gillespie in season 1883/84. Chalmers made 26 appearances that season, keeping six clean sheets. One of those was in a 10-0 thrashing of Abercorn in March 1884. Charlie Heggie, who himself had played in goal since he joined the club, scored six goals in that match. Abercorn must have been sick of the sight of the Rangers attackers; less than a fortnight later, they lost 9-2 although the scorers in that game are not known.

Chalmers was the principal custodian for the next three seasons. In the second of those seasons, Willie endured a 10-2 defeat against Airdrieonians at Kinning Park, Rangers' worst-ever defeat. There had been heavy snow in Glasgow to such an extent that this match was the only one to go ahead in the city. This was at the behest of the Rangers committee, but the visitors mastered the conditions better and doled out a real hammering.

Chalmers was most unfortunate. In the ten games that followed the Airdrie mauling, he conceded a further 27 goals. Among those games were matches against Bolton Wanderers and Blackburn Rovers. And on 6 November 1886, he conceded five goals in a match against Dumbarton. Rangers recovered from 5-0 down to draw the match 5-5, but they got another hiding on 3 January 1887.

They faced Preston North End away from home, and Chalmers was beaten eight times.

But Willie Chalmers does have a place in Rangers' history. He is one of only seven Rangers players to have been an ever-present in what was the club's first and to date only appearance in the English FA Cup. Chalmers kept clean sheets against Everton and Lincoln City as Rangers went all the way to the semi-final. However, the journey ended at that point, Chalmers conceding three goals as Rangers lost 3-1 against Aston Villa at Nantwich Road in Crewe.

Willie Chalmers made his last appearance for Rangers on 17 September 1887. He conceded three goals in a 3-2 home defeat against Dumbarton. A month earlier he had lost eight goals as the first Ibrox Park was opened, visitors Preston North End gate-crashing the party by winning 8-1.

The following season, on 28 May 1888, Rangers faced a team called Celtic in what was the latter's first-ever fixture. Jimmy Nicol was the goalkeeper, and he conceded five goals in a 5-2 defeat. Thankfully, Rangers would fare much better over the years as the Old Firm rivalry evolved.

A couple of years later the Scottish League was formed. Rangers were one of ten teams to contest the first-ever title race, and the man trying to keep out the opposition attackers was, for the most part, David Guthrie Reid.

Born on 7 June 1865 in Milton, Reid made his first appearance for Rangers on 2 May 1885. That was in the second replay of a Glasgow Merchants' Charity Cup first-round tie against Dumbarton at the second Hampden Park. Rangers lost 2-0.

Over the next couple of seasons, Reid would compete with the likes of Willie Chalmers and Jimmy Nicol for the goalkeeper's jersey, but by season 1889/90, he seemed to be the favoured option. He played in all four Scottish Cup ties and four of the five matches played in the Glasgow Cup. Both campaigns ended before the final;

Queen's Park winning 2-0 in the semis of the Glasgow Cup, while Vale of Leven triumphed 3-2 after a replay in the third round of the Scottish Cup. Reid also played in 13 other matches, including a 6-2 thrashing at home to Everton.

In what would prove to be a historical season for Rangers, Reid played in 16 of the 18 league matches in 1890/91, conceding 25 goals. He kept a clean sheet in five of those 16 games. Alick McKenzie took over for the two league matches Reid missed, 1-1 draws against Cowlairs and Abercorn. Reid also played in the play-off that was ordered after Rangers and Dumbarton ended up tied at the top on 29 points. Although Rangers were 2-0 ahead at half-time, the Sons scored twice after the interval and the first-ever Scottish title was shared.

After quitting the game, Reid carried on the family business as a muslin manufacturer. He passed away on 5 November 1941 at the age of 76.

It's fair to say that the position of goalkeeper changed hands numerous times in the first 20 years of Rangers' existence. But that was soon about to change, and as the world saw out the last years of the 19th century, Rangers finally found regularity in the last line of their defence.

Chapter 2

The First Regular Custodians

DAVID REID was succeeded by David Haddow, who came from Albion Rovers, at the start of season 1891/92. Born in Dalserf on 12 June 1869, Haddow can probably be recognised as the first regular Rangers goalkeeper. Over the next three seasons, he missed only three league games, and he was in goal when Rangers won the Scottish Cup for the first time in 1894.

Haddow made an inauspicious start to his Rangers career. In his first full season, Rangers finished fifth in the league, 13 points behind a Dumbarton side that had battered them 6-0 in May 1892. Rangers also lost 5-3 to Celtic in the Scottish Cup semi-final. Haddow made 22 league appearances, played six times in the Scottish Cup, three times in the Charity Cup and twice in the Glasgow Cup. In total, he shipped 66 goals and only kept the opposition out on six occasions.

However, Haddow, who despite being deemed a bit small to be a goalkeeper, was said to have been agile with excellent judgement, and played in some of the most significant games in Rangers' history. On 2 September 1893 he kept a clean sheet as Rangers recorded their first-ever league win over Celtic, a hat-trick from outside-left John Barker contributing to a 5-0 win. And later that same season, Haddow was in goal when Rangers beat the same opponent 3-1 to win the much sought-after Scottish Cup for the first time.

Both clubs were enjoying contrasting fortunes prior to the final which took place on 17 February 1894. Rangers weren't in the best of form, having lost three of their last five league matches, while Celtic had netted an astonishing 26 goals as they saw off Hurlford, Albion Rovers, St Bernard's and Third Lanark en route to the final. They were also top of the league.

The heavens opened on the day of the game and the rain came down in torrents. According to the match report, that made for a 'spongy' surface, but it didn't deter Haddow. Having made a telling contribution in Rangers' semi-final tie against Queen's Park – he was noted in the *Glasgow Herald* as having made a 'splendid' save from a corner kick in the first half of a match that ended 1-1 before Rangers edged the replay 3-1 – he was part of a stoic defence in the first half at Hampden that managed to keep Celtic at bay. Twice in the first half, the Rangers goalkeeper thwarted Celtic, saving shots from Cassidy and Madden, although the match report suggested that there were 'several times' that the Rangers goal 'nearly came to grief'.

Rangers were better after the break, though, and the deadlock was broken ten minutes after the restart when Hugh McCreadie scored. Haddow's goal was besieged after that as Celtic sought an equaliser, but it was not forthcoming. Splendid goals from John Barker and John McPherson sealed the match for Rangers, with a late consolation from Willie Maley after a 'scrimmage' in Haddow's penalty area being Celtic's only counter.

David Haddow thus had a place in the Rangers folklore. He joined Nicol Smith, Jock Drummond, Robert Marshall, Andrew McCreadie, Davy Mitchell, James Steel, Hugh McCreadie, John Gray, John McPherson and John Barker in the XI that won the first of 34 Scottish Cups for the club.

Haddow made his last league appearance for Rangers towards the end of the following season in a 2-1 win over St Bernard's on 27 April 1895. Rangers finished a disappointing third in the league, nine points behind champions, Celtic, and Haddow was also in the team that relinquished the Scottish Cup, Rangers losing 2-1 to Hearts in the opening round.

Haddow won one cap for Scotland, playing in a 2-2 draw against England at Celtic Park in April 1894. After leaving Rangers, he briefly joined Motherwell, making eight league appearances, before moving to England where he turned out for Burnley, New Brighton Tower, and Tottenham Hotspur.

Haddow later admitted in a newspaper article that he was a 'habitual drunkard' having learned to drink alcohol during a short spell with Derby County. He later admitted that football and the adulation it brought in addition to the drinking and swearing had 'shattered [his] principles and weakened [his] determination.' He would spend eight weeks at a Salvation Army barracks in Whifflet in early 1903 after which he stated that, 'I intend, by the grace of God, to become a Blood-and-Fire Salvationist and an out-and-out Soldier for Jesus Christ.'

David Haddow made 141 appearances for Rangers. In addition to winning the Scottish Cup in 1894, he also played his part in two Glasgow Cup triumphs. He passed away at the age of 85 on 14 April 1955.

One of Haddow's deputies was Archie Montgomery. Born in Chryston in Lanarkshire, Montgomery started out with his local side, Chryston Athletic, before he joined Rangers in 1893. He made his debut when he stepped in for Haddow on 21 April 1894, keeping a clean sheet in a 5-0 win over St Mirren in the penultimate league match of the season. He played in seven successive league matches the following season too and also Glasgow Cup ties against Third Lanark RV and Partick Thistle.

The latter was lost 1-0, but a replay was ordered after Rangers lodged a protest. It transpired that the Thistle keeper, who had had a fine match, had played for Duntocher Harp while registered as a Thistle player. Authorities took a dim view on this, resulting in the replay. When that came around, though, David Haddow was back in goal as Rangers won 5-3 to make the Final.

Montgomery left Ibrox in April 1895 and joined Bury in the English Second Division. He made his debut against a club called Newton Heath – the original name of Manchester United – and was part of the side that beat Liverpool to confirm that Bury were champions of England.

Over the next ten seasons, he made 228 appearances for Bury. However, when Bury made the FA Cup Final in 1900 and 1903, Montgomery missed out. He joined Manchester United in 1905 where he was second in command to Harry Moger. After appearances against Glossop, Stockport County and Blackpool, he returned to Bury as manager in 1907. He remained in post until the outbreak of the First World War and later managed Albion Rovers.

Archie passed away on 5 January 1922, 22 days short of his forty-ninth birthday.

The goalkeeper's jersey did the rounds in season 1895/96, with six goalkeepers used in that campaign. James Yuillie, James Nisbet McAllan and Mungo Murdoch, who was signed from Kilmarnock Athletic, each played one league game, while Willie Wilson, who was a bandsman in the Highland Light Infantry, played in three.

John McLeod, who had played 108 times for Dumbarton, was also tried. Described in the *Scottish Referee* ahead of the 1892 international against England as a 'safe and reliable custodian' whose 'feet and hands act in unison with his quick eyesight', McLeod played in five league matches, one of which was 6-2 thrashing at the hands of Celtic. He also played in the two Glasgow Cup ties against Queen's Park, the Spiders winning the replay by three goals to two after the first match had finished 2-2.

And then there was John Bell from Slamannan, a village just shy of five miles outside Falkirk. Bell's Rangers career was actually bookended with games against Hibernian. He made his debut on 26 October 1895 in a 1-1 draw in the league and his time with the club ended after a 3-2 defeat at Ibrox in the Scottish Cup quarter-final on 15 February 1896. The story goes that Bell felt he was culpable for the defeat. At full time, he left the field, got changed in the dressing room without speaking to anyone and walked out the stadium and never returned. The fact that Rangers had missed twice from the penalty spot in the second half suggests that Bell may have been a little hard on himself.

Thankfully, a solution to the goalkeeping challenges facing the club was found with the signing of Matthew Dickie. Dickie came from a club called Renton for whom he had played in the Scottish Cup Final in 1895. Ironically, the match against St Bernard's which Renton lost 2-1 was played at Ibrox.

Dickie had a connection with Rangers even before he signed for the club. He was born on 19 August 1873 in the same village, Rhu on the east shore of the Gare Loch, as Peter and Moses McNeil, two of the club's founding fathers and gallant pioneers.

The hallmark of the next five seasons after Dickie signed for Rangers was his consistency. 'Brave' and 'reliable' are words that have also been used to describe him. Matthew only missed two league games during those five seasons and, over the course of his Rangers career, he was absent for just 17 of the 158 league matches Rangers contested. The goalkeepers who stepped in on those rare occasions were James Yuill (1), William Howden (1), John McPherson (1), Noble McPherson (2), William Wallace (1) and J.G. Watson (11).

Dickie, who picked up four league titles and three Scottish Cups, was also the goalkeeper in the season where Rangers were invincible, winning all 18 of their league matches in season 1898/99. Dickie, one of only five players to play in all 18 games, conceded 18 goals and kept seven clean sheets. He was also an ever-present in the Scottish Cup run, Celtic denying Rangers the double when they won 2-0 at the second Hampden Park in the final.

The last of Dickie's three Scottish Cup medals came in 1903. He kept a clean sheet in a 2-0 win over Hearts in the replayed final, the first match having ended 0-0. Remarkably, it would be a quarter of a century before Rangers laid their hands on the trophy again. That would also be the last Scottish Cup tie that Matthew would play for Rangers.

In season 1903/04, Dickie shared goalkeeping duties in the league with John G. Watson, but it was the latter that played in each of the five Scottish Cup ties, including the 3-2 defeat to Celtic in the final. That match came a couple of months after Dickie's final league appearance for the club, an 8-1 win over Port Glasgow in the penultimate league match of the season on 13 February 1904.

Dickie's last appearance prior to that had been in an epic match against St Mirren on 9 January 1904. Goals from Alexander Mackie and R.C. Hamilton had given Rangers a 2-1 lead at half-time, but in the second half, FOUR penalty kicks were awarded. Dickie faced three of them, all of which were converted by David Lindsay. R.C. Hamilton scored Rangers' penalty, but a further goal from Lindsay rendered a late goal from Mackie meaningless, the Saints winning 5-4.

Matthew Dickie, who kept goal in the last match at the first Ibrox Park, a 6-1 win over Kilmarnock on 9 December 1899, was capped three times by Scotland and lived to the grand age of 86, passing away on 30 December 1959.

* * *

The season after Matthew Dickie left the club, 1904/05, started with William Allan in goal. Allan had arrived from Falkirk, and he played in each of the first eight league matches. In that run was a sequence of five successive victories, including a magnificent 8-1 win over Partick Thistle that featured a Finlay Speedie hat-trick.

But by early October, Allan had been displaced. On 1 October he lost three goals in a 3-2 defeat at home to St Mirren, and seven days later, Allan made his final appearance for Rangers in the Glasgow Cup Final at Hampden. Rangers lost 2-1 to Celtic. He had spells with Albion Rovers and Falkirk before settling at Hibernian. Allan eventually made 264 appearances for the Edinburgh side, including the 1914 Scottish Cup Final.

Initially, John Watson came back in, playing two league matches, a 2-2 draw with Celtic and a thumping 5-0 win over Queen's Park. But the management team must not have been convinced that Watson was the solution as Thomas Sinclair took over for the rest of the season. He played in the last 16 league fixtures and the Championship play-off that was lost against Celtic. Sinclair also played in seven of the eight Glasgow League fixtures. The one he missed was against Queen's Park on 8 May 1905. His place that day was taken by a chap called Karl Pekarna who can lay claim to being Rangers Football Club's first-ever foreign signing.

Born on 7 July 1881 in Oberlaa, Pekarna, who was a postman, had come to the attention of Rangers during a post-season tournament in Vienna to mark the tenth anniversary of First Vienna FC. The Danish club, Bolden Cluben of Copenhagen, were also involved, and when their goalkeeper wasn't fit enough to face Rangers, Pekarna stepped in. He conceded nine goals in the match but is said to have impressed with his 'jumping power'. Pekarna was subsequently offered £3 10 shillings to come to Scotland, and he accepted, travelling to Glasgow in December 1904.

There were high hopes for the lad who had just become Austria's first professional footballer. With Sinclair the chief custodian in the first XI, Pekarna started off in the reserve team. He seemed to be settling well, and early in 1905, he was quoted in the *Viennese Sport-Illustrierte* saying:

> [In Scotland] the goalkeeper has no time to catch the balls nicely because three strikers are immediately on his back. Usually, the ball is not caught but knocked out with the fist. Rangers are happy with me and want to make me the best goalkeeper in Scotland, which doesn't seem out of the question.

But sadly, homesickness robbed Karl of his chance at Rangers. Despite being offered a two-year contract he went back to Austria where he had to apply for reamateurisation. He subsequently moved to Germany where he initially turned out for FC Wacker in Munich. He then moved to Bayern Munich in 1910, making his competitive debut on 18 September 1910 in a 6-0 away win over SpVgg Fürth.

Pekarna's debut season ended with Bayern winning their regional title, the *Ostkreis*. Karl appeared in all 18 matches, Bayern winning 16, drawing one and losing one. They scored 107 goals and Pekarna conceded 21. Winning the title took Bayern through to the *Endrunde Süd-Deutschland* (South German Championship) alongside the other regional winners, Karlsruher FV, Mannheimer FG Union 96 and SV Wiesbaden 1899. Pekarna and his team-mates won three and lost three of their matches and finished second to Karlsruher.

Pekarna drew praise for his displays. The German coach Dr Otto Nerz claimed he was 'the best goalkeeper of his time', while journalist Carsten Germann commented:

> Pekarna demonstrates a goalkeeping game to the astonished Munich audience that had not been seen on the continent until then. With saves on the fly and a powerful fisted clearance.

Pekarna was also department manager of a sporting-goods shop, but his career was interrupted when he was drafted into military service during World War One. He survived the war, but he was to suffer a tragic loss a couple of years after the war was over. In 1920 his younger brother Eduard, also a goalkeeper, died after breaking his neck in an accidental clash as he made a fist save in a match.

Four years later, Pekarna, who had now retired and become a teacher, suffered a stroke that paralysed half of his body and forced him into a wheelchair. He passed away in Vienna on 23 January 1946.

The man Pekarna was expected to vie with for a place in the team, Tom Sinclair, also has a story to tell. Born in Dunkeld in 1880, Thomas Smith Sinclair pushed on after making 34 appearances in his debut season. In season 1905/06, Sinclair didn't miss any of the 30 league matches played, but it was a difficult season for Rangers. They lost 5-1 to Airdrie away and 5-0 against Hearts at Ibrox inside the opening ten league fixtures, and although goals from Kyle, Shaw, and May earned a 3-2 win over Celtic, by the end of the season 48 goals had been conceded. Sinclair and his defence only managed to shut out the opposition on five occasions.

Sinclair also played in the shock Scottish Cup quarter-final loss to Port Glasgow Athletic. The brief report in the *Glasgow Herald* doesn't mention much about the Port's winning goal, focusing instead on the fine display of Sinclair's opposite number, Robert Ward. But Sinclair didn't end the season empty-handed. He kept goal in a thrilling eight-goal Old Firm Charity Cup semi-final at Parkhead – Rangers won 5-3 – and was also in goal when Rangers defeated Queen's Park 3-2 in the final. Jimmy Speirs scored two goals in both the semi-final and final. He would later captain Bradford City in the FA Cup Final, scoring the only goal in the replay against Newcastle United at Old Trafford.

For Sinclair, season 1905/06 would be his last as a first-teamer at Rangers. In season 1906/07, he returned to the reserve team with Sandy Newbigging, who had been recruited from Reading, taking his place in the first XI. And it was early in that season that Sinclair answered an SOS from Celtic.

The Old Firm had met at Ibrox on 16 August for Finlay Speedie's benefit match. Speedie opened the scoring before Jimmy Quinn restored parity before half-time. But second-half goals from Speedie, Smith and Speirs gave Rangers the advantage. Celtic's consolation came via a penalty kick scored by James Hay.

During that second period, Celtic's keeper, Davey Adams, was injured when he caught his hand on a nail that was sticking out of one of the goalposts. With the opening league fixtures just two days later, Rangers agreed to loan Sinclair to Celtic until Adams recovered. And the Rangers reserve did superbly well, keeping clean sheets in eight of the nine matches he played and winning a Glasgow Cup medal when Celtic beat Third Lanark at Ibrox in the final.

As Sinclair was shutting out Motherwell on the opening afternoon of the league season, Sandy Newbigging was conceding two goals as Rangers kicked off with a 2-2 draw at home to Falkirk.

Born in Larkhall on 12 September 1876, Newbigging started out in junior football with Lanark Athletic, and after three years with Abercorn, he joined Queens Park Rangers in 1900. A year later, Sandy moved to Nottingham Forest where he would be the deputy for Harry Linacre. In his four seasons at the City Ground, Newbigging made seven appearances before moving to Reading in 1905.

Results like that draw against Falkirk would be the hallmark of Rangers' season. Only four of the first ten league matches were won, and by the end of the season, Newbigging and his team-mates had registered victory in only 19 of the 34 league matches. Rangers finished third, ten points behind champions Celtic.

Celtic also eliminated Rangers from the Scottish Cup, winning the quarter-final tie 3-0 at Ibrox in March 1907, and Queen's Park ended interest in the Glasgow Cup when they won a first-round replay 3-0. But like Sinclair the season before, Newbigging ended the season with a winners' medal, keeping a clean sheet as Celtic were beaten 1-0 at Cathkin Park in the final of the Charity Cup. This was an important victory, for it denied Celtic a clean sweep of honours for the season.

Newbigging made 50 appearances in season 1906/07. Rangers played in 57 matches, and Newbigging started in all but one of the 51 matches that line-ups are available for. The only match he missed was a 3-3 draw against Hearts on 3 January 1907. This was James Stark's benefit match, and Tom Sinclair was the man listed as goalkeeper.

Newbigging was still number one come the start of season 1907/08. He played in each of the first 15 league matches, a run which featured a 4-4 draw against Falkirk and a 5-3 win over Third Lanark, but between 21 December and 7 March Newbigging played in only one of the nine league matches played. John McArthur (6) and Joseph Hadden (2) stepped in, but it's unclear why Newbigging didn't feature as he played in each of the three Scottish Cup ties played during that spell. He also came back in and kept goal in the final ten league matches. That was in the midst of a run of nine victories in ten matches, but that was too little, too late for Rangers. They finished third again, five points behind Celtic.

Three days after the final league match of the season, Sandy Newbigging made his last appearance for Rangers when Woolwich

Arsenal visited Ibrox on 28 April 1908. The match ended 1-1. Newbigging moved back to Reading in the summer and had spells with Coventry City and Inverness Thistle before he ended his playing career.

Sandy Newbigging was 97 years of age when he attended Rangers' centenary celebrations in 1973 making him the oldest former player in attendance. Ironically, the opponents that night were Arsenal. He passed away in Bangour Hospital in 1976.

* * *

Another goalkeeper who featured in season 1907/08 was the man who would take over from Newbigging in season 1908/09, Henry George Rennie.

Born in Greenock on 1 June 1873 and better known as Harry, Rennie had started out as a half-back in the junior ranks. He excelled in that position and was capped as a Junior International. He joined Morton and it was there that he first tried his hand at goalkeeping.

Rennie was said to be ahead of his time. He was the first keeper to demark his penalty area to help him judge angles, and he would also study the body language of opposing forwards as they prepared to shoot for goal.

He joined Hearts in 1898, making his debut against Rangers at the start of what would be the Light Blues' invincible league season. After a couple of seasons at Tynecastle during which time he was capped by Scotland, Rennie looked set to sign for Celtic, but the deal collapsed, and he ended up at Hibernian instead.

At Easter Road, Rennie played a pivotal role in Hibernian's Scottish Cup win in 1902, and the following season he was part of the side that won the Division One title. Alongside captain Bobby Atherton, Rennie was the only man to play in all 22 league matches.

Between 1900 and 1908, Rennie won 13 Scotland caps, and in May 1908 he left Hibernian and signed for Rangers. He moved into the team immediately, making his debut on 2 May in the opening round of the Charity Cup against Third Lanark at Hampden. The match ended 1-1, and Rennie also featured in the replay – a 3-1 victory – the semi-final defeat against Queen's Park, and a benefit match against Celtic for a R. Robertson.

In season 1908/09, Rennie was the Rangers goalkeeper in 31 of the 34 league matches. But it would be another poor campaign for Rangers. They started superbly, five straight wins being part of a sequence that saw Rangers taste defeat just once in their opening 15 matches. That was a 4-3 loss against Airdrie on 10 October, a match Rennie missed. John McArthur took over in his absence.

But it all started to unravel after that. Rangers won just four of the next ten in the league and won just one of the last six. They finished fourth, six points adrift of Celtic.

Rennie conceded 30 goals in his 31 appearances and kept 13 clean sheets, but it would be in the Scottish Cup that Rennie would carve his name into the history books.

He kept clean sheets as Rangers defeated St Johnstone, Dundee (after a replay), Queen's Park and Falkirk to reach the final against Celtic. And it looked like Rennie was set to add to the cup success he had enjoyed with Hibernian in 1902 when Rangers led 2-1 at Hampden with seven minutes remaining.

Jimmy Quinn had fired Celtic in front after 21 minutes, but goals after 75 and 78 minutes from Tom Gilchrist and Alex Bennett looked to have netted Rangers the trophy for the first time since 1903. But in a frantic late flourish, Jimmy Weir crossed into the penalty area. Rennie is said to have gathered the ball, but seeing Quinn coming, he took a step back and turned his body, and the ball, towards the goal. Remarkably, the referee, Mr J.B. Stark from

Airdrie, deemed that Rennie had carried the ball over the line, and awarded a goal.

The match ended 2-2, and the replay took place a week later. That match ended 1-1 – Jimmy Gordon scored for Rangers – but with newspaper speculation rife that extra time would be played, the fans took umbrage when that wasn't the case. They rioted, setting fires and rampaging for over four hours. The cup was withheld.

For Harry Rennie, that was pretty much that for his Rangers career. Although he played in all three Charity Cup matches in May of 1909 – Rangers defeated Celtic 4-2 to win the trophy – he only featured in two of the last four league fixtures. Both games were lost 1-0 against Hibernian and Third Lanark, and the sum total of Rennie's appearances in season 1909/10 were league games against Aberdeen (1-1) and Airdrie (3-0) and a couple of benefit matches. One of those was for Jimmy Quinn, the result being an 8-4 loss to Celtic on 18 August 1909.

Rennie left Rangers in 1910 and joined Kilmarnock with whom he made 33 appearances in season 1910/11. After a single appearance for Morton, he elected to retire at the age of 38.

Harry Rennie passed away on 17 March 1954. He was inducted into the Hibernian Hall of Fame in 2010. He made a total of 56 appearances for Rangers.

* * *

Rennie's replacement at Rangers in season 1909/10 was an Englishman called Herbert Lock. His recruitment was a landmark moment. It was the first time that Rangers had recruited from an English club, and Lock would hold the fort for the best part of the next ten years.

Lock was born in Southampton on 21 January 1887. He started out with St Mary's Guild before joining Southampton in 1907 where he took over in goal from the retiring George Clawley. Although perhaps a little short for a goalkeeper at 5' 8", Lock didn't let this hold him back as he made a name for himself as a courageous and athletic goalkeeper. He also developed a talent for saving penalty kicks, with eight of the 12 penalties Southampton conceded in season 1908/09 saved by Lock.

Lock made his league debut for Rangers in a 3-0 home win over Kilmarnock on 16 August 1909. But he had an uncomfortable start to his career at Ibrox. Rangers won only four of their next 12 league games, losing to Airdrie, Dundee, Hibernian and Clyde, and Lock was also in goal when Rangers lost 1-0 to Celtic at Hampden in the Glasgow Cup Final.

Matters didn't improve much after that. Although only one match was lost at Ibrox – the final match of the season against Falkirk – away form was abysmal. Only six of the 17 league fixtures played away from Ibrox were won. Twenty-six goals were conceded, a stark contrast to the nine shipped at Ibrox. And that abysmal away form continued in the Scottish Cup too, Clyde winning the second-round tie between the sides by two goals to nil at Shawfield. Clyde also eliminated Rangers from the Charity Cup, but the winds of change were starting to gust, and Lock would be a key figure as Rangers halted Celtic's run of successive titles at six.

Having missed only two league matches in his debut season – a 1-1 draw against Aberdeen on 5 March 1910 and a 3-0 win over Airdrie on 19 March – Lock was an ever-present in season 1910/11. The start to the campaign was dogged once again by inconsistency – Rangers lost three of their first ten matches – but after a humiliating 5-1 loss at home to Morton on 22 October 1910, the Light Blues would only fail to win seven of their last 24 league fixtures. In that run were a 1-0 win over Celtic at Parkhead and 7-1 thrashings of Airdrie and Motherwell at Ibrox. The main man during that spell was Willie Reid – he scored 25 goals – but Lock and his defence played their part too, keeping ten clean sheets and only conceding 18 goals. The only teams to score more than once against Rangers were Partick Thistle and Morton, both matches being drawn 2-2.

That was title-winning form, and Rangers finished four points ahead of Aberdeen. Deposed champions Celtic limped home in fifth place, and their miserable season was completed when Lock and Rangers beat them in the final of the Glasgow Cup (3-1) and the Charity Cup (2-1). Indeed, the only pockmark on the campaign for William Wilton's side was a 2-1 defeat against Dundee in the last eight of the Scottish Cup. Former Ranger R.C. Hamilton was one of the goalscorers for Dundee.

It was more of the same the following season. Rangers burst out the blocks, winning 13 and drawing one of their opening 14 league matches. That whirlwind start left any pretenders to the crown in the slipstream, and despite a couple of chastening defeats – 3-0 at Parkhead on New Year's Day and 5-0 against Hibernian five days later – Rangers retained the title, finishing six points better off than runners-up Celtic.

Herbert Lock was the custodian for all but one of the 34 league matches. The match he missed was a 3-2 defeat against Kilmarnock on 30 March 1912, Thomas Farrington being his replacement. That meant Lock had conceded 31 goals in the 33 league games he had played. He kept 12 clean sheets.

Lock added another Glasgow Cup medal too – Partick Thistle were beaten 1-0 in the final – but interest in both the Charity Cup and Scottish Cup was ended by Clyde. The Bully Wee won 2-1 at the semi-final stage of the former – Farrington kept goal in that one – but their victory in the latter was shrouded in controversy.

Clyde had fired the ball beyond Lock three times inside the opening half hour, but Joe Hendry looked to have got Rangers back into the match with a goal early in the second half. But after 73 minutes, fuelled by a foul committed by Alex Bennett, there was a pitch invasion. The match was abandoned, and in the days that followed, Rangers conceded the tie.

Remarkably, Lock had missed just three league matches since he joined Rangers. But season 1912/13 would see him spend a long spell out of the side. He started six of the first eight league games, but he sustained an injury towards the end of a 1-1 draw against Partick Thistle in a semi-final replay in the Glasgow Cup on 7 October 1912. With the Thistle's English outside-right Tommy Callaghan bearing down on goal, Lock bravely dived at his feet. Callaghan's boot struck Lock's head, and Lock's reward for his courage was a spell on the sidelines. His next appearance for Rangers would be in a Glasgow Cup semi-final against Clyde on 27 September 1913.

With Lock unavailable for selection, John Hempsey stepped into the breach. Hempsey had joined Rangers from Morton, making his debut in the second replay of the Glasgow Cup semi-final against Thistle. He kept a clean sheet in a 2-0 win, and he also played in the final, a 3-1 win over Celtic. He had to bide his time to get into the team for a league match, with Thomas Farrington playing in each of the five fixtures played after Lock was injured before a chap with the surname Gibson took over for three matches. But despite making his first league start in a 3-0 defeat at Airdrie, Hempsey played in the 16 games that remained after that. Rangers lost only one of those matches – a 1-0 defeat against Celtic on 1 January – and just two were drawn.

Hempsey had thus played a pivotal role in the retention of the league title. He conceded 14 goals and kept seven clean sheets. Five of those were in succession between 22 March and 19 April. Hempsey also played in the Charity Cup Final, a match Celtic won 3-2, and in the two matches played against Denmark on a post-season tour.

Hempsey started season 1913/14 as number one too. The number of teams was increased to 20, and Hempsey kept goal in 21 of the opening 22 league matches. In the first ten of those matches, Rangers only dropped five points The 11th league match – a 4-2 win over Third Lanark at Cathkin Park – saw John Glenn take over in goal, but Hempsey was back for the visit of Celtic seven days later.

Goals from Thomas McAteer and Whitehead and a missed penalty from Alex Bennett saw Celtic win 2-0, and although Rangers won eight of their next nine league matches, their season and indeed that of John Hempsey effectively ended on 1 January. Celtic won 4-0, and Hempsey only featured once more in the league after that, a 2-1 win over Ayr United on 10 January.

John Glenn stepped in for a couple of matches before Herbert Lock took over. The Englishman played in 12 of the last 13 league matches and kept six clean sheets. But the damage had already been done. Celtic won the league, finishing six points better off than their Old Firm rivals.

Lock also played in the victorious Glasgow Cup campaign, shutting out Clyde in the semi-finals and Third Lanark in the final. He was also in goal when Thirds gained a modicum of revenge in the Charity Cup, winning the semi-final 4-3 on corners after a 1-1 draw.

Lock started season 1914/15 as the man in possession. On 18 August he was given a benefit match against Celtic – he conceded six goals in a 6-4 defeat – and was the number one for the first eight league matches. Thereafter, he vied with Hempsey for the goalkeeper's jersey in what would be the first season played during World War One. The Scottish Cup was suspended, but in the league, Lock played 26 times, while Hempsey appeared in the other 12 fixtures. Lock played in the only Glasgow Cup tie – a 2-0 loss to Partick Thistle – but Hempsey was in goal when Celtic won 3-2 in the final of the Charity Cup.

The pattern would be the same throughout the war years. Of the 38 league matches played in season 1915/16, Hempsey kept goal for

21, Lock for 16. The only one that neither played in was a 2-0 defeat against Falkirk at Brockville on 20 November. Hempsey was due to play but, along with Joe Hendry and Andy Cunningham, he was unable to travel from Glasgow by train due to fog. Alex Bennett, a forward by trade, was chosen to play in goal in a fixture where Rangers were only able to call upon nine players. The match was lost 2-0.

Lock kept his place for the start of season 1916/17, a campaign that kicked off with seven straight league wins and only three goals conceded. But Lock was helping the war effort too, working in the local shipyards, and that took precedence over keeping goal for Rangers. But when he wasn't available, Hempsey stepped in, and John made 21 league appearances in 1916/17.

Unfortunately, Rangers couldn't build on that fine start. Although they only dropped ten points in their first 24 league matches, a wretched end to the season saw the Light Blues lose six of their last 14. They finished third, 11 points behind Celtic and one adrift of runners-up Morton. There would be no crumbs of comfort in the Glasgow Cup or Charity Cup either. Lock conceded three goals in a 3-0 loss to Celtic in the Glasgow Cup semi-finals, while Hempsey was beaten twice when Celtic won 2-0 at Ibrox in the last four of the Charity Cup.

In what would be the last season played during World War One, 1917/18, Hempsey was to the fore. He was also in goal when Rangers defeated Partick Thistle to win the Glasgow Cup, and his form in the league was excellent. Rangers overcame a sticky start that yielded just five wins in the first ten league games to embark on a 20-match unbeaten run. Indeed, only one of the last 26 league games was lost, a 2-0 defeat at Falkirk on 9 March. Hempsey missed that match and the final seven fixtures too, but in the 25 league fixtures he played, he conceded only 15 goals. He shut the opposition out on 15 occasions too. Rangers were crowned champions, finishing a point clear of Celtic.

John Hempsey's last season as a Rangers player was season 1918/19. This campaign saw a series of titanic battles between Celtic and Rangers. Hempsey picked up another Glasgow Cup medal when Rangers drew first blood by beating their Old Firm rivals 2-0 in the final at Hampden. And a fortnight later, Hempsey and his defence defied the Celtic forwards again, goals from Tommy Cairns, Jimmy Bowie and Robert McDermid earning an emphatic 3-0 win at Parkhead in the league.

That victory was Rangers' ninth in succession. By the halfway stage, only four points had been dropped, and Hempsey had only conceded six goals. At the other end, the forwards were firing on all cylinders, scoring 49 goals in those 17 matches, the last of which was an 8-0 mauling of Kilmarnock at Ibrox.

Hempsey looked set to add another league title medal to his collection. After the New Year Old Firm derby ended 1-1, the Light Blues were three points clear. But Celtic matched them stride for stride, and with four matches to play both teams had accumulated the same number of points. Ultimately a 1-1 draw against Ayr United at Somerset Park would prove costly for Rangers. Celtic were champions by a single point.

Herbert Lock was back by the time Rangers dropped that precious point in Ayrshire, and the Englishman was also the custodian when the season ended with victory in the Charity Cup. Lock kept clean sheets as Third Lanark and Clyde succumbed in the opening two rounds and picked up a winners' medal when goals from Bowie and Brown earned a 2-1 win over Queen's Park in the final.

John Hempsey made his last league appearance for Rangers on 8 March 1919 when Hamilton were beaten 3-0 at Ibrox. He had been a more than able deputy to Lock in his seven seasons as a Rangers player. In that time, he made 147 league appearances, played three times in the Scottish Cup, appeared in seven Glasgow Cup ties, and played eight times in the Charity Cup.

Seven days after facing the Accies at Ibrox in the league, Hempsey made the last of his 178 appearances for Rangers in a 5-1 win over the same opposition in the second round of the Victory Cup. After leaving Rangers, Hempsey joined King's Park in the Central League before making three league appearances for Morton in season 1921/22. He passed away on 2 August 1938 at the age of 49.

One other goalkeeper played for Rangers during season 1918/19: John Blackstock Miller. Born in Dumbarton in 1890, Miller signed for his local club in November 1911, and made his league debut in a 2-0 win over Vale of Leven a month later. He would go on to make 231 appearances for the Sons, including 32 in the season that he played for Rangers.

Miller's one and only appearance for Rangers came on Easter Monday, 21 April 1919. And he kept a clean sheet too, the *Glasgow Herald* report on the 4-0 win over Third Lanark at Cathkin Park saying that Miller 'was given few opportunities to demonstrate his abilities as a sound and resourceful custodian'. David Prophet McLean, who was on loan from the English side The Wednesday scored twice for the Light Blues, and a hat-trick against Clyde on 10 May took McLean's tally for the season to 29. In what was his only season at Ibrox, McLean, formerly of Celtic, was top goalscorer in the Scottish League.

John Miller's spell as a Rangers player was even more brief. Indeed, two days after he played against Third Lanark, Miller was back in goal for Dumbarton as they concluded their season with a 3-0 defeat against Motherwell at Fir Park. Miller would spend another two seasons with Dumbarton before spending a year with Bo'ness. He passed away on 24 November 1932.

* * *

Rangers won the title back in season 1919/20, and it was a fitting swansong season for Herbert Lock. With the league expanded

– there were now 22 teams in Division One – Lock kept 20 clean sheets in 35 league appearances, conceding just 20 goals. Remarkably, only seven goals were lost in the 21 matches played away from Ibrox in the league.

Lock also played in each of the eight Scottish Cup ties. Dumbarton, Arbroath, Broxburn United and Celtic were all shut out as Rangers beat a path towards the semi-finals. Waiting for them there were Albion Rovers. It should have been a formality as Rovers were battling relegation from Division One and had lost both league matches against Rangers without scoring.

The Rangers XI showed only one change for the side that had beaten Celtic in the last eight. Andy Cunningham was absent, so Jimmy Gordon was moved from left-back to centre-forward. Archie Ritchie donned the number three shirt. But Ritchie was to have a torrid time up against the former Celtic player Bill Ribchester. Bert Manderson had a difficult afternoon at centre-half too against the plucky underdogs. The match ended 1-1, but contemporary reports suggest that it was the performance of Lock that ensured Rangers secured a replay.

That took place four days later and ended 0-0. But in front of an estimated crowd of 65,000, Rovers romped home in the second replay. Rangers were lacklustre, and fell behind after 15 minutes, Ribchester's corner kick being turned into the net by William Hillhouse. And before half an hour had elapsed it was 2-0. Reports suggest that Lock was a busy man in the intervening period – the *Coatbridge Leader* stated that he had 'dealt with many shots', but the correspondent writing in the *Glasgow Herald* suggested that the Rangers goalkeeper should have done better with the long-range effort from Guy Watson that gave Rovers a two-goal advantage.

Rangers responded, and Tommy Cairns headed the ball against the crossbar before half-time. And they passed up a golden chance to score ten minutes from the end when Jimmy Gordon saw his penalty kick saved by Joe Short. But despite those efforts, Albion Rovers deserved their victory. They would lose 3-2 against Kilmarnock in the final.

Three days later, on 10 April 1920, Herbert Lock made his last league appearance for Rangers, keeping a clean sheet in a 0-0 draw against Hearts at Tynecastle. He remained with Rangers for another year, playing in benefit matches for James Reid, Bert Manderson and Bobby Orr, before returning to England, joining Queen's Park Rangers. Incidentally, during World War One, Lock had also played for Kilmarnock, Ayr United, St Mirren and Partick Thistle.

After a couple of years in London, Lock went back to Southampton. He was understudy to Tommy Allen and made 13 appearances before finishing his playing career with Boscombe. After he stopped playing, Lock became a carpenter and a joiner with Southern Railway.

Herbert Lock made 317 appearances for Rangers. In 221 league matches he kept 92 clean sheets and conceded 199 goals. He died on 16 March 1957 at the age of 70 after suffering a heart attack while cycling in Bitterne.

Stability and consistency were now what was standing out when it came to the position of goalkeeper at Rangers. And that trend continued between the two World Wars, with the next custodian stringing together almost 250 successive league and Scottish Cup ties for the club.

Chapter 3

The Inter-War Years

THREE DAYS after Herbert Lock made his last league appearance for Rangers, Willie Robb made his debut in a 2-1 win over Ayr United. Remarkably, he would play in each and every league and Scottish Cup match Rangers contested from then until 31 October 1925. That amounts to 217 consecutive league games and 24 Scottish Cup ties.

Robb had good reason for missing the Rangers game on 31 October 1925 though. Despite there being a full league card in Division One – Rangers were in Kirkcaldy to face Raith Rovers – Scotland were due to play Wales in a British Championship match at Ninian Park in Cardiff. Robb was selected and won the first of two caps for his country, keeping a clean sheet in a 3-0 win. His second cap also came against Wales two years later.

Born in Rutherglen on 20 March 1895, Robb had spells with Rutherglen Welfare, Eastern Burnside and Kirkintilloch Rob Roy, before he joined Birmingham in 1913. He made 45 appearances in Birmingham blue before coming back to Scotland when World War One broke out. During the conflict, Robb played for Vale of Leven, Royal Albert, Third Lanark and Armadale before coming to Ibrox in 1920.

He soon established himself as the last line of defence in an impressive side. The regular full-backs were Bert Manderson and Billy McCandless, the half-back line was Davie Meiklejohn, Arthur Dixon and Tommy Muirhead, while the front five was more often than not Sandy Archibald, Andy Cunningham, Geordie Henderson, Tommy Cairns and Alan Morton.

They were formidable going forward, but tight at the back too. In his first full season, 1920/21, Robb conceded just 24 goals in 42 league matches. The opposition drew a blank in 22 of those fixtures. Rangers lost only one league game – a 2-0 defeat to Celtic on New Year's Day at Ibrox – and scored 91 goals to give Robb the first of four league titles he picked up in his Rangers career. Those titles were also the first four of the remarkable Bill Struth managerial era.

Aside from his remarkable consistency, Robb had all the necessary attributes to be a great goalkeeper. He was agile, had good reflexes, and his distribution was very good too. A tall man, accounts of the time say that didn't prevent him from getting down to low shots quickly, and he wasn't averse to coming off his line to thwart attackers. And he also had something that all Rangers goalkeepers need: razor-sharp concentration. With that side always on the front foot, Robb would be inactive for spells in each game, but he received praise for staying focused in a number of games.

If his consistency was impressive during his debut season, then Robb surpassed that in season 1921/22. Rangers played in 66 games that season, and Robb's name figures in each of the 64 for which a full XI is listed in McElroy and Ferrier's *Rangers – The Complete Record*. He played in goal for 63 of those fixtures and turned out as inside-right on 4 January 1922 in a benefit match for Tommy Singleton against Clyde.

The Rangers goalkeeper in that match was William Gould. Born in Ayr in September 1892, Gould had come from Queen's Park for whom he had 42 appearances in league and cup matches. But try as he might, Gould couldn't supplant Willie Robb. He made only one more appearance for Rangers, also against Clyde.

That was a benefit match for Harry Rae that ended 1-1. Rangers' goal was scored by Johnny Rollo. Rollo would only play a further four matches for Rangers before joining St Johnstone. He eventually made a name for himself as a player and coach in the USA.

Season 1922/23 saw much of the same. Although line-ups for the post-season trip to play six matches in France and Switzerland are unknown, Robb was the custodian in all but three of the other fixtures Rangers played. That earned him winners' medals in both the Glasgow Cup and Charity Cup, and he was ever-present as Rangers romped to the league title, finishing five points clear of Airdrie. Twenty-nine goals were conceded, while the opposition was kept at bay 15 times.

Rangers rampaged their way through the next two seasons too. Only four league matches were lost in season 1923/24, with the first of those coming on 5 January at Ayr United. And in season 1924/25, the Light Blues were unbeaten at Ibrox and lost only three times away from home. Robb was only beaten 26 times, and four of those goals had come in one match, a 4-1 defeat against Hibernian at Easter Road in March.

The Glasgow Cup and Charity Cup were also retained, but the one downside of Robb's spell at Rangers was the lack of silverware in the Scottish Cup. Rangers hadn't won the cup since 1903, but they did reach the final in Robb's first two full seasons at Ibrox. They lost both matches, though, against Partick Thistle and Morton. Defeats against Ayr United and Hibernian followed before the nadir of Robb's Rangers career was hit in 1925.

Rangers faced Celtic in the Scottish Cup semi-final at Hampden. But they didn't go into the match in the best of form having won just one of their previous seven league matches. And they capitulated in front of a crowd of 101,714, the first time a six-figure attendance had been recorded at a club fixture in Scotland.

Rangers lost 5-0.

Reports suggest that Robb had little to do in the opening 25 minutes – Rangers were 'monopolising play' – but lacklustre defending allowed Jimmy McGrory to open the scoring. Davie Meiklejohn struck the underside of the crossbar early in the second half before Rangers 'fore and aft lost all cohesion and touch with one another' as Celtic doubled their lead. McGrory and Thomson scored again before David McLean nipped in to intercept Bert Manderson's attempted back pass to Robb to complete the rout.

Despite the result, it seemed as if Robb was still Struth's number one. In the remaining seven league matches after the semi-final, Robb conceded only three goals and kept five clean sheets, and international commitments aside, it looked like Willie Robb was likely to extend his run of games for Rangers in season 1925/26. However, he picked up an injury in a 3-1 win at Fir Park towards the end of November 1925, and although he came back for a run of seven straight league games, he pulled on the goalkeeper's jersey for the last time as a Rangers player in a 2-2 draw against Hearts at Ibrox on 16 January 1926. The Edinburgh side were chasing the championship and led 2-0 at one stage of the game. Reports of the time point the finger of blame for both goals at Willie Robb. It was a sad way to end what had been a wonderful Rangers career.

Robb joined Hibernian in the summer of 1926 and showed the same consistency with the Easter Road side that he had with Rangers. However, a dislocated finger hastened his departure in 1930, and Robb joined Aldershot. He made just short of 200 appearances and, during his time there, Aldershot were elected to the Football League. A spell with Guilford City followed – Robb won the Southern League title with them in season 1937/38 – before he wrapped up his illustrious career with Regent Star.

Willie Robb made 317 appearances for Rangers. He passed away on 18 February 1976 at the age of 80.

* * *

The man tasked with taking over goalkeeping duties from Willie Robb was Tom Hamilton. He deputised for Robb in that Halloween match against Raith in 1925, and from the latter part of that season until the start of season 1931/32, Hamilton showed similar consistency of selection like his predecessor had. He missed a mere seven league matches in that time – William Moyles, Duncan Yuill and a certain James 'Jerry' Dawson stepped in during his absence – as Rangers romped to five league titles on the trot. And he was also instrumental in ending a hoodoo that had lasted for quarter of a century.

In that era, the Scottish Cup carried with it more prestige than the league title, and by the start of season 1927/28 it had been 25 years since Rangers had claimed the trophy. Wins over East Stirling, Cowdenbeath, King's Park, Albion Rovers and a Hibernian side featuring one Willie Robb took Rangers through to another final. The stage was set.

A record attendance of 118,115 watched on as Celtic enjoyed the best of the opening half. And it took a superb save from Hamilton to keep the scoresheet blank at the interval. Paddy Connolly unleashed a goal-bound effort, but he was denied by the magnificent Hamilton. The rest, as they say, is history. Rangers scored four times without reply after the break and a ghost was exorcised.

But Hamilton wasn't the only goalkeeper to play in that successful campaign. The win over East Stirling marked the debut match of Duncan 'Dunky' Yuill.

Born in Old Kilpatrick on 19 March 1901, Yuill had a couple of years with Clydebank Juniors before he joined St Mirren in 1923. A loan spell at Clydebank followed before he established himself as a first-team regular with Dumbarton. Yuill made 40 appearances in his debut season at Boghead – 1926/27 – and had 24 games under his belt in season 1927/28 when Bill Struth came calling for his services.

Dunky made his last appearance for Dumbarton on 14 January, a 1-0 home defeat against Albion Rovers, and a week later he was keeping a clean sheet as Rangers hammered East Stirling 6-0. Jimmy Fleming scored a hat-trick. Yuill played in the next round too, a 4-2 win over Cowdenbeath, in addition to making three appearances in the league. Those matches were a 3-1 win over Bo'ness United, a 2-0 home defeat against Motherwell, and a 3-3 draw at St Mirren.

Hamilton came back in the following Saturday and Yuill ended his brief Ibrox career in July 1928 when he joined Aberdeen. He later moved to England, making 211 appearances for Millwall, and playing a part in the Lions' run to the last four of the FA Cup in season 1936/37. He eventually retired after a season with Dumbarton, his 26 appearances in season 1939/40 taking his total for the Sons to 90 across two spells.

William Moyles was also an able deputy for Hamilton in that era. Although perhaps a little small for a goalkeeper at just half an inch over 5' 8" tall, Moyles arrived at Ibrox in June 1926, a month after he had played for Bridgeton Waverley in the Scottish Junior Cup Final. Waverley lost 2-0 against Strathclyde at Firhill after the first encounter between the sides had been drawn 1-1.

It was thought that Rangers were actually seeking to sign the Strathclyde goalkeeper Willie Stevenson, but they opted for Moyles, and he would stay with Rangers for four years. Over that period, he would feature seven times for the first XI.

His league debut came in a 3-1 win over Dunfermline Athletic at East End Park on 23 February 1927 – Jimmy Fleming scored a hat-trick for Rangers – and Moyles played in a benefit match for Tom Kilpatrick against Ayr United too. He also kept goal in the Charity Cup Final against Partick Thistle at Hampden on 14 May 1927.

His inclusion for that one was due to the fact that Tom Hamilton was bound for Canada with the Scotland team. With Hamilton and team-mates Tommy Muirhead, Tully Craig, Sandy Archibald and Andy Cunningham sailing the wild Atlantic, it's fair to say that Rangers were not at full strength.

The match was 'replete with incident and excitement' according to the report in the *Glasgow Herald*. The report in the *Sunday Post* spoke of a 'fairly open' opening 15 minutes, during which time Moyles dealt 'smartly' with an effort from Jimmy Richmond. But Bobby Grove gave Thistle the lead after 20 minutes before Sandy Hair doubled their advantage five minutes later.

But within a minute, Bob McPhail halved the deficit, and after 37 minutes, Alan Morton restored parity. Hair is then said to have applied a 'nudge' to Moyles which 'took the Ibrox goalkeeper through his own goal as he held the ball'.

Morton scored again to give Rangers the lead at the interval, but Hair beat Moyles again after 65 minutes, and with no further scoring before the end of the regulation 90, extra time was required. In the extra half hour, Hair got the better of Moyles a further three times to give the Jags a 6-3 win.

Although he had conceded six goals, Moyles shouldn't have been too disheartened. Hair had had a superlative season, scoring 49 goals in 46 games for Thistle. Included in his haul were five hat-tricks. It has been reported that Hair could have been a Rangers player too but was rejected by the club for being too small!

Moyles next played for the first XI in a match against East Scotland Juniors at Tynecastle on 19 September 1927 – James Marshall scored four in a 7-2 win – and would feature twice in the league in season 1927/28, a 4-1 win over Clyde at Shawfield, and a 7-2 win over Airdrie at Broomfield.

He spent time on loan at Third Lanark – where he played seven times – and Albion Rovers, and his last appearance for Rangers came on 19 September 1928. Rangers travelled to Rugby Park to take part in a benefit match for Mattha Smith. Mattha, grandfather of Gordon, who would ply his trade at Ibrox in the late 1970s, scored one of the seven goals for a Kilmarnock side that would beat Rangers 2-0 in the Scottish Cup Final later that same season.

Willie Moyles left Rangers in February 1930. He joined Albion Rovers, and in August of that same year he joined Partick Thistle. He was deputy to Johnny Jackson, who featured in a mammoth 313 consecutive games for the Jags between 1926 and 1933. The only game Moyles played for Thistle was a benefit match against King's Park for their centre-half, Robert Baird. The match ended 3-3.

* * *

Back at Ibrox, Tom Hamilton was once again 'Mr Consistent'. He only missed one match over the course of the next three seasons, a 1-1 draw against St Mirren in January 1931. And although he only made 25 league appearances in season 1931/32, he was front and centre when Rangers defeated Kilmarnock 3-0 in a replayed Scottish Cup Final. He also played in the 6-1 win over Third Lanark in the final of the Charity Cup.

The Scottish Cup medal added to the one Hamilton collected in season 1929/30, but the emergence of Jerry Dawson effectively spelled the end of Tom's Rangers career. But he was to enjoy a swansong. On 21 April 1934, Rangers faced St Mirren in the Scottish Cup final. Dawson had played in all the ties leading up to the Final, but he had picked up an injury, so Mr Struth called upon his trusted understudy. Hamilton kept a clean sheet and picked up his fourth Scottish Cup winners' medal, goals from Nicholson (2), McPhail, Main and Smith giving Rangers a comprehensive 5-0 win.

Tom Hamilton left Rangers in 1935 with an impressive collection of medals. He picked up five league championships, the Scottish Cup in 1927/28, 1929/30, 1931/32 and 1933/34, two Glasgow Cups and six Charity Cups. Tom was also capped once by Scotland, keeping goal in a 3-0 defeat against England at Wembley in April 1932. Hamilton's Rangers team-mate Alan Morton, won his 30th cap in that match thus becoming at that time the most capped player for Scotland. The previous record holder was Bobby Walker.

After his departure from Ibrox, Hamilton went to Falkirk, making 25 league appearances for the Bairns in season 1934/35. He passed away in July 1964.

* * *

After Hamilton came the 'Prince of Goalkeepers', James 'Jerry' Dawson. Nicknamed Jerry after the former Burnley goalkeeper, Jeremiah Dawson, Jerry came to Rangers in 1929 but had to wait until August 1930 to make his first appearance for the first team. That came in a pre-season match against Dumbarton at Boghead which Rangers won 3-1. Tom Hamilton came back in when the competitive action got underway, but on 24 January 1931 Dawson made his league debut in a 1-1 draw against St Mirren at Ibrox.

Over the course of the next few seasons, Dawson shared the goalkeeper's jersey with Tom Hamilton and George Jenkins. Dawson played in 13 of the 28 league matches in season 1931/32, and clocked up 20 in season 1932/33 as Rangers reclaimed the title having relinquished it to Motherwell the previous season. But he looked to have established himself as the undisputed number one when he started each of the first 20 league matches in season 1933/34. Dawson also kept goal as victories over Celtic (after a replay) and Clyde had secured the Glasgow Cup, and he restricted Arsenal to a single goal over the two legs of the British Championship that was contested in September 1933. However, when he sustained an injury in a match against Queen's Park at Ibrox on 9 December, Bill Struth elected to pitch his new recruit, Jenkins, in to replace Dawson for the next fixture against Airdrie at Broomfield.

The route Jenkins took to get to Ibrox was a circuitous one. He was born in Stockton-on-Tees in County Durham in September 1904, but a couple of years later his family emigrated to Canada. Jenkins would find himself bitten by the 'soccer' bug, starting out with Montreal CPR in the Canadian National Soccer League. He must have impressed as he soon joined Indiana Flooring in the American Soccer League. But Jenkins wasn't providing the 'wow factor' by stopping goals; it was at the other end of the field he was making a name for himself.

Five goals in nine league games followed, but it seems he became frustrated at the lack of game time so headed back to Montreal. And it was at that point that his career changed. Jenkins picked up a serious knee injury, and when he recovered he elected to resume his career as a goalkeeper. He was as impressive in goal as he was as a forward, but although he played a key role in the Montreal Carsteel team, it is unclear how he came to the attention of Bill Struth.

There is no record of him playing in any of the matches when Rangers toured the USA and Canada at the end of season 1929/30, but what is evident is that Rangers had developed strong links in that part of the world. Players such as Robert Logan 'Whitey' McDonald, George Coubrough, Bob Calder and Bob McAuley had joined the club from either the US or Canada. Indeed, both Calder and McAuley had also played for Montreal Carsteel.

Jenkins arrived at Ibrox in November 1933. One of his last matches for Montreal Carsteel was a 6-3 win over a touring side from Chile called Audax Italiano on 18 October. But a couple of months later, he was in the Rangers first XI.

After starting out with the Alliance XI (the reserve team), Jenkins made his first-team debut against Airdrie two days before Christmas. Rangers won 7-2, and Jenkins remained in the team for the next four league matches. He kept a clean sheet as Hibernian were battered 6-0 at Ibrox and made his Old Firm debut in a 2-2 draw at Parkhead on 1 January 1934, before Dawson returned the week after Jenkins had conceded three goals, as Rangers edged a seven-goal thriller against Cowdenbeath.

Jimmy Fleming put Rangers ahead, but Cowdenbeath, assisted by a strong wind, were 3-1 up after 38 minutes. Jenkins was beaten three times by Stewart Renfrew before goals from Bob McPhail, Jimmy Simpson and Willie Nicholson turned the match in Rangers' favour. To this day, Renfrew is the only Cowdenbeath player to net a hat-trick against Rangers.

Although he played only seven times, Jenkins had played his part in one of the most successful seasons in the club's history. Rangers won the league, the Scottish Cup, the Glasgow Cup and the Charity Cup, but perhaps symptomatic of his time at the club, Jenkins was not involved in the finals of any of the cup competitions. For his part, Dawson was in goal for 41 of the 50 matches played across those competitions. He conceded only 34 goals in those matches, keeping clean sheets in 16 of them.

Until the outbreak of World War Two, Dawson was rarely absent but, when he was, Jenkins stepped in. Dawson would miss just one match in season 1934/35 – a 2-1 defeat against Clyde on 20 October – as the league and Scottish Cup were retained, and it was a similar story the following season. Dawson was an ever-present in the league – he conceded 43 goals as a run of three successive titles was broken by Celtic – Scottish Cup, Glasgow Cup and Charity Cup. The Scottish Cup and Glasgow Cup were won, but Celtic won the Charity Cup Final by four goals to two.

Seventeen clean sheets in 38 league appearances followed in season 1936/37. The league was regained, and the Glasgow Cup retained as Dawson's exemplary reflexes and authority in the penalty area helped defy opposition attackers. At the other end, Jimmy Smith scored 31 league goals and was aided and abetted by Bob McPhail who notched 25. Both scored hat-tricks in one of the matches in which Dawson kept a clean sheet, an 8-0 thrashing of Kilmarnock at Ibrox on 27 February 1937.

In the midst of all of this, George Jenkins was still around, biding his time for another chance to play for the first XI. And that opportunity came during season 1937/38 when he played in 12 of the 38 league games, ten of which were in succession from 4 December until 19 February. But in that run of ten games, Rangers were beaten 3-0 by Celtic, lost 3-1 against Partick Thistle, and were hammered 6-1 by a Dundee side managed by the former Rangers forward Andy Cunningham, at Dens Park.

The latter was Rangers' heaviest defeat in 43 years. Alex Venters put the visitors in front after 18 minutes, but doubles from Arthur Baxter and Archie Coats had Rangers 4-1 down by the interval. From the reports written, it appears that Jenkins was not at fault for any of the goals. In fact, he actually kept the score down when he saved a Baxter penalty a minute after the Dundee man had completed his hat-trick.

That hammering derailed Rangers' title tilt. Jenkins would play once more in the league, a 2-2 draw against Hamilton Accies, but even the return of Dawson couldn't stop Celtic charging to the title. Dawson kept only four clean sheets in the last 11 league fixtures, the last two of which were lost by three goals to two against Hearts and Queen of the South respectively.

Dawson was also selected for the Scottish Cup semi-final against Kilmarnock at Hampden Park. The Ayrshire side, managed by Jimmy McGrory, would eventually finish third from bottom of Division One, but despite losing 4-1 at Ibrox in November, they had beaten Rangers 2-1 at Rugby Park less than a month before the 2 April showdown.

A crowd of 70,833 converged on the sloping Hampden terraces to witness a seven-goal thriller in which defensive errors proved costly for Rangers. The report in the *Glasgow Herald* opined that the Light Blues had dominated 'three-quarters of the play', and with 21 minutes remaining they led 3-2 thanks to a double from Alex Venters and a strike from Willie Thornton. But Jimmy Simpson was penalised for handling inside the penalty area – Benny Thomson converted the spot kick – and the Rangers centre-back was caught out again in the final minute. He stood still expecting a foul to be given, but referee Baillie from Motherwell played on, and when Sammy Ross crossed from the left, centre-forward Allan Collins headed the ball beyond a helpless Dawson.

The season petered out after that defeat. Rangers won just three of their final six league games and finished third, 12 points behind Celtic. And the newly crowned champions inflicted a 2-0 defeat on their Old Firm rivals in the final of the Charity Cup too.

Dawson was mentioned numerous times in the match report in the *Glasgow Herald*. The correspondent felt that, apart from the Rangers goalkeeper, Dougie Gray, Jimmy Simpson and Alex Venters, 'the Rangers players were terribly disappointing', and Dawson was powerless when it came to preventing goals from Jimmy Delaney and John Divers. Indeed, had it not been for some superlative saves, the scoreline could have been even bleaker for Rangers. Dawson is said to have 'dived full length' to thwart an attempt from Divers at his left-hand post. And after Divers had robbed Simpson of possession and released Delaney, Dawson raced from his line and 'threw himself at the Celt's feet and successfully smothered the ball'.

The jousting between Dawson and Jenkins continued in what would be the last full season before World War Two broke out. The league championship came back to Ibrox thanks primarily to the 112 goals scored – Alex Venters netted 35 of them – and an unbeaten season at Ibrox. It perhaps wasn't the best season defensively, with 55 goals conceded – Jenkins shipping five in the five games he played – but Rangers were ruthless at the other end. The margin of victory over runners-up Celtic was 11 points.

Although he saw little league action, Jenkins did play in both Charity Cup matches, the latter earning the English-born Canadian a winners' medal. Queen's Park were beaten 2-1 in the semi-final, and Jenkins kept a clean sheet in the 0-0 draw against Third Lanark in the final. Rangers were awarded the trophy by virtue of the fact they had won seven corners to Third Lanark's four.

With Dawson back in goal, Rangers started season 1939/40 with four wins and a draw in the league. The Glasgow Cup was also secured courtesy of a 3-1 win over Queen's Park in the final. But the declaration of war brought an abrupt end to the season, with football becoming regionalised. Rangers entered the Southern Division, winning the title comfortably. Dawson played in 25 of the 30 fixtures and registered clean sheets in each of the opening five matches. Remarkably, the opposition was shut out in just four of the next 25 fixtures. The Scottish Emergency War Cup was won too, Dawson and his defence keeping Dundee United at bay in the final. Meanwhile, at the other end, Jimmy Smith scored the game's only goal.

Jerry Dawson would make 215 appearances in all wartime competitions, keeping 77 clean sheets. When he wasn't available, George Jenkins would usually step into the breach. One such occasion when that happened came in season 1941/42.

Rangers had burst out the blocks, winning their first seven league games. In the process, 30 goals were scored and only six conceded. However, their perfect start to the season was obliterated on 27 September when Rangers faced Hibernian at Easter Road. Dawson was beaten eight times – four of the goals were netted by Bobby Combe – and found himself replaced by Jenkins for the next two league matches. But despite keeping clean sheets against Albion Rovers (1-0) and Dumbarton (7-0), Jenkins was supplanted by Dawson and only played a further five league matches that season.

Later that same season, a future Rangers manager also took a turn in goal. Neither Dawson nor Jenkins were available for the league fixture against Clyde on 6 April, so James Scotland Symon took over. He conceded two goals, but Rangers scored eight at the other end. Alex Venters netted a hat-trick.

Rangers were dominant in the World War Two years. Of the six Southern League titles played for, Rangers won all of them. In the 180 matches played, they were victorious 133 times. Twenty-five matches were drawn, and Rangers only tasted defeat on 22 occasions.

In addition to playing in the Southern League, Rangers participated in the Southern League Cup too. The Light Blues won each of the first three tournaments but came a cropper in season 1943/44. After topping Section A ahead of Motherwell, Hearts and Airdrie, a 4-2 win over Celtic at Hampden in the semi-final took the Light Blues through to face Hibernian in the final. And it was against the Edinburgh side that Dawson sustained a nasty injury that effectively ended his Rangers career.

After 17 minutes, he collided with the Hibs inside-right, Tommy Bogan, and was carried off on a stretcher. It was later established that Dawson had broken his leg. Given he had played in goal a couple of years earlier, Scot Symon, who had started the match at left-half, took over in goal for the remainder of the match. Hibernian claimed the trophy, winning 6-5 on corner kicks after the match ended 0-0.

A leg break was a serious injury at the time, and it was almost a year later that Dawson made his comeback in a Southern League match against Partick Thistle at Firhill. He only played a further nine league games for the club. His final league appearance was in a 2-1 win over Motherwell at Fir Park, and four days later he played at Ibrox for the last time in the infamous 2-2 draw against Moscow Dynamo in November 1945.

Jerry Dawson played for Rangers for the last time on 15 April 1946. The venue was Petershill Park, and the opposition was Celtic. The match was arranged to raise funds for the George Henry Memorial Fund, Rangers winning 2-1 thanks to goals from Billy Arnison and Murdoch McCormack. The latter sadly passed away at the age of 30 in 1951. He made 27 appearances for Rangers during World War Two, scoring 15 goals. One of them was against Celtic on 1 January 1944, the second goal in a 3-1 win at Parkhead in the Southern League.

Jerry Dawson is among the most decorated goalkeepers in Rangers' history. He played a part in five league title triumphs, three Scottish Cups, one Scottish Regional League Western Division title, one Scottish Emergency War Cup, four Southern League titles and three Southern League Cups. He also claimed seven Glasgow Cup medals and five winners' medals in the Charity Cup. Jerry was also capped 14 times for Scotland, winning his first cap against Northern Ireland in a 2-1 defeat at Windsor Park in Belfast in October 1934. Dawson played in nine wartime international matches too.

Dawson joined Falkirk after he left Rangers and, while there, he played an instrumental role in helping his former club win their first-ever Treble, in 1948/49. On the final day of the league season, Rangers were away from home against Albion Rovers, while league leaders Dundee faced Falkirk at Brockville. Dundee only needed a point to be champions. But Dawson saved a penalty at a vital stage of the game, Dundee lost 4-1, and Rangers won by the same scoreline in Coatbridge.

That match would be one of 78 Dawson would play for Falkirk. He came close to adding to his vast array of medals in 1947/48 too when he was part of the Falkirk side that reached the final of the League Cup. The Bairns had topped Section 2 to progress to the quarter-finals, at which point a 3-1 win over Hamilton Accies took them through to face Rangers in the last four.

Rangers had won the inaugural competition the previous season, but they relinquished the trophy when Archie Aikman netted the only goal of the game, profiting on a rare moment of hesitancy from the Rangers centre-half, Willie Woodburn, to score. Alas, hopes of another winners' medal for Dawson were dashed by East Fife.

After the first match was drawn 0-0 – Dawson was lauded for his performance – a hat-trick from Davie Duncan helped earn East Fife a 4-1 win. While reports after the first game may have been complimentary towards Dawson, they weren't on this occasion. He misjudged Duncan's cross for the opening goal, with the match report in the *Glasgow Herald* going on to say that 'Dawson was an ordinary mortal and not the invincible goalkeeper of a week ago,' before opining that Dawson was 'to blame for at least one more of the East Fife goals'.

Jerry Dawson ended his playing career in 1949, moving into management four years later with East Fife. He took over from his former team-mate and sometime goalkeeping deputy Scot Symon, who had moved south to join Preston North End, and led his side to victory in the League Cup in season 1953/54.

Grouped with Aberdeen, Airdrie and Celtic, East Fife lost Dawson's first match in charge, Airdrie winning 4-1 at Broomfield. But a draw against Celtic and a victory over Aberdeen followed before Dawson's side avenged the Airdrie defeat by winning 5-1 at Bayview. A 1-0 victory at Parkhead followed, which set up a decider in the final round of fixtures against Aberdeen at Pittodrie.

The Dons had six points, East Fife seven. Dawson's side were ahead when it came to goal average too which meant a draw would suffice. But in an enthralling contest, East Fife won 4-3 to book a place in the quarter-finals.

The former Rangers custodian masterminded an emphatic aggregate score at that stage – East Fife defeated Dunfermline

Athletic 9-4 over two legs – and his side came from behind to defeat Hibernian at Tynecastle in the last four.

Many expected Dawson's former club Rangers to provide the opposition in the final, but Partick Thistle, under the stewardship of another Rangers stalwart, David Meiklejohn, upset the apple cart by winning 2-0 at Hampden.

Thus, two Rangers greats went head-to-head at Hampden, and it would be Dawson who would emerge the victor. With future Ranger Andy Matthew playing at outside-left, the Fifers edged a five-goal thriller. Ian Gardiner and Charlie Fleming scored to establish a 2-0 lead at half-time for East Fife, and although goals from Johnny McKenzie and Jimmy Walker restored parity, right-half Frank Christie thundered in the winning goal three minutes from time.

Dawson's side finished sixth in the league table in his debut season, although they exited the Scottish Cup in the opening round, losing 3-0 at home against Queen of the South. East Fife dropped to 11th at the end of season 1954/55 – among their 15 defeats was a 7-2 thrashing by Rangers – while their defence of the League Cup ended when Motherwell defeated them in the semi-final.

A steady decline followed, and at the end of season 1957/58, East Fife were relegated to Division Two. Dawson left the club at that point.

A totemic figure among the goalkeepers that have played for Rangers, Jerry Dawson passed away on 19 January 1977. He was 67.

* * *

With Dawson sidelined in season 1944/45, George Jenkins finally got his chance to shine as the number one. He played in 29 of the 30 Southern League matches, conceding 26 goals. With the aid of his defence, he shut out the opposition 13 times. He also earned himself a Southern League Cup medal when he was in the XI that defeated Motherwell 2-1 in the final at Hampden and completed a cup hat-trick when he added a Glasgow Cup and Charity Cup medal to his collection.

Jenkins would start the first three league matches of season 1945/46. Two of them were lost, and he made what would be his last appearance for Rangers in a 2-1 defeat against Hibernian at Easter Road on 18 August 1945.

Since his arrival in November 1933, George Jenkins had made 114 appearances for Rangers. When he left the club, he had short spells with Kilmarnock and Hamilton Accies before retiring. George, who was married to Grace, lived in Sandyhills in Glasgow. His son, Kenny, made 175 appearances and scored 23 goals for Dumbarton, and was part of the Sons side that won promotion to Division One in season 1971/72.

George Jenkins passed away in January 1985 at the age of 80.

Chapter 4

The Iron Curtain and the Swinging Sixties

IN THE first full season of the post-World War Two era and indeed for the next five campaigns that followed, one man dominated the goalkeeping position for Rangers: Bobby Brown.

Born in Dunipace on 19 March 1923, Brown attended Falkirk High School. One of his teachers there was Hugh Brown, father of future Scotland manager Craig Brown. The latter would also be on the playing books at Ibrox, although a knee injury meant he never played a first-team game.

Despite interest from Falkirk, Bobby Brown joined Queen's Park, making his debut against Celtic in April 1940 while he was still at school. He established himself as the number one with Queen's and, although he moved south to train as a pilot in the Fleet Air Arm at Dartmouth Naval College, he was often granted permission to return to Scotland to play for the Hampden side.

Brown was joined in Dartmouth by six of his fellow students from Jordanhill College whom he had met while they were studying to become PE teachers. He eventually qualified to fly the Fairey Swordfish; the aircraft best remembered for its part in sinking the *Bismarck*. Alas, five of those six students who accompanied Brown were killed while on active service.

Petty Officer Brown never saw active service. During a match in Ipswich for the Combined Services XI, he impressed A.V. Alexander, First Lord of the Admiralty. Alexander arranged for Brown to attend the Physical Training College at Portsmouth, and since he was vice-president of Chelsea, Alexander recruited Brown as a guest player for the club. He made a couple of appearances and turned out for Portsmouth too.

Alexander also saw to it that Brown was transferred to Plymouth as a PT instructor, and while there he made a number of appearances for Plymouth Argyle. He also met his future wife, Ruth, who was a Wren in the Signals Regiment. They married in Plymstock in July 1946, a couple of months after Bobby signed for Rangers.

Brown was a man in demand. Newly appointed Manchester United manager Matt Busby wanted to take him to Old Trafford but, although tempted, Brown declined. He wanted to sign for Rangers and made his first appearance for the club in a 4-0 win over Airdrie at Broomfield in the Victory Cup on 4 May 1946.

In what would be a glut of end-of-season fixtures, Brown also played in a further five Victory Cup matches and three Charity Cup ties. And, remarkably, within a month of joining the club, he had two winners' medals, Hibernian being beaten 3-1 in the Victory Cup Final, while Third Lanark were defeated 2-0 in the final of the Charity Cup. It would be churlish not to mention that Brown also faced Celtic three times, emerging with a 100 per cent win record and only one goal conceded!

However, although Brown was to emerge as the long-term successor, it was actually John Shaw who had initially taken over from Dawson and Jenkins. Shaw had come from Benburb Juniors and played in all but one of the last 19 Southern League matches in season 1945/46.

Those games included an Old Firm shutout on New Year's Day and a run of ten successive victories.

Rangers comfortably won the title – runner-up Hibernian were eight points worse off – and Shaw also played in all nine of the Southern League Cup ties. He kept the attackers of Queen of the South (twice), Motherwell and Morton at bay as Rangers made it through to the final against Aberdeen. The 3-2 defeat at Hampden would, however, be one of the last times Shaw would play for Rangers. He only made one post-war appearance, deputising for Brown in a 2-0 win over Morton in the final match of Section B in the season 1946/47 League Cup.

John Shaw's Rangers curtain call against Morton would be the only match Bobby Brown missed in season 1946/47. By the season's end, he had a League Championship medal, a Scottish League Cup medal and a Charity Cup medal. In 30 league appearances, he kept 12 clean sheets and conceded 26 goals.

Over the next few seasons, Rangers and Hibernian were the front runners for the title. Brown would form the last line of what became the fabled 'Iron Curtain' defence, and that rearguard had to keep at bay the Edinburgh side's 'Famous Five' forward line.

In front of Brown would be full backs George Young and Jock 'Tiger' Shaw, while the half-back line would more often than not comprise Ian McColl at right-half, Willie Woodburn at centre-half and Sammy Cox at left-half.

That formidable and obdurate rearguard was the bedrock upon which the success of the immediate post-war era was built. Their parsimony when it came to losing goals meant that it was very rare that Rangers would concede more than one goal in a match. In the six seasons that immediately followed the cessation of hostilities, that Iron Curtain was only breached more than once in a league game on 46 occasions. That amounts to 25.56 per cent of the league fixtures played.

Hibernian won the title in season 1947/48 – Rangers' challenge faltering when they won only two of their last seven league games

– but Rangers redressed the balance in some style the following season. With Brown an ever-present, Bill Struth's side became the first team in Scotland to win the domestic Treble of League Championship, Scottish Cup and Scottish League Cup. Thirty-two goals were conceded in the league – as a measure, runners-up, Dundee, shipped 48 while third-placed Hibernian let in 52 – and Brown chalked up seven shut outs in the 14 cup-ties played.

What was remarkable about the tall, blond and athletic Brown was his consistency. From 2 November 1946 until 19 April 1952, Brown didn't miss a single first-team match. That amounts to 265 consecutive appearances and, during that time, Rangers won three league titles, three Scottish Cups, one League Cup, three Charity Cups and two Glasgow Cups. But the beginning of the end of Brown's glittering Rangers career came on 9 August 1952.

Rangers opened season 1952/53 with a visit to Tynecastle in the League Cup. By the end of the 90 minutes, the home side had scored five times without reply. Although not pointing the finger of blame at Brown, the match report in the *Glasgow Herald* refers to the fact that a couple of the Hearts goals had come from long-range shots, one of which the reporter reckoned 'appeared to be a goalkeeper's ball'.

Over the next three seasons, Brown found himself up against the man who would eventually supplant him as the number one at Ibrox, George Niven. Those seasons would be transitional ones for Rangers as the Bill Struth era came to an end and the Scot Symon era began. Brown made 44 appearances during that time, the last of which was on 23 January 1956 in a friendly match against San Lorenzo at Ibrox. The team from Argentina came to town for a 'floodlit match' that Rangers won 4-3 on a 'snow-covered pitch'. Johnny Hubbard (2), Don Kichenbrand and Sammy Baird got the goals for the home side. Brown acquitted himself well although he is said to have been 'deceived' by a 'speculative cross-shot' by Sava in the second half.

Bobby Brown would end his playing career with Falkirk before embarking on a career in management. In May 1958 he was selected from a shortlist of four to take over from Johnny Pattillo at St Johnstone.

Brown would guide his side to promotion as Division Two champions in season 1959/60, and although the Saints were relegated at the end of season 1961/62, they bounced straight back up as Division Two champions. And during their first season back in the top flight, Brown's boys had the distinction of winning both league fixtures against a Rangers side that would claim the domestic Treble. In the first of those matches, a 3-2 win at Ibrox four days before Christmas in 1963, one Alexander Chapman Ferguson scored a hat-trick.

Brown's former club would also provide the opposition when St Johnstone reached the last four of the League Cup in season 1961/62. And they gave their illustrious opponents a fright, Rangers requiring a goal from Davie Wilson seven minutes from the end of extra time to progress to the final.

Brown looked set to build something of a legacy at Muirton Park, but in February 1967 his country came calling.

During his playing days, he won five caps for Scotland in wartime internationals before gaining his first 'official' cap against Belgium on 23 January 1946. In doing so he carved a place in the history books as he became the last amateur player and last Queen's Park player to gain a full international cap for Scotland. A further four caps followed. But early in 1967, the SFA were looking for a new national team manager, and Brown fitted the bill.

He would take charge of Scotland in 28 matches, but his first is arguably amongst the most famous in the history of the national team. Brown took his team to Wembley to face world champions, England, and inflicted upon them their first defeat since they had beaten West Germany to win the Jules Rimet trophy. Jim Baxter was in imperious form as the Scots won 3-2.

Bobby Brown would be the last of the famous Iron Curtain defence to pass away. He died on 15 January 2020 at the age of 96.

* * *

Bobby Brown's successor, George Niven, had followed a route to Ibrox similar to many of his contemporaries at that time. Born on 11 June 1929 in Blairhall, he came from the junior ranks, playing for Coupar Angus before he made his way to Glasgow in 1947.

With Brown the main man, Niven had to bide his time in the reserve team. Indeed, it would be 19 April 1952 before Niven made his first-team debut, keeping goal in a 1-1 draw against Aberdeen in the final league match of the season.

But his breakthrough came in season 1952/53. Four days after Bobby Brown had conceded five goals at Tynecastle, Niven was brought in for a League Cup Section C match against Motherwell at Ibrox. Between then and the end of the season he missed only one match, a 2-0 win over Stenhousemuir in a floodlit friendly in November. Bobby Brown was in goal on that occasion, with John Woods scoring twice for the Light Blues.

Niven was part of the last line of a defence that held firm at Ibrox – only 14 goals were conceded in the 15 league matches played there – but he was beaten 25 times away from home. But Derek Grierson and Billy Simpson did the business at the other end, Grierson scoring 23 times, while Simpson grabbed 21.

That combination of goals and a solid home record saw George Niven claim the first of the five league titles he would amass during his Rangers career. But it was his display in the Scottish Cup Final against Aberdeen on 25 April 1953 that grabbed all the headlines.

Rangers had beaten Arbroath, Dundee, Morton, Celtic and Hearts to reach the final, but they went into the game without

Willie Woodburn. He hadn't played since picking up an injury three weeks earlier, so his place went to Duncan Stanners. Willie Pryde was another unfamiliar name in the half-back line too. Up front, Willie Paton wore the number nine jersey as Billy Simpson had been out of action since scoring in a 3-0 win over Hearts on 4 April.

Rangers hit the front after eight minutes, courtesy of a goal from John Prentice, but just short of the half hour Niven had to be withdrawn after bravely diving at the feet of Paddy Buckley. Reporting in the *Evening Times*, 'Olympic' reckoned Niven 'was out cold' and as he was helped off the pitch, George Young took over in goal. However, with his head swathed in bandages, Niven was back in goal at the start of the second half although the *Glasgow Herald* football correspondent opined that he was 'a pale, unhappy looking young man'. But if he was, it certainly didn't affect his game as he produced two fine saves to deny Aberdeen victory after Harry Yorston had scored an equalising goal. The correspondent in the *Glasgow Herald* seemed to think that the efforts from Buckley and George Hamilton 'might have beaten a goalkeeper who had no suffered an injury' but they didn't beat George Niven. Rangers won the replay 1-0.

A 3-1 defeat against Partick Thistle meant that Niven didn't add a Glasgow Cup medal to his collection, but he would make up for that in the early weeks of season 1953/54. Clyde were beaten 2-1 in the opening round, and after a 1-1 draw at Ibrox, Niven shut out Celtic in the semi-finals. A double from Paton and goals from Grierson and Prentice secured a 4-0 victory, and George also kept the Third Lanark attack at bay in the final, Rangers winning 3-0 at Hampden Park.

Niven continued in goal as the competitive action got underway. He featured in the nine League Cup ties played, and also the opening eight league matches. But in what would be Bill Struth's last season in charge, Rangers lost 2-0 to Partick Thistle in the semis of the League Cup and won just three of those eight league fixtures.

But after Rangers hammered Hamilton 8-1 at Ibrox in November 1953, Niven picked up an injury which meant a recall from the wilderness for Bobby Brown. And Brown would keep his place in the team until February when he once again came a cropper, at Tynecastle.

The match was drawn 3-3 and Brown was beaten by a 35-yard shot from Jimmy Wardhaugh. The match report in the *Glasgow Herald* stated that 'Brown misjudged his dive and then had to suffer the ignominy of being pilloried for his mistake by [George] Young and [Willie] Woodburn.' However, later in the piece the reporter reckoned that Brown 'was Rangers' best player'. Nonetheless, Brown was dropped, and Niven was recalled the following weekend as Rangers drew 0-0 with Third Lanark in the third round of the Scottish Cup.

Niven retained the jersey for the next four matches which included an epic 4-4 draw with Third Lanark in the third-round replay and a clean sheet when Berwick Rangers were beaten 4-0 in the last eight of the competition. But that tie, played on 13 March, would be Niven's last appearance until he played in a 1-0 win over Celtic in the Charity Cup on 1 May. He picked up an injury that required his hand to be encased in plaster, so Brown once again stepped into the breach.

Brown would be beaten 18 times in the ten matches he played until Niven was fit again. Four were conceded against Falkirk in a 4-3 defeat at Brockville, and nine in two matches against Aberdeen. Those matches came within seven days of each other, a 6-0 thrashing in the semi-finals of the Scottish Cup and a 3-1 defeat at Ibrox in the league.

Overall, it was a wretched season for Rangers. They couldn't muster any kind of consistent run of positive results, and between

23 January and 26 April, Struth's side won only four of the 13 league matches played. The fact that the manager couldn't select a settled defence due to injuries to Niven, Young and Woodburn was undoubtedly a factor.

Niven's return to the fold couldn't help secure some silverware to end the season on a high. Missing Little, McColl and Woodburn, Rangers were beaten 1-0 by Third Lanark in the final of the Charity Cup. It was a sad way to draw to a close the silver-laden 34 years that Bill Struth enjoyed at the helm.

On 8 May, Niven was part of the travelling party that boarded the *Empress of Scotland* bound for Montreal in Canada. After a crossing that was described as 'rough', Rangers arrived a week after they left Scotland. They kicked off what would be a nine-match tour the following day, beating Chelsea 1-0. That would be the first of three encounters with the Stamford Bridge side, and honours ended even. Chelsea won 4-1 in Toronto before a 0-0 stalemate in New York concluded the tour. George Niven played in all nine matches, keeping seven clean sheets. The hat-trick scored by Chelsea's Roy Bentley accounted for three of the five goals Niven conceded.

Upon their return from Canada, Scot Symon was announced as the new Rangers manager. His first match in charge was a thumping 5-0 win over Stirling Albion in the League Cup. George Niven kept a clean sheet, Billy Simpson scored a hat-trick, and Rangers chalked up four wins from their first six league matches. Stirling Albion were once again subjected to a hammering – four goals from Willie Gardiner helping Rangers to a 6-2 win – and a 5-2 win over Partick Thistle went a long way to avenging the loss to Thistle in the final of the Glasgow Cup. But it was another early season joust with Stirling Albion that will be forever etched in the annals of Scottish Football history.

For Rangers it would be a routine 2-0 win, but with a minute remaining, their talismanic centre-half Willie Woodburn was ordered off. He is said to have retaliated after locking legs with Stirling's inside-left, Paterson. He had been sent off against the same side almost a year earlier, and although that was just the third ordering off of his career, the SFA had warned that a 'very serious view will be taken of any subsequent action'. For 'very serious' read 'draconian'. An SFA Referee Committee met on 14 September and decided to ban Woodburn *sine die* (without limit of time). His list of offences were a severe censure and warning in September 1948, a three-week suspension in April 1953, and a six-week ban in October 1953.

Woodburn knew what fate lay ahead of him. After making what would be his final appearance for Rangers in a 1-1 draw against Hibernian, he told Alan Breck of the *Evening Times* that he expected 'this will be the last match I will play in a very long time.' He added that he 'had no right to retaliate' and that he had 'lost his temper'. However, all things considered, it was an extremely harsh call from the governing body.

Niven was the custodian for the infamous match, but while George McKenzie and Duncan Stanners stepped in to replace Woodburn, George would succumb to injury once again. He missed out when Rangers played the British Army at Ibrox in a floodlit friendly. Bobby Brown, who the club had said they were open to offers for, deputised and did so again when Niven's comeback was aborted after a 3-0 win against Falkirk in mid-November. But Niven came back in for a dramatic 4-3 win over Hearts at Tynecastle and missed just one of the last 17 league games. And he was to end the season with a winners' medal, playing his part in a 3-1 win over Queen's Park in the final of the Charity Cup.

Over the next couple of seasons, Niven didn't miss many games. In season 1955/56, Rangers claimed a first league title in three years, and Niven missed only three matches. He would concede a mere 26 goals in 31 appearances, keeping 14 clean sheets. Bobby

Brown once again stepped in when Niven missed out in the league, but when he wasn't available to face Third Lanark in the Charity Cup on 5 May 1956, it was a fresh face that took his place.

William Ritchie's path to Ibrox came via West Calder High School, Addiewell Hearts and Bathgate Thistle. He had played for the latter while learning his trade as a joiner and had come to the attention of Bill Struth when he deputised for his Bathgate team-mate John Neill in a third-team match. Neill, who had signed provisional forms for Rangers, wasn't available, so Ritchie stepped in. His performance impressed Mr Struth, and he signed for Rangers on 12 August 1954. And for the remainder of Niven's time at Ibrox, he and Ritchie would vie for the goalkeeper's jersey, with Ritchie eventually supplanting his rival as the nation swung into the 1960s.

Scot Symon's second season in charge saw the league title return to Ibrox. After an indifferent start that yielded one win, four draws and one defeat from the opening six league matches, Symon's side were unbeaten from 5 November 1955 until 9 April 1956. Custodian for all but three of those matches was George Niven. During the 23-match unbeaten run, Niven kept 13 clean sheets and conceded only 12 goals.

Success in the cup competitions would prove elusive, though. Aberdeen won 2-1 in the semi-finals of the League Cup, Hearts won 4-0 at Tynecastle in the last eight of the Scottish Cup, and Niven was beaten five times when Celtic clinched the Glasgow Cup in a replayed final.

But winning the Division One title allowed George Niven to make history in season 1956/57. This would be the first time a Rangers side entered European competition, and when they drew OGC Nice in the second round of the European Champions Cup, Niven would become the first goalkeeper to represent the club at that level. During his time at Ibrox, he would play in 15 European matches, including both legs of the semi-final of the European Cup in season 1959/60. He was beaten 12 times by an Eintracht Frankfurt side that would go on to lose 7-3 to Real Madrid in the final at Hampden.

The league title was retained in 1956/57. In a tight race with Hearts, Niven was an ever-present, Rangers ending up two points better off than their Edinburgh rivals. The Glasgow Cup would join the league trophy in the Ibrox Trophy Room, but a 4-0 defeat at the hands of Clyde meant the Charity Cup won in season 1956/57 was surrendered.

Hearts were now emerging as the principal challengers for the league, and they would claim the crown by a margin of 13 points in season 1957/58. That was a blow but did not resonate nearly as much as the 7-1 defeat suffered at the hands of Celtic in the League Cup Final. The phrase 'What's the score? Seven past Niven' was promptly coined, but Niven has never been regarded as the scapegoat for the debacle. That fate befell the young centre-back, John Valentine, who never played for the first team again.

It took Rangers some time to recover from the Hampden hammering. Niven kept his place for the next three league matches, but two of them were lost, both at Ibrox. Hearts won 3-2 and Kilmarnock edged a seven-goal thriller two weeks later. Sandwiched in between was a 4-2 league win over Queen's Park and a 6-3 victory over Partick Thistle in the Glasgow Cup, but Niven had now conceded 19 goals in just five games. He lost his place to Ritchie and would only feature in a further three games for the remainder of the season.

But that wasn't the end of the line for Niven. With Billy Ritchie unavailable due to National Service in Cyprus, George was an ever-present in season 1958/59 as Rangers reclaimed the league title. And in season 1959/60, he missed only one league match, a 2-1 win over Raith Rovers on 26 March 1960. That was due to a back injury that was also to count him out of the Scottish Cup semi-final replay against Celtic and the Scotland team to play England at Wembley.

Despite playing regularly for Rangers, caps for the Scotland national team were not forthcoming for Niven. He was selected seven times for the Scottish League, winning the first of them on 9 September 1953 in a 4-0 win over the Irish League at Ibrox. But Niven was never handed the yellow jersey for Scotland.

He looked set to win his first cap against England in April 1960, but the back injury denied him his opportunity. Celtic's Frank Haffey took his place, and while Niven may have been disappointed to miss out, the blow may have been cushioned when he heard that his replacement had been beaten nine times!

It would be another fine goalkeeper from that era, Tottenham Hotspur's Bill Brown, that would also keep Niven out of the team when the national team went on a post-season tour, playing matches against Austria, Hungary and Turkey. Although Brown conceded 11 goals across the three matches, Niven was not called upon.

Back at Ibrox, Niven recovered from injury to play his part as Rangers added the Scottish Cup and Charity Cup to the Glasgow Cup that had been won earlier in the season.

Season 1960/61 was the last season when Niven got regular game time. He started the opening match of the season – a 3-1 win over Partick Thistle in the League Cup – and also played when Rangers lost out 4-2 to Celtic in the opening round of the Glasgow Cup. But Scot Symon left him out for the next match, a 2-1 defeat against Third Lanark, a decision that mystified Gair Henderson of the *Evening Times* who reckoned Niven had been one of Rangers' better players in the games played.

Niven would not play for the first XI again until November. But when Billy Ritchie sustained a bad ankle injury seven minutes into a 3-1 win over Hearts at Tynecastle, Niven was called for. He would keep his place for the next 29 games Rangers contested.

That sequence of fixtures included the League Cup Final against Kilmarnock at Hampden that Rangers won by two goals to nil.

Rangers won the league title and reached the final of the inaugural European Cup Winners' Cup competition in season 1960/61, but by the time the league was clinched with a 7-3 win over Ayr United and Fiorentina edged the Light Blues 4-1 on aggregate, Billy Ritchie was back in goal. Niven's last match of the season was a 4-3 defeat at the hands of Clyde in the opening round of the Charity Cup.

That wasn't just Niven's last match of the season, it was his last match in a Rangers jersey. Billy Ritchie played in all bar one of the matches in season 1961/62, and in the one he missed, a 4-1 loss to Third Lanark in the last four of the Glasgow Cup in May 1962, Norrie Martin deputised. By then George Niven had left Rangers. In February 1962, he moved across Glasgow to join Partick Thistle.

Thistle were managed by the former Rangers centre-forward Willie Thornton, and Niven would go on to make 257 appearances for the Jags. He made the last of those on 29 July 1968 in a pre-season friendly against Blackpool, a few weeks after his 39th birthday.

In three of his six full seasons at Firhill, 1962/63, 1963/64 and 1967/68, Niven was ever-present in the league. In the last of those seasons, he saved a John Greig penalty after 61 minutes of a 5-2 win for Rangers on New Year's Day 1968.

After he retired from playing, Niven continued to pursue his business interests. Alongside former team-mate George Young, he had run a successful coffee bar in Renfield Street in Glasgow's city centre before running a bookmaker's and a pub back in Fife, the latter with his wife, Nessie.

The Niven's moved north in the mid-1970s, George working on the upgraded A9 and then British Rail. He even found time to play football again, playing for the local amateur side, Carrbridge Welfare. However, according to his obituary in *The Scotsman*,

Niven's stopgap appearance resulted in a fine for Welfare as the wrong forms had been filled out!

George Niven made 400 appearances for Rangers and kept 138 clean sheets. He won five league titles, two Scottish Cups, one League Cup, three Glasgow Cups and three Charity Cups.

A humble man, Niven lived in Dulnain Bridge, a village in Strathspey, where he never boasted about what he had achieved as a footballer. He was diagnosed with lung cancer in 2006, a disease he battled bravely until he passed away on 17 July 2008 at the age of 79.

* * *

From season 1961/62 to season 1965/66, Billy Ritchie was the undisputed number one at Ibrox. Regarded as the quiet man of the dressing room, Ritchie was a vital link in the chain that Scot Symon was building. Indeed, his name is inextricably linked with the XI that trips off the tongue for supporters from that era (although they actually only took to the field as a collective on five occasions):

> Ritchie, Shearer, Caldow, Greig, McKinnon, Baxter, Henderson, McMillan, Millar, Brand and Wilson.

In the second leg of the European Cup Winners' Cup Final against Wolverhampton Wanderers at Molineux in April 1961, Ritchie was quite outstanding. Rangers led 2-0 after the first leg at Ibrox, and two minutes shy of the interval Alex Scott scored to increase their advantage. But teams are said to be at their most vulnerable when they have just scored, and the home side responded by mounting an immediate attack on Ritchie's goal. Writing in the *Evening Times*, Gair Henderson takes up the story:

> But this [Scott's goal] was not the climax of the first-half drama in the mud. That came 30 seconds later when

> the furious Wolves hurled themselves upon the Rangers defence. The defenders were swept away as the human avalanche came through, and when the ball arrived at the feet of left-half [Ron] Flowers, 25 yards out, he hit the most vicious shot I have seen in years. Ritchie looked beaten all the way but by some miracle of acrobatics, he made a flying dive to his left, got both hands to the ball and turned it past the junction of his post and crossbar.

It was a defining moment for Ritchie. Regarded as being consistent and reliable, he was a very good shot stopper, he also read the game very well and was blessed with sound positional sense and anticipation. To illustrate that consistency and reliability, Ritchie missed only 16 of the next 292 matches Rangers played at home and abroad after the Wolves match. In that time frame, he picked up two league titles, four Scottish Cups and three League Cups. Ritchie was also part of the sides that reached the quarter-final of the European Cup twice.

Rangers completed the second clean sweep of the major domestic honours in season 1963/64, and Ritchie played in all 50 league and cup matches contested. In the league, 21 goals were conceded in 34 matches and 14 clean sheets were registered. Five of them were in succession between 14 September and 30 October. A further seven shutouts were chalked up in the cup competitions, and when you add the 11 times Ritchie was beaten to the 21 in the league, he and his defence were only breached 32 times in that half century of matches. As much as the forward line of Henderson, McMillan, Millar, Brand and Wilson and the brilliant Jim Baxter are rightly lauded for their contribution, the input from Ritchie and his defence cannot be underestimated.

Season 1965/66 would be the last campaign when Ritchie was the Rangers number one. He started the following season in goal, playing in the nine League Cup ties and the first six league games. He also played in a heavy 4-0 defeat against Celtic in the Glasgow Cup. But his outing against Aberdeen in the League Cup semi-final on 19 October 1966 would be his last for Rangers.

The match ended 2-2 after extra time, and reports suggested that Ritchie didn't have the best of games. Under the subheading 'Ritchie's Mistakes', Raymond Jacobs, writing in the *Glasgow Herald*, said:

> Ritchie, unlike [Aberdeen goalkeeper Bobby] Clark, had throughout not looked safe in his judgement and catching, and he it was who was substantially to blame for Aberdeen's second equalising goal.
>
> Whyte pitched a high ball from 40 yards out towards the far post, and there [Ally] Shewan outjumped Ritchie's fist and headed home.

It was a somewhat unfitting end to a glittering Rangers career for Ritchie. On 11 November 1967, he signed for Partick Thistle who were managed by Willie Thornton. He had to wait until the following July to make his Jags debut, a 3-3 draw against Bury in a pre-season friendly. Ironically, the man he took over from in goal was George Niven.

Ritchie would make 79 appearances for Thistle, the last of which was a 4-1 league defeat against Morton on 14 April 1970. He joined Motherwell a few months later, and he would make a total of 29 appearances for the Fir Park side. In January 1972, Ritchie broke his leg in a match against St Johnstone after he fell awkwardly shortly before half-time.

Ritchie also had a coaching role with Motherwell, but he swapped Fir Park for Stair Park in 1976 when he signed for his last club, Stranraer. When he retired, he took on a role as a PE instructor at Motherwell College and remained there for the next 30 years.

Billy Ritchie made 369 appearances for Rangers, keeping 125 clean sheets. He passed away on 11 March 2016 at the age of 79.

* * *

By the time Ritchie had joined Partick, Neil 'Norrie' Martin had emerged as his successor. Remarkably, Martin had been on the books at Ibrox since the late 1950s, but such was the form of Niven and Ritchie, this was his first real opportunity for a run in the first XI.

Born in Ladybank on 7 May 1939, Martin and his family had moved to Prestwick in Ayrshire in the 1950s when his father took over the Towans Hotel, a former mansion house that was said to have been designed by a close associate of Charles Rennie Mackintosh. Martin initially played football for Dalry Thistle before making the step up to the senior game with Hamilton Accies in 1957. He played once for the Douglas Park side before Scot Symon brought him to Rangers in 1958.

Ostensibly, Martin was third in line behind Niven and Ritchie, but with Ritchie in Cyprus on National Service and Niven injured ahead of a League Cup tie against Hearts at Tynecastle on 23 August 1958, Martin was given an early opportunity to impress. Alas, the match would sum up how luckless Martin would be during his 12 years as a Rangers player.

Willie Bauld gave Hearts the lead, but Johnny Hubbard did what Johnny Hubbard usually did when Rangers were awarded a penalty kick in the era: he found the net. Parity was restored, but shortly afterwards, with 25 minutes left to play, Martin came off worst in a shoulder-to-shoulder challenge with Bauld. He received a lengthy spell of treatment from physio Dave Kinnear but couldn't continue. Bobby Shearer took over in goal and repelled all that Hearts threw at him until Jimmy Milne scored in stoppage time.

An X-ray taken at the Royal Infirmary a couple of days later confirmed that Martin had fractured his shoulder. He would recover, but it would be 20 December 1960 before Martin played for the first team again. That was in a 2-0 win over the British Army at Ibrox. Martin also played in a 4-1 defeat against Third Lanark in the semi-final of the Glasgow Cup in season 1961/62.

Martin's first league appearance for the club saw him at the centre of controversy. Rangers were in the midst of a glut of fixtures. They had drawn 1-1 with Celtic in the Scottish Cup Final on 4 May, then beaten Airdrie 2-0 two days later. A 1-0 win over Third Lanark followed on 11 May.

Remarkably, with the replay with Celtic set for 15 May, Rangers were asked to play Kilmarnock two days beforehand. Symon's side were cantering towards the title, so the manager elected to rest players ahead of the Celtic match. Martin was one of six 'reserve' players drafted in – Willie Hunter, Jim Forrest, Craig Watson and veterans Harold Davis and Doug Baillie were the others – and it looked like Rangers would be asked to explain themselves to the management committee. If their explanation wasn't satisfactory then a fine was the most likely outcome. In the end, Rangers lost 1-0 at Rugby Park, but, restored to 'full strength', convincingly defeated Celtic 3-0 to lift the Scottish Cup.

Martin was back in the reserves for all of season 1963/64, and it would be September 1964 before he would be elevated to the first team again. He was drafted in to face Partick Thistle in a league match at Ibrox, and he featured in the three matches that followed. The last of those was a damaging 4-1 defeat against Dundee at Dens Park.

Rangers hadn't registered a league win by that point – the opening four matches had yielded two draws and two defeats – but when they ended that run with a thumping 9-2 win over Airdrie, Billy Ritchie was back in goal. For the record, hat-tricks were scored in that game by Jim Forrest and Ralph Brand. The brilliant Baxter also netted from the penalty spot.

It's fair to say that season 1964/65 was an indifferent one for Rangers. They should have won the European Cup – Baxter's leg break in Vienna proving decisive – but at home, although the League Cup was won, Symon's side finished fifth in the league table, six points behind Kilmarnock, who pipped Hearts to the title on goal average on a dramatic final day.

In what would be Rangers' final game against Third Lanark at Cathkin Park, Norrie Martin kept a clean sheet as Rangers ended the campaign with a 1-0 win. Martin had come back into the side at the end of March, replacing an unfit Ritchie for a 1-0 defeat at home to Morton. He played in the six league matches that followed and the 2-1 defeat against Celtic in the opening round of the Glasgow Cup.

The latter would prove to be another eventful night for Martin. He injured his left hand saving a shot from John Hughes, and bandaged up, he ended up playing at right-back with Davie Provan taking over in goal. Although Davie Wilson was magnificent when the pack was reshuffled and he moved to left-back, Celtic scored twice in the last 15 minutes to win the game.

Clearly, Martin impressed the Rangers hierarchy with his performances in the latter part of the season, for he was handed the goalkeeper's jersey when the action got underway at the start of season 1965/66. But once more luck would desert him.

Martin was in goal for the opening three League Cup matches, but in the last of them, a trip to Pittodrie to face Aberdeen on 21 August, he suffered a fractured skull. After 65 minutes, Martin collided with Ernie Winchester and had to be stretchered off the field. The following Monday, the *Glasgow Herald* related that after reporting to Ayr County hospital for an examination on the Sunday, Martin was sent to Killearn Hospital once the nature of his injury had been established. Killearn was one of seven Emergency Hospital Service facilities for military casualties during World War II.

As he seemed to do, Martin bounced back from the setback. He made his first-team comeback against Dundee United at Tannadice on 21 March 1966, but a second-half goal from Billy Hainey earned United a 1-0 win. It would prove to be a costly defeat for Rangers. With Billy Ritchie back in goal, they would win each of their last seven league matches but were pipped for the title by Celtic by two points.

Martin finally nailed down a regular slot in the Rangers first team in season 1966/67, yet it would be a season that would promise so much but deliver nothing.

Martin made 28 league appearances, and among them was a 3-2 defeat against Dunfermline at Ibrox when he was beaten twice by a certain Alex Ferguson. Rangers would only drop two points in their next 16 league matches, and with five games remaining, they were two points behind Celtic. Both sides were showing remarkable consistency, with Martin and his defence only conceding 13 goals in that 16-match run. And three of them had come in one match, a thrilling 4-3 home win over St Johnstone.

But Rangers would win only one of their final five matches. On the same day that Celtic dropped a point at Clyde, Rangers lost 1-0 at home to Dunfermline. Both teams won the following weekend, but Symon's side drew each of their last three games and threw away an opportunity to put pressure on Celtic. With Jock Stein's side not in league action, Rangers would have gone top with victories in their matches at home against Clyde and away at Dundee but drew both 1-1. Celtic then came to Ibrox with a game in hand and a one-point advantage. A 2-2 draw secured the title for them.

But season 1966/67 isn't remembered for tossing away the title. Instead, memories are of two other matches that season, and both sum up the misfortune Norrie Martin suffered at Rangers.

On 28 January, Martin was in the Rangers side that travelled to face Berwick Rangers in the Scottish Cup. At the end of the 90 minutes, he had an unwanted place in the club's history, Rangers suffering a humiliating 1-0 defeat. Sammy Reid scored the goal that rocked Scottish football, after 32 minutes, but in the inevitable inquest that followed, Martin and his defence were kept out of the firing line. Jim Forrest and George McLean were made the scapegoats, and neither played a first-team game for the club again. It would prove to be a costly decision, one that without question had a detrimental effect on Rangers winning the European Cup Winners' Cup.

Martin had made his European debut for the club against Borussia Dortmund at Ibrox back in November and had a marvellous match in the return leg. Rangers won 2-1 at Ibrox, but not many fancied them to progress against a side that had beaten Liverpool to win the trophy a year earlier. And Rangers were dealt an early blow in Dortmund when Bobby Watson sustained a broken ankle; any hope of progression had seemingly evaporated.

With no substitutes in European competition at that time, Rangers, with their backs to the wall, had to see out the rest of the match with ten men. A tall order, but a fine save from Martin shortly after Watson's injury would be the first of many defiant ripostes from Rangers. Horst Trimhold set his sights from ten yards and lashed a shot towards goal. Gair Henderson of the *Evening Times* reckoned that 'the speed of light was dawdling compared to the speed of this drive', but Martin dived across his goal, clenched his fists and made a vital save.

Henderson would later single Martin out for praise. He opined that 'in goal, Martin was a marvel. He knew that to keep his place in the team he had to have an outstanding match. He had more than that. When the defensive set-up in front of him was cracked, he made one superb save after another, even after he was injured in a suicide dive at the feet of [Sigi] Held.'

Martin would also feature in the quarter-final win over Real Zaragoza and kept clean sheets in both legs as Slavia Sofia were beaten in the last four. That took Rangers through to the final against Bayern Munich where the decisions to jettison Forrest and McLean and not select Alex Willoughby and Davie Wilson came back to haunt Rangers.

Reports suggested that Symon's side had around 75 per cent of the play against a defensive Bayern, but their impotency in front of goal cost them the silverware. Roger Hynd, a half-back who was drafted in to play at centre-forward, passed up their best opportunity after 33 minutes, firing in a weak shot from six yards that Sepp Maier saved.

Martin was largely untroubled throughout the match but was beaten four minutes from the end of extra time. A high ball was played forward towards the Rangers penalty area. Reports suggest that it was one of those deliveries that leaves a goalkeeper in a dilemma – should he come off his line and try and claim the ball or stay put? Martin elected for the former, but Franz Roth nipped in ahead of him and lobbed the ball over his head with the outside of his right boot. Once again luck deserted Norrie Martin.

However, as much as it had been a bitterly disappointing season for Rangers, Martin had acquitted himself well, yet he only featured in four competitive matches in season 1967/68. The goalkeeping jersey was handed to Erik Sorensen, a Danish international goalkeeper who had been recruited from Morton.

Born in Odense on 22 January 1940, Erik Lykke Sorensen had started his career as an amateur with Boldklubben 1913. He performed to a high standard and was capped at U21 and U23 level for Denmark before he was rewarded with his first cap for Denmark against Albania on 29 June 1963. He kept a clean sheet too, the Danes winning 4-0.

Sorensen would play his part as Denmark qualified for the 1964 European Championships, but when he elected to turn professional, he was barred from playing for his country in the tournament. At that time, the Danes were very much amateur only, but Sorensen would eventually get back into the team during his second spell with Morton. Between 12 May 1971 and 30 June 1971, he played five times for his country. One of those matches was against Scotland in Copenhagen. Denmark won 1-0, their goal being scored by Finn Laudrup, the father of another of Rangers' Danish imports, Brian Laudrup.

Denmark reached the last four of the 1964 Euros, but by then Erik Sorensen was in Scotland. Tempted to join Morton by the visionary Haldane (Hal) Stewart, he was badged somewhat mysteriously as 'The Man in Black' by Stewart ahead of a trial match he would play in against Third Lanark on 23 March 1964. That was because he played clad top to toe in black, and his arrival in Greenock kicked off a 'Viking Invasion'. He would later be joined by Kai Johansen, Jorn Sorensen, Carl Bertelsen, and Flemming Nielsen. Kai and Jorn would later follow the path that Erik took, by joining Rangers too.

When Sorensen signed for Morton in March 1964, his new side were destined for the top flight. He made his league debut against Alloa Athletic on 28 March, the match ending in a 2-2 draw. The point dropped mattered little, though. Morton had won 29 of their first 33 league games and were top of Division Two, 12 points clear of second-placed Clyde.

The match against Alloa would be the first of 102 league games Sorensen would play for Morton in his first spell. One of the most memorable came on 30 March 1965 – a 1-0 win over Rangers at

Ibrox – but a visit to Parkhead on Christmas Day 1965 didn't end so happily, Jock Stein's side thumping eight goals past the Danish goalkeeper. Celtic scored seven times in the opening 45 minutes, and by the end of the campaign, Morton had shipped 84 goals. They ended up finishing second bottom, their relegation to Division Two confirmed when they lost 2-0 at home to Celtic in their final league game.

Sorensen would spend one more season at Cappielow, helping Morton win the Division Two title in season 1966/67. In that campaign, Morton set a new record for least goals conceded (20 in 38 games), while Sorensen chalked up the most shutouts with 21.

In the summer of 1967, he signed for Rangers for a fee of £25,000. He made his first-team debut on 5 August in a 3-0 defeat against Arsenal at Highbury, and three days later he was beaten three times again in a 5-3 win over Eintracht Frankfurt at Ibrox. Alex Ferguson, signed for a record fee of £65,000, scored a hat-trick for Rangers.

Sorensen, who had to dispense of his black jersey and don the traditional yellow one that Rangers keepers tended to wear, would be the number one goalkeeper at Rangers in season 1967/68. He appeared in all but five of the 68 first-team matches Rangers played. He missed three league games in October after having five stitches inserted in a gashed knee, an injury he had sustained in a car accident, and he was also absent when Rangers drew 3-3 at Cappielow in April due to the effects of a heavy cold. He also missed out on one of the post-season tour matches in Scandinavia.

The season didn't start well for Rangers, though. Three wins, two draws and a defeat were not enough to qualify from their League Cup section, all of which heaped more pressure onto the shoulders of Scot Symon. But when the league action got underway, the Light Blues found some momentum. Six of the first eight matches were won, with the other two drawn. But sensationally after the last of those draws – a 0-0 stalemate at home to Dunfermline Athletic – Symon was relieved of his managerial duties and replaced by David White.

Since taking over from Bill Struth in 1954, Symon had led Rangers to two European finals, six league titles, five Scottish Cups, four League Cups, three Glasgow Cups and three Charity Cups. In addition, he had built one of the most celebrated teams in the club's history. However, the breaking up of that side in 1965 coincided with Jock Stein's arrival as manager at Parkhead. The success Stein enjoyed put Symon under pressure, and the barren season of 1966/67 coupled with the humiliating loss to Berwick Rangers would be the tipping point. Nonetheless, the way he was treated was extremely shabby. Chairman John Lawrence sent one of his business associates, Alex McBain, to inform Symon he had been dismissed. Given the service Symon had given the club as player and manager, he should have been afforded more courtesy and respect than he received.

The managerial shakeup didn't derail Rangers. Twenty-two of the next 25 matches were won, which meant with one game to go, Rangers had won 28 and drawn five of their 33 league games. Title in the bag surely? Alas, no. Celtic had matched them stride for stride, their record showing 29 wins, three draws and one defeat. That defeat had come at Ibrox back in September, Sorensen's fellow Scandinavian, Orjan Persson, scoring the only goal of the game.

That was Sorensen's third Old Firm encounter. He had made a couple of notable saves in his first, a 1-1 draw at Ibrox in the League Cup – then conceded three goals in his second, a 3-1 reverse at Parkhead, also in the League Cup. In that encounter, Rangers led 1-0 with 14 minutes to play. At that point, Kai Johansen struck the underside of the crossbar with a penalty kick. A goal would surely have secured victory, but instead the home side scored three times in the closing stages.

Sorensen also featured in each of the six ties Rangers played in the Inter-Cities Fairs Cup. He made his European debut against Dynamo Dresden on 20 September, and the press were fulsome in their praise of his performance. Reflecting on the game, which ended in a 1-1 draw, Peter Hendry of the *Evening Times* said:

> Goalkeeper Eric [sic] Sorensen was the saviour of his side in the Heinz Steyer Stadium. While other more prominent Rangers players were toppled from their high estate, Sorensen gave a display which nearly broke the heart of Dresden and certainly gave the few Scots in the stadium their only bright moments.

Hendry went on to say that three of the saves made by the Dane were in the 'out-of-this-world category' before summing up by saying that 'the rest of his work was simply brilliant'.

Goals from Andy Penman and John Greig saw Rangers through in the second leg before Cologne were beaten 4-3 on aggregate in the second round. Unfortunately, Don Revie's Leeds United proved too strong in the last eight, winning 2-0 at Elland Road after a goalless first leg at Ibrox.

Back to the last-day drama. With Celtic inactive since their scheduled opponents, Dunfermline, were facing Hearts in the Scottish Cup Final, Rangers had an opportunity to pile on the pressure. A win over Aberdeen at Ibrox would have put them two points in front, although Celtic did have the upper hand when it came to goal average (4.73 to 2.94).

Ahead of the Aberdeen game, Rangers were the only unbeaten team in the UK. But 90 minutes later, that record was in tatters, a 3-2 defeat gift-wrapping the title for Celtic. Writing in the *Glasgow Herald*, Glyn Edwards was particularly scathing about Sorensen's performance:

> Like the rest of his colleagues, Sorensen made mistakes, but whereas those of the outfield players could be rectified, his were punished almost without exception. He was to some extent responsible for the first two goals, was fortunate on another that Greig was behind him when he completely missed Shewan's free-kick just before the interval, and generally caused hearts to flutter any time he was called upon to cut out a cross, be it high or low.

A damning verdict indeed, and Davie White clearly agreed. This would be the last time that Sorensen would play a league game for Rangers. In fact, he only made a further five appearances for the club, the last of which was a 3-1 defeat against Tottenham Hotspur in a pre-season friendly at White Hart Lane on 31 July 1968. It would be another match littered with errors from the Dane. He failed to deal with two corner kicks from Jimmy Greaves, the upshot of which was two goals from Peter Collins. Sorensen was substituted at half-time.

Not surprisingly, Davie White elected to change his goalkeeper when the competitive action for season 1968/69 got underway. Sorensen would be supplanted by Norrie Martin, with another goalkeeper, Gerry Neef, providing the backup. Remarkably, Sorensen had gone from number one to number three inside a year.

In season 1968/69, Norrie Martin made 55 appearances in total. He was his usual dependable self too, keeping 13 clean sheets in the opening 30 league fixtures. One of them was against Celtic at Ibrox on 2 January, John Greig's penalty giving the home side a 1-0 win. That completed the league double over Jock Stein's side – Martin playing his part in a 4-2 win at Parkhead earlier in the season – but points dropped against other sides would be decisive in the title race. For example, Martin was beaten six times in the two matches played against Kilmarnock – both were 3-3 draws – and St Johnstone, St

Mirren, Dundee United, Aberdeen, Dundee and Airdrie all scored victories over David White's side.

Rangers' cause wasn't helped either when their new £100,000 signing, Colin Stein, was banned for six weeks after an ordering off against Clyde. The absence of Stein, who had scored 13 league goals in 18 league appearances following his transfer from Hibernian, coincided with a run of form that saw the Light Blues win three, draw two and lose two. That equates to six points dropped and when you consider that Celtic's title-winning margin was five points, you can see just how significant that loss was.

Stein also missed the Scottish Cup Final against Celtic. Martin had played in each of the four ties that had taken Rangers to the Hampden showdown, wins over Hibernian, Hearts, Airdrie and Aberdeen. The latter match was arguably Rangers' best performance of the season, Willie Johnston scoring a hat-trick as the Dons were battered 6-1.

Martin was also chosen to keep goal in the final, but once again a major domestic honour would elude him. Alex Ferguson replaced the suspended Stein at centre-forward in what would be his last competitive game for the club. Although in the team to score goals, Ferguson was also tasked with marking Billy McNeill at set pieces. But the Celtic captain was afforded a free header from a corner kick in the second minute, and he duly punished Rangers by opening the scoring. It would be the first of a litany of errors in the opening half by the team in blue jerseys.

A minute shy of the interval, an errant pass from Orjan Persson was intercepted by George Connelly, and he released the ball to Bobby Lennox who had clear run in on goal. He beat Martin with ease, and within seconds it was 3-0. Martin tried to play a short pass to John Greig, but it caught the Rangers captain unawares. He was robbed by Connelly who proceeded to take the ball round Martin and despatch it into the net.

There was no way back for Rangers. Stevie Chalmers made it 4-0 with 14 minutes remaining, and Rangers had lost a Scottish Cup Final for the first time in 40 years.

Although battered and bruised, there was still an opportunity for Rangers to win a major honour in season 1968/69. Wins over Vojvodina Novi Sad, Dundalk, DWS Amsterdam and Athletic Bilbao took Rangers through to the semi-finals of the Inter-Cities Fairs Cup, the predecessor of what is now known as the Europa League. Newcastle United stood between David White's side and a place in the final.

Martin had played in each of the eight ties leading up to the Battle of Britain clash, but White chose Gerry Neef as his number one for both legs. Martin had been left out of the sides that had played out the two league matches that followed the cup final, and Neef obviously impressed the management team enough to retain his place. In the end, though, Rangers would be left to rue a missed penalty by Andy Penman in the goalless first leg at Ibrox. Newcastle won a second leg marred by crowd trouble by two goals to nil and went on to defeat Ujpesti Dosza in the final.

Norrie Martin would play only two more first-team games for Rangers. The first was a 3-1 league defeat at Easter Road on 11 October 1969 – Neef was ruled out after sustaining a hand wound in a Glasgow Cup win over Queen's Park – and his final appearance came on 16 December 1969 at Palmerston Park in a 5-2 friendly win over Queen of the South. He was released on a free transfer at the end of season 1969/70.

After short stints with East Fife, Queen of the South and Hamilton Accies, Martin announced his retirement, at which point he took over the running of the Towans Hotel. Tragically, it was destroyed by fire in 1996.

Norrie Martin must be one of the few players to have been on the books at Ibrox for over ten years to never win a major medal. He picked up numerous medals with the second XI – three Reserve League titles, three Second XI Cups and four Reserve League Cups – but major success proved elusive. He died at his home in Prestwick on 10 October 2013 just six weeks after he had been diagnosed with lung cancer. He made a total of 126 appearances for Rangers and kept 41 clean sheets.

Erik Sorensen's time at Rangers ended when he was transferred back to Morton in August 1970. He would initially provide back-up to another Dane, Leif Nielsen, but when Nielsen suffered a career-ending injury, Sorensen was elevated to number one once again, retaining that status until the start of season 1972/73. At that point, new signing Roy Baines took the gloves, which gave Sorensen the opportunity to focus on coaching goalkeepers while playing for the reserve team.

Across two spells, Sorensen made 262 appearances for Morton and recorded 68 shutouts. He was appointed Morton manager in February 1974, remaining in charge until August 1975. Under his guidance, Morton won just 15 of the 65 matches they contested.

After leaving Morton, Sorensen had a spell as assistant manager at St Mirren before he returned to Denmark. Now aged 82, Sorensen was said to still be coaching back in his homeland as recently as 2019. He made 54 appearances for Rangers, conceded 59 goals, and kept 15 clean sheets.

It would be another foreign goalkeeper that moved ahead of Sorensen in the pecking order at Ibrox in 1968.

Born on 30 October 1946 in Hausham, Germany, Gerhardt Neef was a policeman playing amateur football in Dusseldorf when the Aberdeen manager, Eddie Turnbull, brought him to Scotland for a trial in July 1968. The Dons were suitably impressed and were set to offer Neef a contract when Rangers stepped in and signed him instead.

With Norrie Martin back as number one, Neef spent much of his first season at Ibrox in the reserves. He would make only three league appearances, the first of them coming against Morton on 19 April 1969, reward for a series of impressive displays in the second XI.

Perhaps with a nod towards the next season, Neef was selected for each of the three matches Rangers played on a post-season tour that saw them play Tottenham Hotspur and Fiorentina in Toronto before facing *Lo Viola* again in New York.

The Spurs match saw Colin Stein score twice before he was sent off for the FOURTH time in season 1968/69. At the other end, Jimmy Greaves, who had previously netted goals against Rangers when the two sides met in the European Cup Winners' Cup in 1962, went one better than Stein, netting a hat-trick as the English side won 4-3.

Despite conceding eight goals across the three matches, Neef had done enough to convince Davie White that he should be number one for season 1969/70.

In his second appearance of the season, Neef picked up a Glasgow Cup winners' medal when Rangers defeated Partick Thistle 3-2, but nine days later, he was culpable when Celtic won 1-0 at Parkhead in a League Cup tie.

Drawn alongside Celtic, Airdrie and Raith Rovers, Rangers were in the driving seat going into the match at Parkhead. Three wins out of three including a 2-1 win over Celtic at Ibrox saw them top the section. But after 67 minutes of the match came what Gair Henderson of the *Evening Times* described as 'a moment of horror' for Neef.

Henderson reckoned that up until that point Neef had 'given the impression that he had washed his hands in glue' as his handling of crosses and shots had been assured. But when he tried to clutch Bobby Murdoch's free kick, he couldn't hold onto the ball, and when it slipped from his grasp, Tommy Gemmell headed in the only goal of the game.

The teams were now level at the top of Section 1, but when Rangers contrived to draw 3-3 at home to Raith three days later, Celtic edged to the top. The quest for a first major honour for the Light Blues since 1966 would be extended once again.

Neef redeemed himself for his Old Firm faux pas when the two sides met in the league at Ibrox in September. Although Rangers lost 1-0 against the ten-men visitors, Neef was said to have 'distinguished himself with several magnificent saves', and his performance showcased the exceptional agility that he had.

The loss to Celtic in the league seemed, however, to be a minor bump in the road. With Neef missing only one of the next 22 league games, Rangers won 16, drew four and lost two. One of the draws came at Parkhead on 3 January, a game in which Neef once again showed the good, bad and indifferent sides of his game.

The game ended in a no-score draw despite Billy McNeill finding the net a minute before half-time. However, referee John Paterson reckoned that Neef was impeded so ruled the goal out. In the second half, Celtic came close again when Neef got in a fankle when trying to clear a Bertie Auld corner kick; rather than clear the ball to safety, the German goalkeeper's attempted clearance struck the post. But moments later, Neef demonstrated great bravery when he came off his line to foil Bobby Murdoch. The resulting collision left Neef dazed, but his intervention undoubtedly helped secure a point for Rangers.

Neef's display may have been influenced by stories doing the rounds that the Rangers manager, Willie Waddell, was on the lookout for a new goalkeeper. Waddell, who had replaced Davie White at the helm when White was dismissed in the wake of a 6-2 aggregate hammering at the hands of Gornik Zabrze in the European Cup Winners' Cup, was reportedly interested in bringing the Aberdeen goalkeeper Bobby Clark to Ibrox. The move never materialised, but the writing was on the wall for Neef. He played a further ten games for the club in season 1969/70 before he lost his place to Peter McCloy in March. Among those games was a 3-1 defeat at Parkhead in the Scottish Cup quarter-finals.

It was a match that Jim Parkinson of the *Glasgow Herald* described as 'one of the most hateful confrontations between the Glasgow sides for years'. Although an own goal from Jim Craig gave Rangers the lead early on, Neef was the busier of the two goalkeepers, and when Alex MacDonald was ordered off after 62 minutes with the score tied at 1-1, the German had more work to do as Celtic laid siege to the Rangers goal. In one attack, he made a fine save from Bobby Lennox, but he was powerless when David Hay sent a searing shot into the net with four minutes left to play. Jimmy Johnstone's goal a couple of minutes later only served to rub salt into Rangers' wounds.

Incidentally, Neef and McCloy were not the only players to keep goal for Rangers in season 1969/70. On 19 January 1970, a Rangers XI featuring Jim Baxter, Orjan Persson and Sandy Jardine travelled to Methill to play East Fife in a friendly. In goal was Danny Stevenson. Rangers lost 1-0 – Colin Jackson scored an own goal – and Stevenson would eventually move to St Mirren without featuring for the first team again.

However, Stevenson, who is held in high regard by the St Mirren supporters and would also teach PE at Renfrew High, will always have a place in the Rangers history books for he was in the team that contested Jim Baxter's last-ever match for Rangers.

Baxter had been brought back to the club by Davie White at the start of the season, but it's fair to say that Slim Jim wasn't so slim anymore. He rolled back the years on a couple of occasions but had only featured once since Waddell had taken over. After pulling up in training and missing Waddell's first match in charge – a 2-1 win over Dundee United on 13 December – he had played in a 3-2 win against Aberdeen at Pittodrie but hadn't played since. With a Scottish Cup tie against Hibernian looming, it would appear that the East Fife match was his last chance to prove his fitness. Evidently, he didn't. He was released on a free transfer at the end of the season.

Having spent the most part of season 1969/70 as the Rangers number one, Gerry Neef actually found himself displaced, not by McCloy but by a youngster recruited from junior football for the early part of the following season. Neef started the first match of the pre-season tour of West Germany against Hamburg but was replaced ten minutes after the interval by a 20-year-old called Bobby Watson.

Watson had come from Ardrossan Winton Rovers, and according to Malcolm Munro of the *Evening Times*, he was 'fast and brave and imaginative' on his debut. Neef on the other hand blundered once more, conceding a cheap goal at his near post. It was, opined Munro, 'rank bad goalkeeping'.

Watson retained his place for the 1-1 draw against Kaiserslautern and also the 2-0 defeat against Spurs at White Hart Lane. And when the competitive action got underway with a League Cup tie at home to Dunfermline Athletic, it was Watson who kept goal. But just two days later, the promising Rangers career of Bobby Watson shuddered to a halt.

The Glasgow Cup had not been concluded in season 1969/70, so Rangers faced Celtic at Hampden in what was badged as that campaign's final on 10 August 1970. Watson made his Old Firm debut, but Celtic won 3-1 and the finger of blame of their second and third goals was pointed in the young goalkeeper's direction. Although he was perhaps deceived by the run of Lou Macari, he allowed Tommy Gemmell's cross to get past him and the ball hit the net via the inside of the post. And when Jimmy Quinn netted early in the second half, it was felt that Watson had been badly positioned.

Clearly Willie Waddell concurred. Watson was dropped for the League Cup tie against Motherwell at Fir Park, and when Peter McCloy was absent for three league matches in January 1971, Gerry Neef was called upon.

Tragically, the first of those matches was the league match against Celtic on 2 January 1971.

Neef hadn't been named in the original 18-man pool for the matches against Falkirk on New Year's Day and Celtic 24 hours later. But when Peter McCloy was injured in the match at Brockville, Neef was called in for the Old Firm match.

The match itself was pretty uneventful, but with 90 seconds remaining, Bobby Lennox shot for goal. Neef dived and managed to divert the ball onto the crossbar, but the rebound fell to Jimmy Johnstone, and he looked to have snatched the points for the visitors when he knocked the ball into the net. But there was time for one more attacking foray from Rangers and Colin Stein rose to restore parity.

Honours ended even, which seemed to hand the title advantage to Aberdeen, who led the race by four points albeit they had played one game more than Celtic. Rangers? They were sitting in third place, 12 points adrift of the Dons.

Very soon, though, it emerged that league placings mattered little; people were losing their lives as a crush barrier had collapsed on Stairway 13. In one of the worst disasters in British football history, 66 people went to a game of football and never returned home.

Willie Waddell was colossal in the aftermath. He made sure that the club were represented at all the funerals and pushed ahead with plans to redevelop Ibrox Stadium. It was his mission to ensure that this would never happen again. The Ibrox amphitheatre that is in place today is his legacy.

For a while, football seemed irrelevant. Yet just a fortnight later, Rangers played Dundee United at Ibrox. Neef was selected again, and he acquitted himself well in a match that ended in a 1-1 draw.

He would feature again a week later in a 2-1 win over Motherwell, but for the remainder of his time at Ibrox, opportunities to displace McCloy were rare.

Neef played in the third/fourth-place play-off in the Gothenburg Alliance Jubilee Tournament against Orgyte in July 1971 and in the Paisley Charity Cup against St Mirren in May 1972, but although he was on the bench for the European Cup Winners' Cup Final in Barcelona, that was the sum total of his first-team action that season. And in what would be his last campaign at Ibrox, 1972/73, he made what would be his last appearance for Rangers in a 2-1 in over Arbroath at Gayfield on 21 October 1972.

After leaving Rangers, Neef went back to Germany, where Hans Tilkowski, the West Germany goalkeeper in the 1966 World Cup Final, signed him for 1. FC Nuremberg. He would end his playing career there, but the Neef name would resonate again in Scotland when Gerry's daughter, Melanie, excelled as a 400-metre runner. Melanie would win the AAA championship in 1994 and 1995 and claim gold in the 1995 European Cup, clocking a time of 51.35 seconds in Villeneuve-d'Ascq, France.

Gerry Neef made 59 appearances for Rangers and kept 17 clean sheets. After battling against throat cancer, he passed away on 23 February 2010 at the age of 63.

Once more it seemed that the goalkeeping position at Ibrox was in a state of flux. Not since Billy Ritchie had the club had a consistent and reliable goalkeeper. All that was about to change, though, as the man that was number one at the start of the 1970s would go on to rack up a record number of post-war appearances over a 16-year Rangers career. His name was Peter McCloy.

Chapter 5

Triumph, Trebles and Tough Times

IT IS unlikely that any Rangers goalkeeper, current or future, will match the number of appearances Peter McCloy made for Rangers in the post-war era. After making his debut against Dunfermline Athletic on 14 March 1970, McCloy kept goal on 646 occasions.

He last pulled on the gloves for the first team in a friendly against Falkirk on 30 July 1986. In those 646 appearances, he conceded 640 goals and kept 249 clean sheets. Yet when people list the great goalkeepers, McCloy's name is rarely mentioned. But you don't make that many appearances for Rangers and remain in the first-team squad for 16 years unless you are of a high standard in the position you play.

Born in Girvan on 16 November 1946, McCloy would eventually follow in the footsteps of his father, James, and become a goalkeeper. McCloy senior had played for Petershill, Clyde, St Mirren, Bradford City and Swansea Town. He was beaten five times in the 1934 Scottish Cup Final when Rangers routed St Mirren 5-0.

'At school, I played outfield,' said McCloy. 'I would play two games on a Saturday – one for the school team and one for the youth club – and after that I went into amateur football at the age of 15. That was with Crosshill Thistle, but it was only then that I thought about becoming a goalkeeper.'

McCloy must have excelled when he did go in goal. He impressed scouts from Motherwell and signed for the Fir Park side on his 17th birthday. And just over a year later – on 28 November 1964 – McCloy made his first-team debut against Morton.

'I was part-time for my first year,' recalled McCloy. 'Bobby Ancell was the manager that signed me, but he left to take the Dundee job and Bobby Howitt took over. I was in and around the first team in season 1964/65, and I remember playing in the Summer Cup. All the teams in the First Division apart from Rangers and Celtic took part and we had Kilmarnock, who had just won the league, in our section.'

Motherwell topped that section, though, and that took them through to face Hibernian in the semi-finals.

McCloy recalled, 'We lost 2-0 at Easter Road, but beat them 6-2 at Fir Park the following Wednesday. That took us through to play Dundee United in the final. We beat them 3-1 at home on the Saturday, then lost 1-0 at Tannadice on the Wednesday night.'

McCloy turned in some impressive performances in the competition, and when he did likewise in season 1965/66, there were rumours that Liverpool manager, Bill Shankly, was interested in signing him. Nothing came of that, but McCloy did earn a call-up to the Scotland national team.

'I was brought in as backup to Bobby Ferguson for games against Brazil and Portugal,' said McCloy. 'They were both looking for games to prepare for the World Cup in England. I was only 19, but to get to watch Pelé up close and be in the same Scotland squad as the likes of Jim Baxter and Billy Bremner was really good for my confidence.'

During his time at Fir Park, McCloy would make 184 first-team appearances. A number of them were against Rangers, notably in season 1966/67 when Motherwell conceded ten goals in the two league fixtures the sides played. Rangers won 5-1 at Ibrox in

November and repeated the scoreline at Fir Park in March. Jim Forrest scored six of the ten goals.

The following season would be a difficult one for Motherwell. They won only six of their 34 league games and were relegated to Division Two when they finished second bottom of the Division One table. But in the midst of that, McCloy found himself selected for the Scottish League representative squad.

He had won his first Scottish League cap on 7 September 1966, keeping a clean sheet in a 6-0 hammering of the League of Ireland at Celtic Park. And a year later he was chosen again when the Scots defeated the Irish League 2-0 at Windsor Park. A certain Alex Ferguson donned the number nine jersey for the Scottish League, while John Greig played at left-half. Ferguson and Greig were both on the scoresheet that evening.

McCloy would add two more league caps to his collection. He played in a 2-0 defeat against the English League at Ayresome Park on 20 March 1968, and he faced the English League again on 27 March 1973. That match ended 2-2, John Duncan scoring twice for the Scots. As an illustration of the calibre of player that McCloy was featuring alongside, Sandy Jardine, Danny McGrain and Derek Johnstone were in the Scottish League XI, while Peter Shilton, Howard Kendall and Bobby Moore played for the English League.

Winning 50 per cent of his league caps while playing for a side that was battling relegation shows how highly rated McCloy would be, but he shared goalkeeping duties with Keith McCrae as Motherwell bounced straight back up to the top flight, winning the Division Two title in season 1968/69 in some style, losing only two matches and finishing 11 points clear of runners-up Ayr United.

McCloy started season 1969/70 in goal, helping Motherwell finish top of their League Cup section. In the last eight they faced Morton but looked to be heading out of the competition at the quarter-final stage when a double from Joe Harper helped

Morton win the first leg 3-0. But McCloy and his defence shut the Cappielow side out in the return leg, and goals from McInally, Muir and Forsyth forced a play-off at Ibrox.

Motherwell won the play-off 1-0, and McCloy played in the subsequent semi-final defeat against St Johnstone at Hampden Park, but by early December he had lost his place to McRae. He was relegated to the reserves, so it came as a surprise to him when he found out in March 1970 that the recently appointed Rangers manager, Willie Waddell, wanted to make him his first signing.

'When Willie Waddell left Kilmarnock and went into journalism, he would go around the clubs and watch training,' recalled McCloy. 'I remember him coming to watch us at Motherwell one day so maybe I made an impression on him.'

He continued, 'I was playing in the Motherwell reserves at the time and had played against Rangers reserves at Fir Park the Saturday before I signed. We had a young team, but the Rangers team had the likes of Baxter and Davie Provan in it. It was a bit of an onslaught, but we drew the game 1-1. The following Tuesday when I went in for training, Bobby Howitt told me that Rangers were interested and that I had to make my way across to Ibrox on the Friday to discuss personal terms. A deal was done that meant Bobby Watson and Brian Heron would go to Motherwell while I went to Rangers.'

By the time McCloy arrived at Ibrox, Rangers were out of Europe, both cups and were out of contention for the league title too. With seven league matches left, that gave McCloy time 'to break in and get to know the guys'. He played in all of those remaining matches, but it wasn't the best of starts as Rangers won one, drew two and lost four of them. And McCloy had a false start to season 1970/71 too.

He recalled, 'Rangers went to West Germany in pre-season, but I couldn't go as I had a virus. Gerry Neef and Bobby Watson were the goalkeepers that played in the matches out there, and Bobby also played when we lost 3-1 to Celtic in the Glasgow Cup Final. That was on a Monday night, and on the Wednesday I came back into the team when we beat Motherwell 2-0 at Fir Park in the League Cup. It really took off for me after that.'

Indeed it did. Rangers didn't lose a goal in their next seven matches, and McCloy would miss only three matches for the remainder of the season. That meant he was part of the XI that ended a five-year wait for a major trophy when 16-year-old Derek Johnstone towered above Jim Craig and Billy McNeill to net the only goal of the League Cup Final. But it would be during season 1971/72 that McCloy would achieve immortality.

Although the season started badly with heavy defeats in the League Cup against Celtic, the Glasgow Cup was won when Clyde were beaten 2-0 in the final. But four of the first five league matches were lost, which left any hopes of a challenge for the championship in tatters.

'It was a strange season,' recalled McCloy. 'Our league form wasn't up to much, yet we were beating real top-quality opposition like Torino and Bayern Munich in Europe. We played a different system in Europe that suited us, but as it was maybe a bit too defensive, we couldn't play like that in Scotland.'

He continued, 'Barcelona was my most memorable moment as a Rangers player for a lot of reasons. Obviously winning the game was massive, but it was nice to have people close to me there too. My mother and father had never been on an aeroplane before, but I managed to get them on one to get over there. And since the club allowed you to take one person as part of the travelling party, I took my wife-to-be. We got married a week later.'

Season 1972/73 saw changes at Ibrox. Within weeks of the season starting, the goalscoring heroes, Colin Stein and Willie Johnston, had left, while Willie Waddell moved 'upstairs' to become general manager. Jock Wallace took over as manager.

'There wasn't much difference between the two of them to be honest,' said McCloy. 'In those days the managers ruled the roost. There weren't any agents around, and if you didn't sign a contract then you could effectively get put out of the game. But that could work in your favour too as there were a number of the players that played in Barcelona that played over 500 games for Rangers.'

The 1972/73 campaign would be another memorable one for Rangers. Although they lost to Hibernian in the semi-finals of the League Cup, they defeated Celtic 3-2 in the Scottish Cup Final – Tam Forsyth infamously netting the winner from a matter of inches – and ran them close in the title race.

'We actually started the season very poorly,' recalled McCloy. 'After we lost 1-0 at home to Hearts in December [the fourth league defeat of the campaign], big Jock spoke to us and said our bonus would be doubled if we didn't lose another game. And that's exactly what we did. We didn't lose again, yet still missed out on the league by a point.'

He continued, 'We nearly got them. Our last game was at home to East Fife and Celtic were away at Hibs. We won 2-0, but in the end, Celtic won quite easily and that was it. We got our bonus money, but I would have liked to have had a league medal too.'

In the run McCloy refers to, Rangers won 18 and drew two of the league fixtures they played. McCloy was in the team for each of those matches, keeping eight clean sheets. Indeed, the only match he missed that season was a 2-1 win over Arbroath in the league in October. Gerry Neef deputised as McCloy had dislocated a finger.

But that remarkable run of consistency was conspicuous by its absence in what turned out to be an abject season 1973/74. McCloy missed only four league games – Stewart Kennedy and Donald Hunter deputised – and the emphatic 8-0 win over Queen's Park in the third round of the Scottish Cup, but Rangers finished third in the league, and were beaten comfortably by Dundee and Celtic in the Scottish Cup and League Cup.

'Terrible, probably the worst season during my time at Rangers' was McCloy's immediate recollection. 'It was difficult to put your finger on what went wrong. We should have kicked on from the end of the previous season, but it didn't happen.'

One of McCloy's deputies that season, Donald Hunter, has an interesting story to tell. Signed from Vale of Leven, he would only make four appearances for Rangers, the last of which was in a pre-season friendly against Amal Alliance on 23 July 1974. When he left Rangers in 1975, he had a number of clubs interested but was swayed by the intervention of one Alex Ferguson. Ferguson was in charge of St Mirren, and Hunter would be an ever-present when the Saints won the First Division title in season 1976/77, Ferguson's first piece of silverware as a manager. Hunter later joined Dumbarton where his manager was the Rangers legend Davie Wilson. He made his debut on 23 September 1978 in a 2-0 win over Hamilton Accies and made 30 appearances for the Sons before finishing his career with Alloa Athletic. After he retired, Hunter joined the police force.

Peter McCloy had rarely missed a game since he came to the club, but a spot of knee trouble meant he only played eight first-team games in season 1974/75. And they all came on the post-season world tour.

'I had to get the full cartilage removed from my left knee,' said McCloy. 'When I was fit again, I went into the reserve team and was part of the team that won the Treble. We won the Reserve League, the Second XI Cup and the Reserve League Cup.'

Meanwhile, McCloy's replacement, Stewart Kennedy, was helping the first team stop Celtic doing ten-in-a-row, and for the next three seasons, McCloy and Kennedy would compete for the number one jersey.

Born in Stirling on 31 August 1949 and recruited from Stenhousemuir in April 1973, Kennedy had started out in junior football with Camelon Juniors before signing for Dunfermline Athletic. He made his Pars debut on his 19th birthday against Clyde in the League Cup. Harry Hood scored a hat-trick for Clyde in a 3-0 win.

That would be Kennedy's one and only first-team match for Dunfermline. He was released by Dunfermline on 30 April 1969, at which point he returned to junior football with Linlithgow Rose. He did well enough at that level to earn a move to Stenhousemuir in 1970, and after making 68 league appearances for the Ochilview side, Jock Wallace made his move.

Kennedy made his first-team debut on 29 August 1973 in a League Cup sectional tie against Falkirk at Brockville. Peter McCloy was rested by Jock Wallace for that one, but when the Rangers number one sustained an injury to his left hand in training a couple of weeks later, Kennedy came back in for the 2-1 win over Dumbarton at Boghead. However, he would make his third and last appearance of the season three days later when Rangers were beaten 1-0 at home by East Fife.

But he was back in business at the start of season 1974/75. With McCloy sidelined, Kennedy was in goal throughout pre-season. That meant he featured in the final of the Drybrough Cup – Celtic won 4-2 on penalties after a 2-2 draw at Hampden – and also played in the Nou Camp in the final of the IX Trofeo Joan Gamper against a Barcelona side that included one Johan Cruyff. The crowd is recorded as being 100,000, and bizarrely the game started one day and ended the next! It kicked off at 10.45pm, which meant that after 90 minutes had elapsed midnight had been passed.

Kennedy was the last line of defence when Rangers burst out of the blocks at the start of the league campaign. Although home and away defeats to Hibernian had ended interest in the League

Cup, the Light Blues won ten and drew two of their opening 12 league fixtures. In that spell, Kennedy conceded ten goals and kept four clean sheets. The run was ended by a 1-0 home defeat against Hibernian, but Rangers would lose just one of their next 16 in the league. That was a remarkable 4-3 defeat against Airdrie at Broomfield four days before Christmas.

That is Championship-winning form, and the title was duly clinched with a 1-1 draw at Easter Road on 29 March. Rangers eventually finished seven points ahead of runners-up Hibernian, and 11 clear of deposed champions Celtic.

The role played by Stewart Kennedy that season cannot be underestimated. In 34 league appearances, he conceded 33 goals and shut the opposition out on 11 occasions. His form was such that he earned a call-up to the Scotland national team, winning his first cap in a 1-1 draw against Sweden on 16 April 1975. Kennedy was riding the crest of a wave, but he came crashing down from it on 24 May 1975 at Wembley. He was beaten five times as Scotland lost 5-1 to England. It would be Kennedy's fifth and final appearance for his country.

Since he was made the scapegoat for that thrashing, Jock Wallace elected to take Kennedy out of the limelight. McCloy was handed the gloves for the opening matches of season 1975/76, playing in the first eight league fixtures and the first nine League Cup ties. But a freak accident in France counted him out of action for a couple of months.

'I got injured in the warm-up when we played Saint-Etienne in the European Cup,' recalled McCloy. 'I broke my finger stopping a shot from Colin Stein, but I came back in on New Year's Day against Celtic. We won 1-0 and went on to win the Treble.'

McCloy kept possession of the number one jersey at the start of season 1976/77 too. He kept goal in the Glasgow Cup Final – goals from Sandy Jardine, Colin Jackson and an Alex Miller penalty gave

Rangers a 3-1 win – and made five league appearances, two in the European Cup against FC Zurich, and played seven matches in the League Cup. Rangers won once and drew four times in those five league matches, exited the European Cup, and in one of the League Cup ties, Rangers drew 3-3 with Clydebank at Ibrox. A certain Davie Cooper was Rangers' chief tormentor that night. But when flu ruled McCloy out of the second leg at Kilbowie, Stewart Kennedy came in, and then stayed in the team for the rest of the season.

'Jock had this thing when it came to the goalkeepers, which meant that if the person playing was doing alright then he stayed in the team,' said McCloy. 'I disagreed with that as I felt if you had been in good form before you went out the team, then you should have come back in. It used to annoy me as if you weren't in the first team then your career pretty much stopped at that time.'

The pattern was much the same in the Treble season of 1977/78. McCloy played in the opening five league games, the first three ties in the European Cup Winners' Cup, and both legs of the 6-1 aggregate win over St Johnstone in the League Cup. But in that spell, Rangers conceded ten goals in the league, and after a 3-3 draw against St Mirren at Love Street, Jock Wallace decided to bring Kennedy back into the team.

McCloy only featured in one of the next 23 league matches. That was a 1-0 win over Clydebank on 4 February. He also missed the League Cup Final win over Celtic, but after Rangers lost 2-0 at Parkhead on 25 March, a defeat that saw Rangers' lead at the top of the table cut to a single point, McCloy was back for the visit to Edinburgh to face Hibernian.

Writing in the *Evening Times*, Hugh Taylor reckoned McCloy had a 'splendid game' at Easter Road, and he was desperately unlucky not to save the penalty kick from Ally McLeod that earned the home side a point. Aberdeen's win over St Mirren meant they leapfrogged Rangers at the summit, but with McCloy in place, the Light Blues won five and drew two of their last seven matches to pip the Dons by two points. Shutting out the opposition in each of the last four league games was significant in that final push for the title.

McCloy then picked up a Scottish Cup medal when the third leg of the domestic Treble was completed, when Aberdeen were beaten 2-1 at Hampden. Somewhat unfairly, most recall McCloy swinging from the crossbar in that match when Stevie Ritchie's mishit shot looped into the air and over McCloy's head into the net. But given how tight things were when McCloy returned to the starting XI, the fact that that was one of only six goals he conceded in the ten matches he played during the run-in illustrates how important his presence was at that time.

Just a few months later, the winds of change blew through the corridors at Ibrox. Jock Wallace shocked everyone by quitting and moving to Leicester City, while John Greig hung up his boots and took over as manager of Rangers.

'It started off very well for John,' recalled McCloy. 'We came close to winning the Treble again and had a good run to the quarter-finals of the European Cup. But after that we had a pretty poor time of it.'

In Greig's first season, Peter McCloy was the undisputed number one at Ibrox. He missed only one first-team game – the 3-1 win over Celtic in the Glasgow Cup Final – and picked up winners' medals in the League Cup and Scottish Cup. And he went one better in season 1979/80, pulling on the number one jersey in each of the 65 first-team fixtures played. That included matches in Calgary, Toronto, Montreal, Dubai and Kuwait, but domestically and in Europe that campaign was an abject one.

The season started with a memorable win over Celtic in the final of the Drybrough Cup, a match that featured sublime goals from Sandy Jardine and Davie Cooper. But Aberdeen bumped Rangers out of the League Cup in the third round, and in the league only five of the first 15 matches were won. Things didn't improve much after that, and Rangers eventually finished fifth on 37 points. That was only four points better than Kilmarnock who finished eighth. The season ended with the infamous riot at Hampden after Celtic won 1-0 after extra time in the Scottish Cup Final.

By the end of that season, Stewart Kennedy had left the club. After making 152 appearances for Rangers and keeping 47 clean sheets, he was given a free transfer and ended up at Forfar Athletic. Kennedy would establish himself as their first-choice goalkeeper for a number of years, and such was his status, he polled 76 per cent of the vote when the BBC were looking for the club's all-time Cult Hero in 1976.

Kennedy played against Rangers in the second round of the League Cup in season 1980/81, Rangers winning 5-1 on aggregate. Remarkably, Kennedy faced FOUR penalty kicks in the second leg at Ibrox. He saved the first one taken by Sandy Jardine, but the referee, Bob Valentine, ordered a retake as he was of the opinion that Kennedy had moved before the ball was struck. Despite pleas from manager John Greig for the taker to be changed – Greig later revealed that Kennedy had faced numerous penalties in training while he was at Ibrox so knew Jardine's style too well – Jardine took the penalty but struck the post. Ten minutes later, Davie Cooper was tripped in the box and Alex Miller stepped up to score from 12 yards. Rangers' third penalty award came ten minutes into the second half and Colin McAdam, who had scored twice in the first leg, stepped up to seal a 3-1 win for Rangers.

The sides were drawn together in the Scottish Cup the following season, meeting at the semi-final stage. Kennedy initially kept his former side at bay in the first match at Hampden which ended 0-0. However, goals from Derek Johnstone, Jim Bett and Davie Cooper edged Rangers through in the replay. Kennedy was also in goal the following season when a John MacDonald double earned Rangers a 2-1 win over Forfar in the fourth round of the Scottish Cup at Ibrox.

Stewart Kennedy would make over 300 appearances for Forfar before he retired in 1991. His testimonial match took place against Rangers at Station Park on 26 February 1985, and it would prove to be a big night for a certain Alistair McCoist.

Just ten days earlier, McCoist had sunk to the nadir of his Rangers career in a Scottish Cup tie against Dundee at Ibrox. He had dropped down to the reserves, but a double in a 5-1 win over Hearts reserves at Ibrox and another brace in Kennedy's benefit match earned him a first-team recall. He didn't look back. Ten goals in the last nine league games kick-started his Rangers career. It's fair to say he did more than okay after that!

Rewinding back to 1980, Peter McCloy started season 1980/81 as the man in possession of the number one jersey. George Young and Gordon Marshall would provide the competition. However, only Young played for the first team, and Marshall would actually enjoy more top team action with Celtic, making over 100 appearances for them between 1991 and 1998.

Irrespective of the competition for the yellow jersey, Rangers weren't faring much better. Aberdeen ended interest in the League Cup again, winning 3-2 on aggregate this time, and although they made a promising start in the league with a 15-match unbeaten run, five defeats and three draws in the next 11 effectively ended hopes of winning the title.

'If you manage either Rangers or Celtic, it's a difficult job, but you have to remember John also went into the job straight after he finished as a player,' said McCloy. 'It may have been better had he gone away and then come back. John had to replace international players too like Colin Jackson, Sandy Jardine and Tom Forsyth. John also didn't have the budget that Graeme Souness had for example, and although the players he brought in were good players, they didn't make it at international level. That meant slowly our team got weaker rather than stronger.'

One of the players Greig signed that did have international caps was goalkeeper Jim Stewart. He arrived from Middlesbrough in March 1981 and went straight into the team for the last ten league matches plus the semi-final and final of the Scottish Cup.

'At a club like Rangers you have to expect there will be competition for places,' said McCloy. 'I was also 34 at that time so I always expected to see another goalkeeper come in. Once I dropped out the team it was just a matter of keeping my head down and working away until I got a chance to get back into the team.'

That chance came at the start of the following season. Stewart injured his ankle in training, and McCloy deputised while he recovered, playing in the opening four league fixtures, a couple of League Cup ties and also a heavy 3-0 defeat against Dukla Prague in the opening round of the European Cup Winners' Cup. Stewart came back and played the next five in the league before McCloy was in again following a 2-0 defeat at home against Partick Thistle. He looked to be in for the long haul this time, but a thigh knock picked up in a 3-3 draw against Celtic at Parkhead forced him out of the League Cup Final. He would only play twice more in the league that season.

Stewart was the main man at the start of season 1982/83, but McCloy had been the hero during a pre-season match against St Etienne. He came off the bench when Stewart picked up an injury and proceeded to save four penalty kicks in an epic 18-kick shoot-out. McCloy foiled Johnny Rep, Thierry Oleksiak, Alain Moizan and Flemming Christensen, although the latter scored when his kick had to be retaken. The referee felt McCloy had moved before the ball was struck.

Stewart recovered to take his place in goal when the competitive action got underway, but after Motherwell inflicted a 3-0 defeat on Rangers at Fir Park on 3 January 1983, McCloy was back in business. He played in each of the last 17 league games, and the six Scottish Cup ties, the last of which was a 1-0 defeat against Aberdeen in the final.

Season 1982/83 would also feature the first-team debut of Andy Bruce. Bruce joined Rangers from Linlithgow Rose and had played for Scotland Schoolboys at Wembley against England Schoolboys in 1980. Scotland won 5-4, and the match featured the likes of Paul McStay and John Robertson, while future Rangers forward Paul Rideout scored a hat-trick for England.

Bruce played youth and reserve-team football at Ibrox until, at the age of 18, he was drafted in for the penultimate league match of the campaign, a 2-1 win over Hibernian at Easter Road. But up against the likes of McCloy, Stewart and, latterly, Nicky Walker, Bruce found first-team opportunities limited. He next played for the first team on 31 October 1984 when he came on as substitute for McCloy in a 5-0 win over New Zealand at Ibrox – the match was a benefit game for Billy Mckay – and featured in four other matches that season. Bruce appeared in all three matches played in the Middle East coming on as substitute for McCloy in the first and last matches of the tour and starting the middle one. Four days later, Jock Wallace selected him for the league fixture against St Mirren at Love Street. Rangers lost 2-1.

Andy Bruce, who also played twice for Partick Thistle during a loan spell in March 1984, would make only one more appearance for the Rangers first team. That was in the final of the Glasgow Cup on 9 September 1985. He kept a clean sheet as a strong Rangers XI defeated Queen's Park 5-0. He left Rangers in 1986 when Graeme Souness came in as player-manager, moving along the M8 to join Hearts. With Henry Smith the main goalkeeper at Tynecastle, opportunities were once again few and far between. His only league appearance for Hearts came at Fir Park on 15 April 1987, a goal from Sandy Clark giving the Edinburgh side a 1-0 win. He decided to retire from football at the age of 23 and join the police force.

Incidentally, Andy Bruce isn't the only goalkeeper with the surname Bruce to play for Rangers. On 5 May 1917, Rangers lost 1-0 against Morton in a benefit match for the Greenock Infirmary. The goalkeeper in that match was Robert Bruce. It would prove to be the one and only time Robert played for the Light Blues.

Remarkably, at the age of 36, Peter McCloy was the Rangers number one again. He picked up a Glasgow Cup medal at the start of season 1983/84, played in all the pre-season friendlies, and played in all but two of the first 17 league matches. But after a shambolic start to the season – Rangers lost eight of their first 12 in the league – John Greig resigned, and Jock Wallace returned to the club. And although McCloy played in the first seven league matches under Wallace, he brought in Nicky Walker who he had worked with at Leicester City and Motherwell.

'They kept trying to replace me,' joked McCloy. 'As one of the few that had been at the club during Jock's previous spell as manager, we knew what to expect. We all had the greatest respect for him, as he was a great man-manager and motivator. He came back and took over a team that had been failing, but things soon picked up and we won the League Cup. But Jock couldn't get the consistency out of the team to make a challenge for the league.'

With Walker cup-tied, McCloy played in that League Cup Final victory over Celtic, and also the last ten league games. Only one of those matches was lost, but the sequence also included a run of five successive draws. Rangers eventually finished fourth, 15 points adrift of Celtic.

Walker started season 1984/85 as the number one but dropped out after a horrendous night on and off the park in Dublin in the UEFA Cup in October. McCloy enjoyed a run of 17 league matches as a result and also played in the 1-0 victory over Dundee United in the League Cup Final. And McCloy also played when Wallace took his squad to the Middle East in March 1985.

'Even games like that counted,' said McCloy. 'Most folk say I played 534 games for Rangers, but if you include matches like that then I actually played 646 times for the club. That included world tours in 1975 and 1984. After the one in 1975 we came back and won the Treble and I think he was hoping for something similar in 1984. We didn't get much time to ourselves given the number of games we played, but the squad in 1984 didn't have the same quality overall as the one in 1975.'

He added, 'In terms of the Middle East, can you imagine going to play in Baghdad? I think we were only out there about two weeks before the war between Iran and Iraq started.'

Nicky Walker had a firm grasp on the number one jersey in season 1985/86 but come April major changes were afoot. After losing 2-0 against Tottenham Hotspur in a friendly at Ibrox, Wallace was gone. In his place came the club's first player-manager, Graeme Souness, who was ably assisted by Walter Smith.

'When Walter came in, he spoke to me and said I would be playing,' said McCloy. 'I played against St Mirren and Aberdeen, but when Graeme Souness arrived in time for the Glasgow Cup Final against Celtic, he told me that Walter had said I had done well but he wanted to take a look at Nicky.'

He added, 'Graeme told me that he was bringing in Chris Woods, but he wanted me to stay on and work with him as a coach. I was almost 40, so I didn't expect to be Graeme's first choice, but I was still retained on a playing contract in case emergency cover was required.'

Peter McCloy's record for Rangers is impressive, but he can also lay claim to a number of goalscoring assists too. In addition to saving shots, McCloy also had another string to his bow; the distance he could get when kicking the ball out was phenomenal. The clearances were effective at times too, none more so than in Barcelona in 1972. McCloy's 'hoof' up the park went all the way through to Willie Johnston, and Bud expertly tucked the ball away to score the goal that effectively won the European Cup Winners' Cup.

During his 16 years as a Rangers player, McCloy won two league titles, four Scottish Cups, four League Cups and was in the XI that won the European Cup Winners' Cup in 1972. He also picked up three winners' medals in the Glasgow Cup and one in the Drybrough Cup. He was capped four times by Scotland, all of his appearances coming between 12 May 1973 and 30 June 1973. His last cap came against Brazil in a 1-0 defeat at Hampden Park.

Chapter 6

Turbulence and Transition

THE EARLY to mid-1980s was a doleful period for Rangers. Too often title challenges petered out in the early months of the New Year, and since they were unable to put together a string of positive results, they developed a reputation as a cup team. The Scottish Cup was won in 1981, with League Cups added in 1982, 1984 and 1985. The Scottish Cup Final was also reached in 1980, 1982 and 1983, while Celtic edged the League Cup Final 2-1 in 1983. Thus, between 1980 and 1985, Rangers played a part in eight of the 12 domestic cup finals contested.

During that era, the main competition provided to Peter McCloy came from two goalkeepers, Jim Stewart and Nicky Walker.

Stewart was 27 years of age when he joined Rangers in March 1981. By the time he arrived, he had been capped by Scotland, been part of a World Cup squad and sampled life in the English First Division. But his career had started some 12 years earlier when he signed as a schoolboy for Kilmarnock.

'I went to Kilwinning High School, and initially played outfield,' said Stewart. 'But I was soon advised that I'd be better off playing in goal! I must have done okay, though, as I was selected to play for Ayrshire Schools and Scotland Schoolboys.'

While playing for Ayrshire, Stewart came up against a future team-mate, Derek Johnstone.

'Ayrshire met Dundee in the final of the National Counties Schools competition, and DJ played up front for Dundee,' recalled Jim. 'It ended up 7-7 over two games, and DJ delights in telling everyone he scored a hat-trick against me. But what he doesn't share that often is that I saved his penalty kick in the last minute!'

He continued, 'I went to Leeds United and Rangers on trial. Perhaps at that time my confidence level wasn't as high as it could have been and things didn't work out, so I decided to sign for Kilmarnock who I had been training with.'

At that time there were no youth academies so promising youngsters like Stewart were signed on schoolboy forms instead. Referred to as 'S' forms, Jim signed his in January 1969. He made history when he did so, becoming the first player in Kilmarnock's history to be recruited in this way.

Jim would enjoy a year with Bellfield Boys Club and spent season 1970/71 with Troon Juniors, but during those spells there were opportunities to play for Kilmarnock too. For example, he pulled on the gloves for the reserves early in season 1969/70. Raith Rovers reserves provided the opposition at Stark's Park and won 2-0. The win maintained Raith's 100 per cent winning start; Kilmarnock meanwhile were rooted to the bottom of the table, this being their third successive defeat. And while with Troon, Stewart made four appearances for the Kilmarnock second XI.

At the end of the season, Stewart got the news he was waiting for; he was offered a professional contract with Kilmarnock.

'I had left school by then and I was working as a Mechanical Engineer with ICI,' said Stewart. 'Kilmarnock had just reverted from full-time to part-time, and I would remain part-time until I left to join Middlesbrough when I was 24.'

In season 1971/72, Stewart played for the reserves, coming up against some of the leading lights of the Scottish game in the process. When Kilmarnock lost 3-1 to Celtic on 3 December, Lisbon Lions such as Bobby Murdoch and Tommy Gemmell were in the Celtic side, and three months later, Jim played well at Ibrox in a 1-0 defeat. Derek Parlane got the goal for Rangers.

Stewart must have impressed with his displays over the course of the season as he was handed his first appearance for the first team towards the end of the campaign. And it was a baptism of fire, a local derby against Ayr United in the first leg of the Ayrshire Cup Final at Somerset Park. Ayr's Davy McCulloch scored the only goal of the game after 13 minutes.

Stewart next played for the first XI in a pre-season friendly against Brora Rangers ahead of season 1972/73, and a few weeks later when Ally Hunter picked up an ankle injury in training, Stewart was handed an opportunity to stake a claim. Up against the likes of Derek Dougan and John Richards, he kept a clean sheet in the second leg of a Texaco Cup tie against Wolves at Rugby Park on 26 September 1972.

The match was held up for some 20 minutes when the floodlights failed, but Stewart shone enough in the match to keep his place for the visit of the European Cup Winners' Cup holders, Rangers, four days later.

Kilmarnock won 2-1 to arrest a run of four successive league defeats.

Stewart was between the sticks again the following week for a pulsating 3-3 draw against Arbroath at Gayfield, but Hunter was fit enough to return to action for Kilmarnock's next fixture. Stewart returned to the reserves, but it wouldn't be long before he got an opportunity for a prolonged run in the team. Towards the end of January 1973, Ally Hunter signed for Celtic, and Walter McCrae chose Stewart as his replacement.

'Kilmarnock were struggling at the time,' recalled Stewart. 'The transition from full-time to part-time was a difficult one, and we ended up getting relegated.'

Jim had played in a 3-3 draw against Arbroath in October 1972 and that result saw Kilmarnock rise to 15th in the old 18-team top flight. But they would go no higher than that. Instead, come the final day of the campaign they faced Falkirk at home with their hopes of survival hanging in the balance.

Going into the match, it was between Kilmarnock and Dumbarton for the final relegation place. Both teams were level on 21 points, with Kilmarnock ahead (only just) on goal difference. Both teams were at home – Dumbarton faced Dundee United – so it looked like all-out attack would be the order of the day.

'We were 2-0 up at half-time, but Falkirk scored twice in the second half and the game ended 2-2,' noted Stewart. 'Dumbarton won their game, so we went down. But the key game for me was a few weeks earlier when we lost 4-2 against Dumbarton. Ross Mathie, who had been at Kilmarnock, scored against us that day. Getting relegated at the end of my first full season as a number one was a downer.'

Despite suffering relegation, Stewart had enjoyed a fine season. He had made 24 appearances and won an Ayrshire Cup medal, Kilmarnock retaining the trophy with a 2-1 aggregate win over Ayr. And Jim also won the first of five caps for Scotland at U23 level. That came against Wales at the Vetch Field in Swansea on 14 March 1973. Danny McGrain, Jim Holton, Kenny Dalglish and Derek Parlane were in the Scottish side, and after Dalglish opened the scoring, Asa Hartford netted the winner in the closing seconds.

Somewhat bizarrely, Stewart made all his U23 appearances and won his first full cap before he was picked for the U21 side for the first time. That came in September 1977 at Ibrox against Switzerland, with the likes of George Burley, Willie Miller, Paul

Sturrock and Davie Cooper wearing Dark Blue. Scotland won 3-1, and Stewart had now earned another place in the history books of Kilmarnock as no other player has been capped at both U21 and U23 level while at Rugby Park.

Kilmarnock made an inconsistent start to life in Division Two, and Walter McCrae was eventually replaced by Willie Fernie.

'Willie changed the way we played,' recalled Stewart. 'We became a wee bit more expansive and seemed to gel together as a team. The likes of Davie Provan and Gordon Smith were coming through at that time too.'

The change in playing style galvanised the Ayrshire side. Kilmarnock reached the last four of the League Cup – they lost to eventual winners Dundee – and scored goals with breathtaking regularity as they finished as runners-up to Airdrie.

But as much as the likes of Ian Fleming and Bobby Morrison grabbed the headlines at the sharp end of the pitch, Stewart had an excellent season too. He made 51 appearances, and his performances were of such a high calibre that they caught the eye of the Scotland national team manager, Willie Ormond. Despite not having been capped at full international level, Stewart was one of the three goalkeepers named in the final squad that would travel to West Germany for the 1974 World Cup.

'I had done alright in the games I had played for the U23s, and I had also made my debut for the Scottish League against the English League at Maine Road,' said Stewart. 'That was at the time of the miners' strike, and we got beaten 5-0 by an English team that had the likes of Colin Bell and Ray Clemence in it.

'But being part-time and getting a call to go to the World Cup was phenomenal. At that time David Harvey of Leeds United was the recognised first-choice goalkeeper for Scotland, and Thomson Allan, who was at Dundee, was his number two. I knew that I wasn't going to play but getting to go along and experience being part of a World Cup squad and learn from the likes of David and Thomson was invaluable for me.'

From the high of West Germany, Stewart came back to earth with a bump when he was part of the Kilmarnock sides that were hammered by the Old Firm in the opening league games of season 1974/75. A 5-0 opening-day defeat at Parkhead was followed a month later by a 6-0 thrashing from Rangers at Rugby Park.

Kilmarnock managed to steady the ship, finishing the season in 12th place. That should have been enough to keep them in Division One for the following season, but league reconstruction kiboshed that. Teams that finished in the top ten would form the new Premier Division in season 1975/76, but Kilmarnock's points tally of 31 was two shy of tenth-placed Motherwell. Winning just one of the last five league games would ultimately prove costly.

However, Jim Stewart wasn't in the team at that point. He played in each of the first 18 league games, culminating in a 3-2 loss on New Year's Day against Ayr United.

'I had a disagreement with the manager, not something I would recommend,' said Stewart with a smile. 'I missed half a season, so I learned my lesson, you never contest the manager's point of view.'

But all was eventually forgiven, and after he got his place back, Stewart was rarely out of the team. Indeed, in his final two seasons with Kilmarnock, he missed only one league match. That was a match against Rangers at Rugby Park on 13 November 1976, although Stewart had good reason for being absent. He had been called up to the Scotland squad.

But at the end of season 1977/78, it was time for a change. After 220 competitive appearances for Kilmarnock, Stewart decided to sign for Middlesbrough in the summer of 1978.

'I had been selected in the initial 40-man squad for the World Cup in Argentina, but I didn't make the cut,' said Stewart. 'Alan Rough, Bobby Clark and Jim Blyth were selected. I was disappointed, but the move to Middlesbrough came about on the back of me being considered in the first place. Rangers were reported to be interested too, but I heard that the former Celtic player Bobby Murdoch had recommended me to Boro. John Neal was the Middlesbrough manager at the time, and eventually the two clubs agreed a fee.

'Jim Platt was the goalkeeper at Ayresome Park, but I was told I would be coming in as the number one. Middlesbrough were full-time and playing in the English First Division, so it was a good opportunity for me. I came in and played around 30 first-team games, and we were sitting mid-table. But the club wanted better than that, and I remember being left out the team on my birthday. From then until the end of the season results improved so I found it difficult to get back into the team.'

It would be 19 April 1980 before Stewart made his next league appearance for Middlesbrough. He played in five of the last six games, the last of which was a 5-0 thrashing of European Cup Winners' Cup finalists Arsenal at Ayresome Park. That helped Middlesbrough finish the season in ninth place.

But when season 1980/81 kicked off, Jim Platt was back in goal, and Stewart was back in the reserves. He would make only two more league appearances, the last of which was on 27 September 1980 against Stoke City at the Victoria Ground.

Stewart looked set to continue for the rest of that season in the reserves at Ayresome Park when out of the blue he got a phone call. John Greig wanted him to sign for Rangers!

Rangers lost 2-1 against Hearts at Tynecastle on 14 March 1981 to extend their abject run of form away from home. This was a third successive away defeat in the league, and since the start of the season only four of the 15 matches away from Ibrox had been won. When you consider that three of those successes had come in succession at the start of the campaign, then you can understand why enough was enough for John Greig. He admitted to being a long-time admirer of Jim Stewart, and that Saturday evening he called the Boro boss, John Neal, to see if Jim would be available for an immediate transfer.

Time was tight as the transfer deadline was looming, but the transfer fee was set at £110,000, which at that time made Stewart the most expensive Scottish goalkeeper ever.

'The old transfer window closed in March each year,' said Stewart. 'We were coming back on the bus after we had played Wolves in the quarter-finals of the FA Cup and I remember speaking to a journalist and saying that it looked like I would need to wait until the next window opened before I got a move. But shortly after that, I got a call from Davie Provan, who was part of John Greig's backroom team at Rangers. He asked me if I was interested in joining the club, and given I wasn't playing for Middlesbrough, it was a no-brainer.'

He added, 'Davie wasn't sure if the move would go through in time, but assured me that if it didn't, the club would come back in for me in the summer. But we managed to get the deal done, and it was made clear that if I was fit and available, I'd play.'

Remarkably this was the third time that Jim had reportedly had the chance to join Rangers.

'When I was linked with Rangers in 1978, it was only speculation,' admitted Stewart. 'Colin Stein had been on loan at Kilmarnock, and there was talk about a possible swap deal that would see me go to Rangers and Colin go to Kilmarnock. But it never progressed any further than just being a rumour.'

Irrespective of what had happened before, Stewart was a Rangers player now, and he was pitched into the action immediately when Rangers welcomed Dundee United to Ibrox. Greig had been raging in the wake of the loss in Edinburgh and he made changes for the match. Stewart replaced Peter McCloy in goal, and there was no place in the defence in front of him for Derek Johnstone or

Sandy Jardine. Both had been substituted at Tynecastle, but their exclusion didn't affect a change in fortune for a ragged Rangers side.

One of the changes saw the return of Gregor Stevens. He had last played for the first team on 7 February against United at Tannadice. He was sent off for dissent after 81 minutes, the upshot of which was a four-game ban. And he didn't last the 90 minutes on his return from suspension either, picking up another red card with 20 minutes remaining. By the time Stevens saw red, Rangers were 4-1 down although Stewart wasn't at fault for any of the United goals. Indeed, in his post-match musings, Greig actually said that 'The only bright spot was the performance of Jim Stewart, who had some very good saves.'

Stewart renewed some old acquaintances in Rangers' next match, a 2-0 win over former club Kilmarnock, and after the conclusion of the match, he was on his travels. John Greig elected to take his squad on a four-day break to Estoril in Portugal in a bid to get them ready for the forthcoming Scottish Cup semi-final against Morton. But this was not a holiday. On the front page of the *Rangers News*, Greig was quoted as saying that 'We're out [in Portugal] to work, to build up morale and to get the team spirit right for the last few weeks of the season.'

Rangers played one match during their time in Portugal – a Sandy Jardine goal sufficient to earn victory over GD Estoril Praia – but upon their return, Rangers lost 2-1 at Love Street. The run of consecutive away defeats was now at four, and it would be the opening day of the following season before Rangers tasted league victory on the road once again.

In contrast, home form was excellent. Rangers won all but one of their last six home matches in the league, with Stewart keeping clean sheets in four of them. But the away form was Rangers' undoing and they eventually finished third in the title race, 12 points adrift of champions Celtic.

Silverware was salvaged, though, in the shape of the Scottish Cup. Stewart made his cup debut in the semi-final at Parkhead, and he recalls a rather tempestuous encounter that Rangers edged by the odd goal in three.

'I remember that Bobby Thomson and Jim Holmes of Morton were sent off,' said Stewart. 'It was a typical hammer and tongs cup tie and we won 2-1.

'Personally, I was delighted as only a few weeks earlier I had been playing my last game for Middlesbrough reserves against Lincoln City on a works pitch and here I was going to play in a national cup final for Rangers.'

Given he had made his debut against Dundee United, it was ironic that Stewart and Rangers would face Jim McLean's men in the final.

They had finished fifth in the league, a point behind Rangers, but they were emerging as a force to be reckoned with. The league head-to-head that season was level at two wins apiece, so the stage was set for an epic joust.

'I had ambitions to win trophies and when I signed for Rangers, my focus was on making sure we won the Scottish Cup,' said Stewart. 'The first game wasn't the best, but we had a chance to win it when we got a penalty in the last minute. Unfortunately, Reddy [Ian Redford] smashed it down the middle and Hamish McAlpine saved it with his legs.'

Stewart added, 'We brought back Solo [John MacDonald], DJ, and Coop for the replay. It worked perfectly. Coop, a great pal of mine, was magnificent, scoring one and laying on the second for Bobby Russell. Wee Solo got two and we won 4-1.'

The Scottish Cup win should have been a launch pad for a title challenge in season 1981/82, and initial signs were promising.

Pre-season took Rangers to Sweden. Four matches were played, Jim featuring in three of them. He was between the sticks for the two home friendlies too, a defeat against UEFA Cup holders Ipswich Town, and a 2-0 win over Manchester City.

Stewart played in the first five League Cup sectional ties too – Rangers winning four and drawing one – but sustained an ankle injury in training that would rule him out of action until late September. He returned for a routine League Cup win over Brechin City, and later joked that he wished he had been given an umbrella as he was largely inactive in a 1-0 win played out in torrential rain.

But league form was topsy-turvy. With Stewart on the sidelines, Rangers won only one of their first four league games. And although Jim came back in to feature in 26 of the last 32 league matches, Rangers couldn't muster a decent run of results. For example, after beating St Mirren 3-2 at Love Street on 10 March, Greig's men won only five of their last 14 league matches. Rangers finished third, and the season was summed up when runners-up Aberdeen fired four goals past Stewart on the final day to finish ten points better off.

A week later, Stewart was beaten four times by the Dons again, but on this occasion, Rangers were most unfortunate. Leading 1-0 in the Scottish Cup Final thanks to a John MacDonald goal, Aberdeen restored parity when Alex McLeish rather fortuitously curled a right-foot shot into the top corner.

'Alex told me afterwards that he did that kind of thing in training every week,' laughed Stewart. 'I thought we played well on the day, but extra time took its toll on us.'

Aberdeen scored a further three goals, and Jim tasted defeat in a cup final for the first time. Earlier in the season, he had picked up his second winners' medal when Rangers defeated Dundee United in the League Cup Final, but he wouldn't complete a double.

Season 1982/83 kicked off with Stewart as the main man in goal. He played in each of the first 18 league matches, and also all 11 League Cup ties. In the latter, he tasted defeat in a cup final again, Celtic winning 2-1 in December.

But prior to that, it looked like Rangers were all set for a sustained title challenge and an extended run in Europe. Greig's men were undefeated after eight games and Jim and his defence had also shut out Borussia Dortmund over two legs in the UEFA Cup. But it would be a false dawn. League form soon deteriorated, and another season of inconsistency was played out. And the UEFA Cup run was halted abruptly too.

'We had too many draws to begin with [five in the first eight games], but we were unbeaten before we went to Parkhead to play Celtic,' recalled Stewart. 'We lost that one 3-2, and four days later we got battered against Cologne. We beat them 2-1 at Ibrox, but we conceded the first goal over there after only seven minutes. Less than 15 minutes later, we were 4-0 down, and I remember looking at the scoreboard and thinking we could be in for a long night.'

Cologne eventually won 5-0, and the body blow of that result effectively derailed Rangers' challenge for domestic honours. Dundee United won the league, Celtic won the League Cup, while a late Eric Black goal saw Aberdeen retain the Scottish Cup. Rangers were beaten in both of the cup finals and finished fourth in the league table, a massive 21 points adrift of United.

Jim Stewart had a difficult season too. He kept a clean sheet in seven of those opening 18 league games, but inside three days, in January 1983, his time in the first team came to an abrupt halt.

He recalled, 'I played in the Old Firm game at Ibrox on 1 January, but I conceded a poor goal and we lost 2-1. We then went to Fir Park to play Motherwell two days later, and I knew I needed to play well. But as a team we were poor, and we lost 3-0, Brian McClair scoring a hat-trick.'

John Greig decided it was time for change, and the following week Peter McCloy was back in goal for the league match with Dundee United while Jim was selected for the reserves.

'Back then you found out who was playing when the first-team and reserve-team line-ups were put up in the dressing room on the Friday after training,' said Jim. 'Ahead of the United game, the two sheets went up, and I wasn't in the first XI. I hadn't spoken to the manager or been asked to go and see him. That was just how it was, although Greigy did speak to me later to explain why he was leaving me out. He felt that he needed to make changes as we had lost a couple of games, and although I was disappointed, I had to take a bit of responsibility. Greigy did say that he felt a couple of games for the reserves might help rebuild my confidence and that would then give me a chance to get back in.'

Stewart played 12 times for the reserves in the closing months of season 1982/83. With confidence restored, he was looking to get back into the first team in the new season. But after an awful start that saw Rangers win just three of their opening nine league games, Greig resigned. He was eventually replaced by Jock Wallace. Would the return of Wallace see Stewart appearing with more regularity for the first team?

'Before Greigy left, I had come back into the team in the second leg of the European Cup Winners' Cup tie against Valletta,' recalled Stewart. 'I also played in a League Cup tie against Hearts when Derek Ferguson made his competitive debut. I had featured the previous Saturday when we lost 2-1 against Motherwell at Ibrox – Andy Ritchie scored with a penalty kick – and the following week, wee Tommy McLean took the team when we lost 3-0 against St Mirren at Love Street.'

He added, 'We were playing Porto in our next game, but I did something to my elbow. I had to get fluid drained from it, so I didn't even make the bench. Jock came in after that and since he had been rumoured to be interested in signing me when he was last at Rangers, I hoped he would give me an opportunity.'

Unfortunately, that opportunity never arose.

'My mindset at that time was that I was a number one goalie,' admitted Jim. 'I knew Jock had worked with big Peter before, though, and he went into the team. We then went on an unbeaten run, so Peter remained in possession. But my chances of getting back in were hampered when I had to undergo a cartilage operation in January 1984. By then Jock had decided to bring Nicky [Walker] in so with my contract up in the summer, I knew my time at Rangers was almost up.'

To help with his recovery and match fitness, Stewart was loaned to Dumbarton in February 1984. Under the guidance of Billy Lamont, the Sons were pushing for promotion to the Premier Division. Stewart featured in two league matches and a Scottish Cup tie before he returned to Rangers. Each of his three matches for the Sons ended with a victory, and Dumbarton would eventually reach their promotion goal when the former Rangers winger Davie Wilson took over from Falkirk-bound Lamont.

Jim returned to Ibrox, but although back to fitness, he didn't succeed in supplanting Peter McCloy. With his contract up at the end of the season, it was time for pastures new.

'There was interest from Motherwell and St Mirren,' said Stewart. 'Tommy McLean was manager at Motherwell, but they were in the First Division at the time. Alex Miller was at St Mirren, and they were doing well in the Premier Division. Alex told me that I would be coming in to support Campbell Money who had just taken over from Billy Thomson who had moved to Dundee United. I knew therefore that I was going to St Mirren as back up for Campbell.'

Stewart would spend two seasons with the Buddies. He made his debut on 20 October 1984 in a 4-0 defeat against Aberdeen at Pittodrie and played in nine league fixtures for the Love Street side. The last of those proved to be a chastening experience, a 5-0 thrashing at the hands of Celtic that handed David Hay's side the title on goal difference at the end of season 1985/86.

That would be Stewart's last league appearance for St Mirren. In the summer of 1986, he took the decision to go and help out an old team-mate at Partick Thistle.

'DJ had just got the Partick manager's job and he called me up and asked me if I would go there,' said Stewart. 'I was 32 at the time and was full-time with St Mirren. I didn't have an issue going part-time, but with hindsight it wasn't the right move, and at the end of that season, I decided to call it a day.'

After making his debut against Celtic in a friendly, Stewart made 12 appearances for Thistle. He kept a clean sheet in what would be his last senior league appearance, against Queen of the South, on 27 January 1987, and the following week pulled on the gloves for the last time when Thistle exited the Scottish Cup losing 3-1 against Motherwell at Fir Park.

With a young family to support, Stewart joined the Ministry of Defence when he retired from playing. He would be there for eight years as a serving police officer. But a new career path would emerge with the advent of the role of goalkeeping coach.

'Alan Hodgkinson was coaching the Scotland national team goalkeepers, and he ran a couple of goalkeeping seminars that I decided to go along to,' said Stewart. 'I went along more out of interest than anything else, but I got bitten by the bug as I still wanted to put something back into the game. I was doing training with the MOD at the time which meant travelling from Scotland to England. But after that was finished, I was posted in Beith. Jim Fleeting was manager of Kilmarnock at the time, and he asked me to come in and work with the goalkeepers on a part-time basis.'

That was in 1989, and Jim would remain at Rugby Park until 1994. He even managed to play a couple of games for Kilmarnock – an Ayrshire Cup semi-final victory over Girvan, and two friendly matches in the Joe Meldrum Memorial Trophy which was hosted by Glenafton Athletic in August 1989.

Jim Fleeting left Kilmarnock in 1992. Tommy Burns took over and he retained Stewart's services. They would work together again when the pair were part of the backroom staff assembled by Walter Smith when he became Scotland manager in 2004.

'I decided to leave the MOD and become a self-employed goalkeeping coach,' said Stewart. 'I had some opportunities working with some clubs, doing a couple of days here and there, and then Craig Brown asked me to come and work with the Scotland U21s. I was eventually promoted to the senior side when Berti Vogts became the Scotland manager, and when Walter took over from him, he kept me on. I had never worked with Walter before, but over the years we developed a great relationship on and off the park.'

But as Stewart recalls, he thought he had blotted his copybook with Smith even before their first match together.

'We were playing Italy in the San Siro,' said Stewart. 'I had heard that Walter was a stickler for everything being set up on the pitch before the players came out to train. Coisty, Tommy and I left early in a taxi to sort that out, and I remember Coisty telling us about the chance he had missed back in 1984 when he had played for Rangers against Inter Milan at the San Siro.

'When we arrived, Tommy started to get excited as we walked along the corridor as it looked like the Italy team were still out on the pitch training.

'But as we got outside, we quickly noticed that it wasn't the Azzurri, it was Walter and the Scotland players! I don't know what route the taxi driver took to the stadium, but it was a longer one than the gaffer and the boys.

'Walter walked towards us and said to me that I had better have a good reason for being late and getting myself involved with Coisty and Tommy. As I didn't know Walter at the time, I didn't know if he was being serious or not, but we had a good laugh about it all when we went back to the hotel for dinner after training.'

Evidently, Smith wasn't too perturbed as Stewart would play a key role in his coaching team for the next seven years. And when Walter left to rescue Rangers in 2007, Jim went with him, which afforded him the opportunity to coach the goalkeeper Allan McGregor.

'He's the best goalkeeper I've worked with,' said Stewart proudly. 'He's the first one in every morning and one of the last ones to leave. I worked a wee bit with the late, great Andy Goram when the Scotland U21s trained with the full team, and everything Andy had, Allan tried to replicate. He's focused, dedicated, and hates to lose. He's a brilliant shot stopper. I know Allan looked up to Andy, and I can't pay Allan a higher compliment than saying he's up there when people talk about the greatest Rangers goalkeepers of all time.'

Jim Stewart made 107 appearances for Rangers and kept 40 clean sheets. After serving under Walter Smith, Ally McCoist and Mark Warburton, he left Rangers in 2017. His son, Colin, is the current goalkeeping coach at Ibrox.

* * *

When Jim Stewart left Rangers for St Mirren, Nicky Walker was the man entrusted by Jock Wallace to compete with Peter McCloy for the number one jersey. Given that Walker had played under Wallace at Leicester City and Motherwell, it was no surprise that he followed big Jock to Ibrox.

Born in Aberdeen on 29 September 1962, Joseph Nicol Walker started out as a right-back at primary school in Aberlour before deciding that his best position was goalkeeper.

'When I was still at primary school, I was playing for the U13 and U14 teams,' said Walker. 'I also played for our village team – Aberlour Villa – in the Welfare League and Elgin Boys Club. I was playing three or four games a week, and I got a chance to go to Keith who were in the Highland League. But they had an experienced goalkeeper which meant I wasn't going to get many games. At that stage, I decided to join Elgin City, and I started to get games for them when I was maybe 16 or 17.'

Walker's performances for Elgin soon attracted a number of suitors, including Jock Wallace who had taken over the reins at Leicester City following his shock departure from Rangers in the summer of 1978.

'When you played for the school team and in the Highland League, there were lots of scouts at the games,' recalled Walker. 'I remember going to Derby County and Dundee United on trial, and there were lots of opportunities. But I had stayed at school to do my Highers and I planned to be a PE teacher until Leicester showed an interest, and I agreed to sign a four-year deal with them.'

When Walker arrived at Filbert Street, Mark Wallington was the Leicester number one. He had signed for the club in 1972 and hardly missed a game. But a sequence of 331 successive appearances was broken when Wallington was injured during Leicester's 5-2 win over Shrewsbury Town in the sixth round of the FA Cup.

'Back then the FA Cup was massive,' said Walker. 'Mark got studded in the thigh but had to play on as there was no sub goalies in those days. We lost a couple of goals to go 2-1 down, and our centre-forward, Alan Young, eventually had to take over in goal. But Alan got injured too, so Steve Lynex, who was a winger, stepped in.'

Wallington's injury meant Walker was handed his Leicester debut on 9 March 1982 against Chelsea at Stamford Bridge. The visitors lost 4-1, but Walker played in the five league matches that followed. City won four and lost one of those games before Wallington returned to action when the Foxes faced Tottenham Hotspur in the FA Cup semi-final at Villa Park.

'I thought I did reasonably okay in the games I played,' said Walker. 'But Jock pulled me aside before the semi-final and said that he thought it was too big a game for me. Mark came back in, and we were beaten 2-0.'

He added, 'Years later when I was at Rangers, Jock told me he regretted not playing me at Villa Park. He was trying to protect me and went for Mark's experience, but as an 18-year-old, it was a sore one at the time. However, in hindsight, I think the manager probably made the right call.'

At the end of the season, Jock Wallace was heading back to Scotland. He became manager of Motherwell and Walker would soon follow him to Lanarkshire.

'Big Jock phoned me straight away,' said Walker. 'He knew that Sheffield United and a couple of other clubs were trying to sign me, but he told me not to do anything as he wanted me at Motherwell.'

Walker was signed by Motherwell in January 1983. The Motherwell number one at that time was Hugh Sproat, and he had created something of a reputation for himself as he would sport a green jersey when facing Rangers then don a blue one when Celtic provided the opposition.

Motherwell's new recruit didn't have to wait long for his debut, as the day after he put pen to paper – 15 January 1983 – he made his league debut. Celtic were the visitors to Fir Park, but they left defeated, two Brian McClair goals earning the home side a 2-1 victory.

Walker played in 14 of the 15 league matches that followed. In that run, Motherwell were hammered 5-1 by Aberdeen, 4-1 by Dundee United and 4-0 by St Mirren. But Wallace's side did enough to secure their Premier Division status, finishing eighth, seven points better off than ninth-placed Morton who were relegated along with Kilmarnock.

Although he missed out on the opening league match against Dundee United, Walker was the undisputed number one at Fir Park in the early months of season 1983/84. He was enjoying his football and looked set for a run of games until a bombshell was dropped in November 1983. John Greig resigned, and, eventually, Jock Wallace succeeded him as manager of Rangers.

Bobby Watson took over from Wallace at Motherwell, but he and Walker didn't have the best of relationships. Before 1983 had ended, Walker was Rangers-bound, and for a third time in his career, Nicky would soon be part of Jock Wallace's playing squad.

After watching from the stands as Rangers defeated Dundee 2-1 at Ibrox on 17 December, Walker made his league debut in a 2-0 win over Hibernian at Easter Road three days after Christmas. His appearance was unexpected – even Walker didn't know he was playing until he was told on the bus journey from Glasgow to Edinburgh – but an injury to Peter McCloy in training the previous day saw the new boy thrust into action.

Jimmy Nicholl, on loan from Toronto Blizzard, was ordered off against Hibernian, and a Rangers player saw red in Walker's next match – Ally Dawson was dismissed on this occasion – but the Light Blues continued their fine form under Wallace by earning a 1-1 draw against table-topping Aberdeen.

With heavy snowfall hitting Scotland and forcing fixtures to be postponed, Jock Wallace decided to take his squad away to Majorca for a sunshine break towards the end of January 1984. They departed after Walker chalked up another clean sheet when he shut out St Johnstone in a 2-0 win at Ibrox.

Upon their return, a refreshed Rangers struggled to defeat Dunfermline Athletic in the Scottish Cup at Ibrox before Walker had to step aside when Wallace's side faced Dundee United in the semi-final of the League Cup. Having played in the competition for Motherwell earlier in the season, he was cup-tied, which meant a recall for Peter McCloy.

'We had big Peter, Jim Stewart and young Andy Bruce as the goalies when I came to the club,' recalled Walker. 'Peter was great, and it was clear he still wanted to play. I was full of respect for him, and we got on really well. Alongside the likes of Ally Dawson and Derek Johnstone, he was very helpful when it came to schooling me about the club and how I should live my life.'

He added, 'Jim Stewart was amazing. He was a Scottish internationalist, but I think he knew his time was up at Rangers. But it showed the mark of him as a man that he was so supportive and respectful when I came in. I also spent time with him when I was at Hearts and Partick Thistle and Jim was the goalie coach. The word "gentleman" is often overused, but that term applies perfectly to Jim Stewart.'

After embarking on a fun-filled but gruelling post-season world tour, Walker appeared to have won the battle for the number one jersey. After playing in all the pre-season matches, including a 2-2 draw against former club Leicester City, Nicky was selected in the team in each of the opening six Premier Division matches. He kept five clean sheets in those games, shutting out St Mirren, Celtic, Dundee, Hibernian and Aberdeen. However, a dreadful evening in Dublin on 18 September 1984 brought the stellar start to Nicky's season to a shuddering halt.

'That was a disaster,' was Walker's rueful recollection. 'We played Bohemians in the UEFA Cup, and it was just a poisonous atmosphere. The first half was okay, but it all flared up at half-time. I spent most of the time standing about five to ten yards outside my box. The supporters were lobbing everything they could get their hands on onto the pitch. There were bricks and boulders, bits of masonry, bits of terracing, and at one point a dart flew past my face.'

Understandably, under such a barrage Nicky did not have the best of performances that night. Rangers lost 3-2, and he found himself relegated to the reserves. That restored his confidence and Walker was eventually reinstated to the first team on 19 January when Rangers faced league-leaders Aberdeen at Pittodrie. However, it was an afternoon to forget; Frank McDougall scored four times in a comprehensive 5-1 win for the home side.

Nicky played in seven of the last 12 league games, but season 1985/86 proved to be his breakthrough year. At the age of 23 he finally claimed the number one jersey, missing only two of the 36 Premier Division matches. He was an ever-present in the Scottish Cup, League Cup and UEFA Cup too.

But that campaign would be one of the worst in Rangers' history. League form was wretched, Hearts eliminated Rangers at the first hurdle in the Scottish Cup and Hibernian won the Skol League Cup semi-final 2-1 on aggregate. And matters came to a head when Tottenham Hotspur came to Ibrox for a friendly in April 1986. Rangers lost 2-0 and Wallace was dismissed shortly afterwards.

Having worked with him since he was 17, Walker was upset when his mentor was sacked.

'Jock was unbelievable, just a fantastic fella,' said Walker. 'Back in those days there were motivators and tacticians but there were none better at man-management than big Jock. He knew how to get the best out of his players. I'm still in touch with his son, John, who is the same age as me.'

Wallace's place in the manager's office was taken by Graeme Souness, and the Souness era started with silverware. Six days after clinching the Premier Division title, Celtic arrived at Ibrox for the Glasgow Cup Final. Walker wore the number one jersey in front of a full house at Ibrox and watched his buddy Ally McCoist net a match-winning hat-trick.

'I didn't think I'd be playing,' revealed Walker. 'Big Peter had played in the first game [at St Mirren] when Walter Smith picked the team, but I was picked, and it was great to get a winners' medal. That atmosphere was incredible too, probably the best and loudest I experienced during my playing days. I came in after the game and my ears were actually ringing because of the noise.'

But for the remainder of his time at Rangers, Nicky Walker would be second in line when it came to the position of goalkeeper for the Rangers first team. Among the first of Souness's signings was England international goalkeeper Chris Woods, who arrived from Norwich City for £600,000, and Walker knew instantly that the writing was on the wall for him.

'I was on holiday in Spain with my mates and in those days you got the paper a day late,' said Walker. 'When I read we had signed Chris, that pretty much confirmed for me that I wouldn't be getting a game the following season. We came back for pre-season and played in Paul Miller's testimonial against Tottenham and after the game Souness said I had played well. But Woodsie was a very good goalkeeper so I knew if he was fit, then he would play.'

In what proved to be a Championship-winning season for Rangers, Walker made just two appearances in the league. Supplanting Woods was an impossible task. The only action Walker saw was in a 2-0 win over Motherwell in September and a 4-0 win over Clydebank a week later, deputising when Woods injured his back.

The lack of top-team game time eventually saw a loan deal set up in January 1987, with Walker joining Falkirk. There were rumours of permanent switches to Chelsea and Tottenham Hotspur too.

'Derek Ferguson and I were supposed to be going to Stamford Bridge as part of a swap deal for Tony Dorigo,' said Walker. 'That fell through, as did a move to Tottenham when Terry Venables decided to sign Bobby Mimms instead.'

He added, 'I went to Falkirk on loan for about a month and really enjoyed it. They were struggling, but we had a good dressing room. We lost most of the matches I played, but I felt I acquitted myself well.'

It was much the same for Walker in season 1987/88. Another loan deal was struck in January 1988, this time with Dunfermline Athletic, but it was cut short after just one match. Woods fractured his ribs in a 2-0 defeat at Parkhead, so Nicky was recalled to Ibrox.

Walker started four successive league matches to add to his only other appearance that season. This had come in October against Aberdeen at Hampden.

'The week before the Skol Cup Final I injured my knee playing for the reserves at Parkhead,' said Walker. 'Woodsie got sent off in the first-team game at Ibrox which meant he was suspended for the final. I hardly trained that week, but when Souness asked if I'd be fit, I said I was. I probably wasn't 100 per cent fit, but you might never get a chance like that again, so I said I was okay.'

The final was among the most memorable in the history of the competition. Rangers took the trophy by edging a nerve-shredding penalty shoot-out after an epic 3-3 draw. One of the standout moments, though, was a stunning free kick from Davie Cooper.

'I still remember the noise when the ball hit the net,' recalled Walker. 'Wee Durranty was absolutely brilliant that day, but I had mixed emotions. For the first goal I gave away a penalty although I still maintain that Willie Falconer stood on my hand and went down.'

A further league appearance followed in a 1-1 draw with Hibernian at Ibrox in April to take Walker's tally of first-team appearances to six. But he would enjoy more game time in season 1988/89 after Woods was struck down by labyrinthitis.

'I came in and played 12 games,' said Walker. 'I did okay but got caned for a couple of goals I conceded at Tynecastle and Tannadice. I was under a lot of pressure because no matter what I did or didn't do I knew Woodsie would come back in when he was fit again.'

Season 1988/89 was Nicky Walker's last in a Rangers jersey. With his contract expiring, he signed for Hearts on 23 August 1989.

'I was offered a two-year contract, but as much as I loved Glasgow Rangers, I wasn't going to get too many games,' said Walker. 'My last involvement with Rangers was the Scottish Cup Final. We lost 1-0 against Celtic and we went back to Ibrox afterwards. When we were there, the canteen staff, who I got on really well with, presented me with a colour team photograph and I left Ibrox with that tucked under my arm. Apart from Masters games in the future, that was my last involvement for Rangers.'

He added, 'I was supposed to go to Ipswich Town, but that didn't happen. Wee Doddie [Alex MacDonald] phoned me and asked me if I wanted to come to Hearts. He told me he had a decent goalie [Henry Smith] but I had the chance to come in and fight for the jersey.'

And fight he did, but Walker did not make a league appearance for Hearts until 16 February 1991. His arrival galvanised Henry Smith and it was season 1992/93 before Nicky enjoyed a decent run in the team, playing 18 times in the league. He vied with Smith for the gloves again in season 1993/94, making 17 Premier Division appearances and also played in the 2-1 defeat against Rangers in the Scottish Cup semi-final at Celtic Park.

Walker – who had a loan spell with Burnley in 1992 – left Hearts in October 1994 to join Partick Thistle. Before he departed, he won the first of two caps for Scotland, and he was one of three goalkeepers selected in the squad for Euro 96.

'It was amazing to play for Scotland,' said Nicky. 'I won my first cap at Ibrox, but I would have loved it if one of my caps had come at Hampden.'

He added, 'Before the Euros, the talk was about who was going to play – Goram or Leighton – so I knew I was never going to get a game, but I trained hard and loved it.'

After the Euros, Walker had a season with Aberdeen before returning home to spend the latter years of his career in the

Highlands with Inverness Caley and Ross County. He retired in the summer of 2004 at the age of 42.

Walker was only part-time with Inverness and Ross County, splitting his time between football and the family shortbread business and he is still based in Aberlour today where he undertakes the role of managing director.

'To be a Rangers goalkeeper, you need self-confidence and concentration,' concluded Walker. 'I was at Rangers at a time when we weren't winning the league, so I was probably busier than others have been, but there were still games with long periods of inactivity. You've got to have a thick skin too. If you make a mistake, there's no hiding from it, it's headline news. It gets magnified, so you have to be robust and confident in your own ability.'

Nicky Walker made a total of 136 appearances for the Rangers first team. He won a Skol League Cup winners' medal (1987/88) and two Glasgow Cup medals (1985/86 and 1986/87).

Chapter 7

Rangers Reborn

WHEN DAVID Holmes came to Ibrox in November 1985, the season was all but over for Rangers. After a promising start, they had started to tumble down the league table and had exited the League Cup at the semi-final stage. Their European odyssey had also ended abruptly, CA Osasuna winning 2-1 on aggregate in the opening round of the UEFA Cup.

The New Year didn't affect a change in fortunes either. Rangers eventually finished fifth in the league and were beaten by Hearts in the third round of the Scottish Cup which meant a season without silverware.

Rangers were in a state of disrepair. But Holmes took decisive action to rectify that when he appointed Graeme Souness as the club's first-ever player-manager, in April 1986. Souness, who had had a glittering playing career, came in and the wind of change started to blow through Ibrox at hurricane force.

The former Liverpool captain was intent on restoring Rangers back to the top in Scotland as well as making them a force to be reckoned with in Europe. A major overhaul was required, and integral to that rebuilding process was the improvement of the spine of his team. In Ally McCoist, Souness had a prolific goalscorer, and in Ian Durrant he had one of the most promising box-to-box midfielders in the country. But he lacked a commanding centre-back and also reckoned he needed a top-class goalkeeper. The England captain, Terry Butcher, filled the void for the former, while the latter position went to Christopher Charles Eric Woods.

Born in Swineshead in Lincolnshire, on 14 November 1959, Woods is regarded by many as one of the finest goalkeepers ever to play for Rangers. But the genesis of his career in that position came after he picked up an injury while playing for his school team at the age of 14.

'I had always played outfield and I used to take the goal kicks as the goalkeeper couldn't kick the ball very far,' recalled Woods. 'But I tore my thigh muscle so in order to keep playing I went in goal. That's where it all started for me.'

Woods obviously excelled as he attracted the attention of a number of clubs who were keen to sign him.

'It looked like I would sign for Derby County,' said Woods. 'The youth-team manager there was a guy called Alan Hill, but he moved to Nottingham Forest to work with Brian Clough, so I ended up going there instead.'

Woods was 17 when he joined Forest in 1976. The other goalkeepers at the club at that time were John Middleton and Peter Wells, but it would be the signing of Peter Shilton in 1977 that would offer Chris the chance to get into the first team.

'I always considered working under Shilts as being an apprenticeship for me as he was the best goalkeeper in the world at that time,' said Woods. 'But when he signed, he was cup-tied for the League Cup, so Mr Clough selected me to play in all but one of the League Cup matches that season.'

John Middleton played in the opening-round win over West Ham United, but Woods was handed his Forest debut on 25 October 1977 in the next round against Notts County at the City Ground. A couple of goals from Ian Bowyer helped Forest win comfortably, 4-0, and Woods would play in each of the six matches that followed in the competition.

Wins over Aston Villa, Bury and Leeds United took the youngster to Wembley for the first time as a player. Forest would face the all-conquering Liverpool side of that era, and Woods would keep two clean sheets as his team emerged victorious, winning 1-0 in a replay at Old Trafford which handed Woods the first of many honours he collected in his playing career.

Woods remained with Forest for another season and was a non-playing substitute when they won the first of two successive European Cups in season 1978/79. But with Shilton cementing his status as the world's best goalkeeper, opportunities to play were limited for Woods. It was time to move on.

'After winning the League Cup I went back into the reserves at Forest,' recalled Woods. 'But I eventually decided that it was time for me to go to a club and become a number one. I could have gone to Watford, but I went to QPR as at that time it felt that that was the right move for me. Tommy Docherty was the manager, and I had some good times in the 18 months I was there.'

Woods made his QPR debut against Bristol Rovers on 18 August 1979 at Loftus Road. QPR won 2-0, and that would be one of 14 clean sheets young Woods would keep in the 41 league matches he played that season. Woods started the first 22 league matches of season 1980/81 too, but a 2-1 win away at Bolton Wanderers on 19 December 1980 would be the last time he would keep goal for QPR as a managerial change signalled the beginning of the end of his time in London.

Woods recalled, 'Terry Venables took over from Tommy and he brought in his own guys like John Burridge who he had worked with at Crystal Palace. Terry did say that he thought I would be a very good goalkeeper, but John was his man, so it was at that point that I decided to leave QPR and join Norwich.'

That move was rubber-stamped in March 1981 when QPR recouped the £250,000 they had spent on Woods when they sold him to Norwich City. The move to East Anglia would prove to be the launch pad for Chris Woods's career.

In five seasons at Carrow Road, Woods barely missed a game. After making his debut in a 3-0 defeat against Wolverhampton Wanderers at Molineux, he played in every league game Norwich played until 29 September 1984. That amounts to 143 successive league matches.

During Woods's time at Carrow Road, he was part of a side that was relegated twice and promoted twice. He was also in the XI that won the League Cup in season 1984/85. And during his spell with Norwich, he won the first of his 43 caps for England in a 5-0 win over the USA on 16 June 1985. Ironically, his last cap was also against the USA, on 9 June 1993.

It was in fact after an England game that the seeds were sown for Woods's move to Rangers. Woods was on the bench when England defeated Scotland 2-1 at Wembley on 23 April 1986. Terry Butcher and Glenn Hoddle scored for the home side, with Scotland's goal coming from the man that had just been announced as the new player-manager of Rangers, Graeme Souness.

'I jokingly asked Graeme after the game if he was looking for a goalkeeper,' said Woods with a smile. 'Things escalated from there, though. He went away and did his homework on me then called me up and before I knew it, I was a Rangers player.'

The fee paid for Woods was reported to be £600,000, making him the most expensive goalkeeper in Britain at that time. But the fee didn't burden him; he was just looking forward to a new challenge in his career.

'If I'm being honest, I didn't know a lot about Rangers before I signed,' said Woods. 'One of the main reasons for me going there was Graeme Souness. I've got the upmost respect for him. He sold his vision to me, and I have to say that everything he told me came true.'

He added, 'I knew when Graeme signed me that I was going to be number one, but I also knew that if I didn't produce the goods then I wouldn't be in the team.'

Woods made his Rangers debut in a 2-0 win over Union Solingen on a pre-season tour of West Germany, and less than a month later played in his first Premier Division match against Hibernian at Easter Road. To say it was a tempestuous start would be an understatement. Souness was ordered off and a melee ensued that Woods was part of.

'It was interesting,' said Woods. 'I was one of the 21 players that got booked and we lost 2-1. It was an eye-opener. It was at that point that I realised that everyone who played Rangers wanted to beat them, and that was made even more clear when we played Dundee United a week later.'

Two goals from Ally McCoist had Rangers cruising, but a double from Kevin Gallacher and a strike by former Rangers player Ian Redford earned United a 3-2 win.

'I remember I made a save in that match but United scored on the rebound,' said Woods. 'All of a sudden people were starting to ask questions about me and Graeme. But after that things settled down, and we went on to have a very good season.'

The United defeat was followed by four straight wins, including a 1-0 victory over Celtic at Ibrox in the first Old Firm match of the campaign. Woods missed the last of the wins in that sequence – 2-0 away at Motherwell and 4-0 at home to Clydebank – with a back injury, but they would be the only league matches he would miss all season.

Inconsistency was still the order of the day, though, for Rangers. Although Woods swelled his League Cup medal collection to three when Celtic were beaten 2-1 at Hampden, Rangers found themselves trailing in the title race. But helped by some obdurate defending at one end and lethal finishing at the other, a pre-Christmas gap was bridged, and Rangers hit the front after a 2-0 win over Hamilton Accies in January.

Woods was a key player in that run, and he was now showing consistently why he was regarded as one of the best goalkeepers in the British Isles. Accomplished in all aspects of the art of goalkeeping, he had superb reflexes and was comfortable dealing with cross balls.

Woods was the last line of an impressive defence that primarily featured the likes of Terry Butcher, Graham Roberts, Dave McPherson, and the often-underrated Stuart Munro. And that quintet played their part when Woods became a world-record holder.

After conceding a goal to Uwe Rahn of Borussia Monchengladbach on 26 November, he wouldn't fish the ball out of the net again until 31 January. Twelve successive clean sheets were recorded and a world-record 1,196 minutes without conceding a goal was chalked up.

'That run wasn't just about me or the defenders,' said Woods. 'Defending starts from the front, so that record was down to the whole team. I still think the record stands today too. Edwin van der Sar went 14 games without conceding, but they weren't in consecutive games like I did.'

The run was ended by a goal from Adrian Sprott in a shock 1-0 win for Hamilton Accies in the third round of the Scottish Cup. But as cataclysmic as some reckoned that result would be, it didn't derail Rangers' title tilt. And on 2 May 1987, after nine years, the Light Blues were crowned champions of Scotland once again.

'I think we were nine points behind Celtic at one point, but we ended up winning the league by six points,' recalled Woods. 'Once we started to get into the swing of things, we thought we would win every game. There was a confidence about the whole club.'

He continued, 'At Pittodrie, I remember nearly having my hand pulled off. The supporters came onto the pitch and some of them were trying to get my gloves off, but the Velcro around my wrist was still tight. I happened to be in the goal that was furthest from the dressing room, so I couldn't make a quick dash down the tunnel.'

Woods could understand the exuberance of the supporters, and there was a party atmosphere among the players and staff on the team bus too as it journeyed back to Glasgow.

'It was a great trip back,' said Woods. 'There were supporters everywhere, and we even stopped to pick a few of them up and bring them on to the bus. It was really special for all of us.'

Woods made a total of 55 appearances in his debut season at Rangers. In 42 league appearances, he conceded just 23 goals and kept 25 clean sheets. Numbers like that allied to the predatory partnership formed between Robert Fleck and Ally McCoist were the main reasons why the season ended with the League Championship trophy back inside a cabinet in the Ibrox Trophy Room.

The goal was now to retain the title and have a shot at winning the European Cup. But a series of unfortunate events would scupper those ambitions. The first of those came on 17 October 1987.

Rangers had had a poor start to their title defence. They won only one of their first five league matches, although a run of five wins in seven had steadied the listing ship prior to the visit of Celtic for the second Old Firm match of the season. During the first one, Graeme Souness had been ordered off, and players would see red in this one too. Woods was one of them.

'The whole thing was surreal,' recalled Woods. 'Frank [McAvennie] popped me into the back of the net early in the game, and after that there was an incident where we squared up to each other. There was a push here, a push there, but when the referee, Jim Duncan, sent Frank off, I knew I'd be going too.'

He continued, 'I thought it was ridiculous. I think I grabbed Frank around the neck, and he swung his arms to take mine away. I still had the ball in my hand when Terry [Butcher] and Graham [Roberts] got involved. It was farcical, and the fact that it ended up in court was unbelievable.'

On the field, the upshot was that Woods missed out through suspension when Rangers faced Aberdeen in the League Cup Final. Nicky Walker deputised, and Rangers won an epic contest 5-3 on penalty kicks after a 3-3 draw after extra time. But Woods had the gloves back when the sides met again in the league less than a month later. Rangers lost that one 1-0, but the broken leg sustained by Terry Butcher would arguably cost the Light Blues the title and perhaps the European Cup too.

'Terry was a leader on and off the pitch,' said Woods. 'He was a great centre-half, and you knew that most of the balls that came into the box he was going to head clear. It was a pleasure to play alongside him. We were room-mates for five years, so we got to know each other really well.'

Woods would have his own injury problems in season 1987/88. He played in each of the first 27 league matches but fractured his ribs during a 2-0 defeat at Parkhead on 2 January. He missed four matches as a result, but even short spells of absence such as that were rare for Woods. However, in season 1988/89, he would find himself out for a much longer period of time when he picked up labyrinthitis.

'That was one of the most frightening things I've ever gone through,' said Woods. 'I used to play a lot of squash and I remember coming home after playing on a Sunday afternoon and sitting down to have a cup of tea. I bent down to put my cup on the floor, but when I sat back up, I felt woozy and dizzy. After that it was about three-and-a-half weeks before I could even get out of bed. I was out for three months, but even when I came back in, I was still struggling. If I came for a cross, when I landed and my feet hit the ground the ball looked as if it was juddering.'

Prior to his spell out of the team, Woods had added another League Cup medal to his collection when Rangers beat Aberdeen 3-2, and when he came back into the team at the end of February, he was on course to pick up another League Championship medal too. But hopes of a domestic Treble were dashed when Celtic eked out a 1-0 win in the Scottish Cup Final.

'Gary Stevens went to play a back pass to me but left it short and Joe Miller came in and beat me in a one-v-one,' recalled Woods. 'It was disappointing to lose, and that was the one domestic competition I didn't win at Rangers. It would have been nice to have a complete set of medals.'

Season 1989/90 saw the arrival of Maurice Johnston and Trevor Steven. The signing of Johnston was a seismic moment. Just a few weeks earlier it looked like he was all set to return to Celtic after a spell in France with Nantes, but when it became apparent that wasn't a done deal, Souness made his move.

For years, Rangers had been criticised for not signing Roman Catholics, now they had done that and also struck a psychological blow to their Old Firm rivals too. Johnston's arrival divided opinion, but for Woods, his arrival meant that the quality of the playing squad had been enhanced.

'When Mo came in, he added a little bit more quality to the team,' said Woods. 'We all heard the rumbles going round that he wouldn't score against Celtic, but although he didn't score in his first game, he got the winner at Ibrox, and after that the supporters really took to him. But the players recognised from the start that he would make us a better side.'

The winning goal Woods referred to was in November 1989 and took Rangers top of the league. But they had had to overcome a wretched start to reach the summit. The season started with two successive defeats and only two wins from the first eight league fixtures. And in the opening game of the campaign, a 1-0 defeat against St Mirren, Woods picked up another injury that would keep him out of the team for a period of time.

'A cross came in and Kenny McDowall came in from behind me and hit my right shoulder,' said Woods. 'That displaced my acromioclavicular which meant I missed eight matches. I was in a lot of discomfort – even driving the car was painful – but I wanted to play that much that I took some injections to get through it.'

With Nicky Walker moving to Hearts, the man that looked set to step in for Woods was Lindsay Hamilton.

Hamilton had joined the club in November 1986 from Stenhousemuir for £25,000. He had joined Stenny after two years with Thorniewood United, making his debut as a trialist on 27 December 1982. Hamilton played three more times that season, and for the next three years, he made the number one jersey at Ochilview his own. Hamilton missed only 11 of the 127 league matches Stenhousemuir played, and he sealed his move with a fine display against Rangers in the Skol League Cup early in season 1986/87.

In essence, Hamilton came to Ibrox as the third-choice goalkeeper behind Woods and Nicky Walker, although the latter was on the transfer list at his own request when Hamilton joined. That meant access to the first team was limited primarily to friendly matches, although he did make his debut in a Glasgow Cup semi-final against Clyde on 28 April 1987. Previously a sought-after honour, the competition was now viewed as an opportunity to blood promising youngsters, and Hamilton was joined in the Rangers team that night at Firhill by the likes of Gary McSwegan, John Spencer and David Kirkwood. Spencer scored Rangers' goal in a 1-1 draw, the match being settled when Rangers won 5-4 on penalties. Hamilton saved three of the seven penalties taken by Clyde.

Hamilton's next first team opportunity came almost 18 months later. He came on as substitute for Walker in a testimonial match for Charlie Kelly of East Stirling. One start and two further appearances from the bench followed, the latter of which was a 2-1 defeat against Gretna. That fixture was arranged to raise funds for the Lockerbie disaster.

When Walker left for Hearts in 1989, Hamilton was elevated to number two goalkeeper, and he started two of the friendly matches ahead of season 1989/90. In the first of them – a 4-2 win over Clydebank – Rangers fielded a couple of South African trialists, Thomas Madigage and Augustine Makalakalane. Madigage scored one of the goals, but neither player made enough of an impression to be offered a permanent deal.

Given he appeared to be next in line for the gloves if Woods got injured or suspended, it would not have been a major surprise had Hamilton been handed his competitive debut three days after Woods dislocated his shoulder against St Mirren. Rangers were due to play Arbroath in the second round of the League Cup at Ibrox, and even the match programme had Hamilton listed as goalkeeper for the evening.

However, Hamilton's hopes of a first-team debut in front of the Rangers supporters at Ibrox would be cruelly dashed. Graeme Souness dipped into the transfer market and signed an Israeli goalkeeper called Ben-Zion Shabbtai Ginzburg. He'd become better known as Bonni, but his registration was rushed through so that he could play against Arbroath. He kept a clean sheet as Rangers won 4-0. Ally McCoist scored a hat-trick and missed a penalty.

Ginzburg, who would eventually win 68 caps for Israel, was less than convincing the following weekend when Rangers lost 2-0 at Easter Road before he was handed an Old Firm baptism at Parkhead. Rangers drew 1-1 to register their first point of the season, and Ginzburg played in a further two league matches, two

League Cup ties, and the second leg of the European Cup tie against Bayern Munich. The latter match was drawn 0-0 – the tie was all but over following Bayern's 3-1 win at Ibrox – and that was one of only three clean sheets Ginzburg kept in his eight competitive appearances that season.

He would make a further six appearances for Rangers, all in friendly matches. The last of them came at Dens Park on 4 August 1990 in a pre-season friendly against Dundee. Mark Hateley netted his first goal for Rangers in that match.

With opportunities to displace Woods scarce, Ginzburg returned to Israel where he would play for seven clubs before announcing his retirement in 2001. Post-retirement, Ginzburg moved into the media, becoming the main presenter of a football highlights show and today he works as a commentator for the Israeli sports channel Sport 5. And in what must be a first for a Rangers player, Ginzburg also took part in Israel's version of *Dancing with the Stars*.

Lindsay Hamilton never did make a competitive appearance for Rangers. His final top-team game for the club came in a 5-2 win over Clyde at Firhill on 8 August 1989, exactly a week before he was due to play against Arbroath. He had spells on loan at Stirling Albion and Leeds United – he didn't play any games for the latter – before signing for St Johnstone in the summer of 1990.

Hamilton soon established himself as the number one goalkeeper, making 77 league appearances over two seasons for the Perth side. He was transferred to Dunfermline Athletic in July 1992 where he initially vied with John Hillcoat for the gloves. Hamilton was eventually supplanted by Ian Westwater, and moved on, playing for Portadown, East Fife, Queen's Park and Partick Thistle before finishing his career where it started with Stenhousemuir. He is currently the goalkeeper coach at East Fife.

As far as Woods was concerned, he came back into the team following his shoulder injury on 14 October 1989. He wouldn't miss another competitive game for Rangers until he left to join Sheffield Wednesday in the summer of 1991. That amounted to 83 consecutive appearances.

The League Cup Final was lost to Aberdeen in season 1989/90, but the league title was retained. Woods and his defence once again played a significant part in that achievement. In 36 league games, only 19 goals were conceded. Woods kept 18 clean sheets, with a run of six in succession between 23 December and 27 January.

'Everyone in that team was good at what they did,' said Woods. 'We had a lively dressing room, and that helped us achieve the success that we did. Nobody got an easy ride, and there would be arguments, but in the end hands would be shaken, and we got on with it.'

Another big hitter was thrown into that dressing-room mix in the summer of 1990. Mark Hateley had played with Woods for England, and after a ropey start, he would have the final say in an enthralling title race that went right to the wire.

But before the final-day drama unfolded, there would be two other major moments that season: the departures of Terry Butcher and Graeme Souness. Butcher left to join Coventry City in November, and Souness took over from Kenny Dalglish as Liverpool manager five months later.

'I was surprised when Graeme left us,' admitted Woods. 'But given the success he had enjoyed with Liverpool as a player, becoming their manager was obviously something he always wanted to do. It was great for us that Walter [Smith] took over from Graeme, though. Walter was the first person I met when I came to Scotland as he picked me up from Edinburgh Airport. We built up an excellent working relationship and were good friends away from the club as well.'

Smith took over for the four games that remained. Rangers won the first two – both by 1-0, against St Mirren at Love Street and Dundee United at home – but then contrived to lose 3-0 away from home against Motherwell on the penultimate weekend of the campaign. That allowed Aberdeen to edge ahead on goal difference which meant it was win or bust for Smith's men when they faced the Dons at Ibrox in the final league match. The pressure may have been on, but for Woods, there was never any doubt about the outcome.

He admitted, 'We knew what we had to do. As a squad of players, we never doubted ourselves and we knew if we played to the best of our ability, we would win the game. Aberdeen did have a couple of chances early on in the first half – one of them was a one-v-one with me – but after that I remember Mark Hateley's header. After that went in, I was sure Aberdeen wouldn't come back.'

That dramatic afternoon would be the last time Chris Woods wore the Rangers goalkeeper's jersey in a competitive match. One of the first challenges facing Walter Smith was the advent of the 'three-foreigner rule' in European competition, and that saw him seek out more Scottish players to bolster his squad. One of his signings was Andy Goram from Hibernian, and that pretty much sealed Woods's exit.

'Because of the relationship I had with Walter, I knew he was going to sign Andy,' said Woods. 'I also knew that Andy would be the number one and my time at Rangers was up. I completely understood Walter's decision, but I was still disappointed to leave. I loved being at Rangers – it was a great place to be – and my family were settled in Dunblane. We loved Scotland and it was hard to leave, but these things happen in football. There were certainly no hard feelings.'

Woods was still around as the pre-season action got underway ahead of season 1991/92. He played in a couple of pre-season friendly matches with the first team – a 1-0 win over Morton at Cappielow and a 3-2 victory over St Mirren in Campbell Money's testimonial – and Woods also played in a number of games for the reserves as they toured the Highlands. But it was only a matter of time before he left the club, and the opening match of the Premier Reserve League campaign, a 3-1 win over St Johnstone Reserves at McDiarmid Park, would prove to be his final appearance as a Rangers player. On 14 August 1991, he signed for Sheffield Wednesday for a fee of £1,200,000.

Woods would be an integral part of the Wednesday side that finished third in what would be the last season before the introduction of the Premiership. That secured European football for the Owls for season 1992/93, and Woods would also emerge from the shadows of Shilton and become England number one.

'Shilton was my idol and I thought when I played, he was the best goalkeeper in the world,' said Woods. 'When we trained together for England, I felt I was getting closer and closer to his level, so when he retired after the World Cup in 1990, I got the opportunity to be number one. Unfortunately, it didn't last very long.'

Woods would win 43 caps for England, 20 of them while he was a Rangers player. He was in goal at what was a disastrous European Championship finals for England in 1992, and a year later he played for his country for the last time. Injury and a loss of form saw him left out of the squad, and although Graham Taylor encouraged him to fight to regain his place, a recall was not forthcoming.

Woods came close to adding medals to his collection in season 1992/93 when Sheffield Wednesday reached the final of the League Cup and FA Cup. Both were lost to Arsenal, and in the replay for the latter competition, the Gunners won 2-1 after extra time – Woods, who had had an excellent season, being unable to deal with a late header from Andy Linighan.

Chris eventually lost his place in the Wednesday team to Kevin Pressman, and after a spell on loan at Reading moved to the USA to play for Colorado Rapids. He would return to England in October

1996 when Graeme Souness brought him to Southampton on loan to provide cover for Dave Beasant. Alas, Woods didn't have the best of times on the south coast, conceding seven goals in a 7-1 thrashing against Everton then sustaining a broken leg against Blackburn Rovers. Short stints at Sunderland and Burnley followed before he hung up his gloves in 1998.

Since retiring, Woods has held goalkeeper coaching roles with, among others, Everton, where he worked with Walter Smith once again, Manchester United, West Ham United and Scotland.

If you speak to Rangers supporters who saw Chris Woods in action for the club, then you will struggle to find many that are anything other than effusive in their praise of him. He is quite rightly talked about in the same breath as Goram, McGregor and Klos when debate rages over who has been the finest Rangers goalkeeper in the past 50 years. Including non-competitive matches such as friendlies and testimonials, Woods made 262 appearances for Rangers and kept 128 clean sheets. He won four league titles and two League Cups.

'There were that many highlights during my time at Rangers that it's difficult to pick out just one,' concluded Woods. 'Obviously setting the shutout record was significant, but just being part of that team that won that first title, we'll always be remembered for that. And just being part of such a huge club was memorable too. Everyone was so friendly. You had Stan who was on the front door and the kitchen staff, and when I do go back and visit, I try and catch up with as many of them as I can, although a couple are no longer with us. We were like one big, happy family.'

Chapter 8

The Goalie

ANDREW LEWIS Goram was born on 13 April 1964, and the art of goalkeeping was in his genes.

His father Lewis had also been a shot stopper, starting his career with Leith Athletic before moving to Hibernian in 1948. Up against Tommy Younger, Goram found first team opportunities limited, and he moved on loan to Third Lanark in season 1949/50. And during his time with Thirds, he played a part in one of Rangers' 55 title triumphs.

On the final day of season 1949/50, Rangers travelled to Cathkin Park needing a point to edge out Hibernian and clinch the Division One title. And Rangers romped to a 2-0 lead inside the opening 20 minutes of the game. The first of those goals, scored by Billy Williamson, fell, however, into the controversial category, and illustrated how little protection goalkeepers were afforded in that era.

A cross from Willie Thornton was attacked by Williamson, and the Rangers number ten succeeded in despatching both the ball and Goram over the line. The *Glasgow Herald*'s 'Football Correspondent' reckoned the referee, a J.S. Cox from Rutherglen, was 'in perfect position' to deem that Williamson's challenge of Goram had been 'fair', and although the home side fought back to earn a 2-2 draw, Rangers had the point they needed.

Goram senior made 11 appearances for the 'Hi-Hi', and his displays are said to have brought confidence to their defence as they fought to avoid relegation. Thirds succeeded in their mission, with Goram winning many admirers among their support.

At the end of that season, Goram moved to Bury, making over 100 league appearances for them before finishing his career with spells at Macclesfield Town, Mossley and Buxton.

The family were still based south of the border when Goram junior started his career, playing in goal for a team called Marauders on a Saturday, then at the other end of the pitch as a centre-forward for Walton 24 hours later. He would top score for Walton but had more of a fondness for saving goals than scoring them.

Regular game time in goal for Tottington High School and the Greater Manchester County Select earned Goram a trial for the England Schoolboys – he wasn't successful – but he also caught the eye of Roy Horobin who was a scout for West Bromwich Albion. He was signed by WBA as an apprentice in 1978, but at that time, Goram's preference was actually to make a career as a cricketer.

He had captained Lancashire Schoolboys and was on the ground staff at Lancashire when the legendary Clive Lloyd was a regular at the crease. Like Goram, Lloyd was a left-handed batsman, and a career with his hands wrapped around a bat made out of English willow beckoned.

But the pulling power of the beautiful game would eventually prove too strong, even though the move to WBA didn't work out. Goram spent a year there working under the flamboyant Ron Atkinson, but when Atkinson left to join Manchester United, his replacement at the Hawthorns, Ronnie Allen, told young Goram that he had no future as a goalkeeper as he was too small.

But Jimmy Frizzell, the manager of Oldham Athletic, didn't agree with Allen, and offered 5ft 11in Goram the opportunity to cut his teeth as a professional footballer. He handed Goram his debut in a 1-0 win over Charlton Athletic on 4 May 1982, and the youngster kept his place for the two league games that remained.

Frizzell left Oldham a few weeks later, and he was replaced by Joe Royle. Initially, the arrival of the former Everton centre-forward looked to have put the brakes on the fledgling career of Goram. He recruited Martin Hodge, but when Hodge was struck down by a chest infection early in season 1982/83, 17-year-old Goram was back in. And he was rarely back out after that. Apart from a stop-start season in 1983/84, Goram was the number one at Boundary Park from that moment until he left to join Hibernian for £325,000 in October 1987.

Goram didn't just impress the Hibernian manager, Alex Miller, though. On 16 October 1985, Alex Ferguson, on the recommendation of Joe Royle, picked him in his Scotland squad for a friendly against East Germany at Hampden Park. Although born in Bury, Goram's father was born in Edinburgh, and when he replaced Jim Leighton after 52 minutes, he won what would be the first of 43 Scotland caps Goram would earn in what was a chequered international career.

Goram made his full debut the following March in a 3-0 win over Romania and kept another clean sheet in a friendly against Holland in Eindhoven. A certain Alistair McCoist won his first cap in the latter encounter. Clearly, Goram impressed Ferguson as he was selected in the squad that travelled to Mexico for the 1986 World Cup, although he was an unused substitute in the matches against Denmark, West Germany and Uruguay.

The man he replaced in the World Cup squad was the man he also took over from when he signed for Hibernian, Alan Rough. Rough played in the opening 11 league matches, but after making his debut against Dunfermline Athletic in a 4-0 win at Easter Road, Goram didn't miss a game. He even managed to score a goal on the final day of the season, his long clearance catching out the Morton goalkeeper David Wylie in a 3-1 win for the Easter Road side.

Goram kept the consistency going in season 1988/89 too. He played in all 36 of Hibernian's league games, registering six shutouts in the first seven games and 12 in total. He also played a key role as Hibernian reached the last four of the Scottish Cup and the quarter-finals of the League Cup.

Goram's run of successive league appearances ended at 84, a failed fitness test counting him out of a 0-0 draw against Dunfermline in December 1989. His 34 league appearances yielded ten clean sheets, though. Significantly, three of them came against Rangers.

In addition to featuring for Hibernian, Goram also played for Scotland. But it was a much smaller ball that he was handling as he represented his country in cricket matches against Ireland, Yorkshire, Sussex and Australia. The latter appearance didn't go down too well at Easter Road, though, as Goram defied orders not to play, to face the mighty bowling of the moustachioed Merv Hughes. The inevitable fine from Hibernian was no doubt well worth it for the experience of coming up against one of the finest bowling talents in the game.

By the end of season 1990/91, a campaign that would be Goram's last as a Hibernian player, he had missed only three league games since signing from Oldham. That amounts to 138 league appearances. And Goram's ability to repel Rangers was at the forefront of that campaign too, with two clean sheets kept in the four league encounters against his future employers. The latter of those two – a 0-0 draw at Ibrox – featured the long-awaited first-team comeback of Rangers midfielder Ian Durrant.

Historically in Scotland, if you excel against the Old Firm, then invariably you end up signing for one half or the other, and that is most certainly the case with Goram. He had been on the Rangers radar for a while having impressed not just Walter Smith but also Smith's predecessor, Graeme Souness.

'Graeme and Walter had identified Andy as a player they wanted about four or five months before he joined the club,' said Sir David Murray who was the chairman at that time. 'I had already started speaking to Hibs about the transfer so after Graeme left and we won the title, Andy became one of Walter's first signings. At that time, he was the best Scottish goalkeeper around, he was keen to join us, so he was an obvious signing given the three-foreigner ruling had just been introduced.'

The players at the club were also consulted. Scott Nisbet, who played at the heart of the Rangers defence in Goram's first two seasons with Rangers, recalls a discussion with the management team one day when he was asked for his opinion on Goram.

'I got called in to have a chat with Graeme Souness and Walter about Andy. Souness had heard I was good pals with Andy, so he asked me what I thought about him as a goalkeeper. I told him that Andy was brilliant, but Graeme seemed concerned as he felt that Andy had a bit of a reputation. I said to him not to listen to all that, he simply needed to know that Andy was a great goalkeeper.'

Skipper Richard Gough was also enlisted to help Goram settle in when he eventually arrived at Ibrox.

'When we stayed in hotels on a Friday night before games, I didn't like to share a room with anyone,' said Gough. 'But on one occasion, Walter asked me to share with Andy to show him the ropes so to speak and talk to him about playing for Rangers. We had a chat and after that I wanted to get some sleep as I always liked to get a good kip the night before a game. But that night I struggled as Andy was on the phone chatting away for most of the night. The next morning, I went to see Walter and told him I wanted to go back to having a room to myself. Andy and I developed a great relationship, but we both knew after that first night that we wouldn't be sharing a room together again.'

But although he would eventually achieve greatness in the eyes of the Rangers fans, Goram endured a rough and ropey start to his Rangers career. After making his debut in a pre-season friendly against Queen's Park, he kept clean sheets in each of his first two league matches, wins over St Johnstone and Motherwell at Ibrox. However, on the first away trip of the league campaign, Goram was deceived by a looping long-range effort from Scott Crabbe of Hearts.

Hearts won 1-0, and although Celtic were shut out in the season's first Old Firm encounter, a few weeks later the new Rangers goalkeeper was caught out again in the semi-final of the League Cup against Hibernian. He came off his line to the edge of his penalty area to punch clear a long ball that had been played forward. However, his clearance only went as far as Mickey Weir, who chipped the ball over Goram to leave Keith Wright with a simple chance to score. There would be another high-profile error in the opening round of the European Cup too, Goram fumbling the ball into his own net to give Sparta Prague what proved to be a decisive away goal.

'The Goalie knew he was having a shocker,' admits Scott Nisbet. 'He said as much to me when we were driving back to Edinburgh one night.'

Nisbet then added with a smile, 'I told him that he needed to get his act together as I had vouched for him!'

Ally McCoist, who himself had endured an indifferent start to his own Rangers career, was in no doubt that Goram would come good, he knew he was 'made of stern stuff'.

'There's a great story about the semi-final when Hibs knocked us out,' said McCoist. 'We were sitting in the dressing room a couple of days later and The Goalie said, "It's typical, if I had stayed at

Hibs, I'd be in the cup final." My response was "Andy, if you had stayed at Hibs, we'd be in the cup final!" In all seriousness, though, we knew Andy was a different breed. We had been blessed with Chris Woods, and the big fella was an excellent goalkeeper. But Goram was a different animal. I had never seen a goalkeeper like Andy. He was a winner with a great attitude. He hated losing goals, and he used to chase me around the training ground if I scored past him.'

He added, 'It was a brave decision from Walter to bring him in. Your goalkeeper, centre-back and centre-forward are probably your three most important positions on the park, and Walter was looking to change one of them straight away. But Walter was a very astute and clever man, and he felt that bringing Andy in wouldn't weaken his team or his squad.'

The last of those mistakes would be a watershed moment for Andy Goram. From that moment on, errors from Goram were few and far between as he established himself as one of the key component parts of the successful team that Walter Smith was building. And perhaps his coming of age as a Rangers player came on New Year's Day 1992 when Rangers visited Parkhead.

A typical predatory finish from Ally McCoist put Rangers ahead, but Tony Mowbray equalised for the home side. A penalty from Mark Hateley squeezed Rangers ahead, but it took a series of wonderful saves from Goram to keep them in front. The pick of the bunch was a diving save to parry away a powerful effort from Paul McStay. A late goal from John Brown sealed the points for the visitors, but the interventions of Goram had been key. It wouldn't be the last time he would break the hearts of Celtic either.

Rangers would lose just one of the 17 league games that followed the success at Parkhead, ironically against Celtic at Ibrox. The season ended with a fourth successive league title, 101 goals scored and just 31 conceded. Goram and his defence had shut the opposition out on 20 occasions. There was also the small matter of a first Scottish Cup success since 1981.

'Bouncing back from those early mistakes just showed the character that Andy had,' said Richard Gough. 'Like a lot of players that come to a club like Rangers you come in and try and prove yourself and maybe try a bit too hard. I remember speaking with Andy at that time and just advising him to do what he was best at. He was trying things like coming off his line to catch crosses, but I remember when he played for Hibernian that he was a really good shot stopper. I knew if he focused on that he would be alright.'

Gough added, 'I had known Andy since he broke into the Scotland team in 1985. He was always a bundle of fun and straight down the line. I knew he would be fine when he came to Rangers, and he was. He was soon flying, and while he may have made some mistakes in his first couple of months with the club, for the six years that followed, I don't recall many more.'

Scott Nisbet echoed the sentiments of the former Rangers captain. 'As a defender, having Andy behind you was brilliant,' said Nisbet. 'He always communicated with you during games, bawling out instructions and telling us where the opposition players were as he could see the whole game from his position. And you knew if a forward got the better of you that we had a world-class goalkeeper that was among the best in a one-on-one situation. I had played with Chris Woods who was another top-class goalkeeper. He used to catch cross balls whereas Andy preferred to punch the ball away, but Andy was the better of the two in a one-v-one. He was superb at spreading himself to narrow all the angles.'

Nisbet added, 'After those early mistakes, Andy just got better and better each week. We became really close. I used to pick him up at the Maybury Roundabout in Edinburgh, and we would usually take it day about to drive through for training. But pretty soon I ended up doing all the driving as Andy needed to sleep as he had been out the night before. I'd wake him up when we got to Ibrox, and he'd pop some chewing gum into his mouth. But once he got out on the training pitch, he would be absolutely phenomenal in every session.'

Goram had enjoyed a superb debut season. The only ever-present in the squad, he made 55 appearances across all competitions.

'Andy's reflexes were amazing,' recalled Sir David Murray. 'That was helped by his days playing cricket, and he was only one of three who played football and cricket for Scotland. The others were Scot Symon and Donald Ford. He wasn't the tallest, but Andy had great positional sense and agility.'

Although Goram had been fit to play each week in season 1991/92, you still need a backup goalkeeper. When Goram joined Rangers, the other goalkeepers at the club were youngsters, Colin Scott (aged 21) and Neil Inglis (aged 17). Bonni Ginzburg had departed in the summer of 1991, so it looked like Scott, who had been at Ibrox since 1986, would be Goram's number two. However, when he suffered a knee injury that required surgery in the USA, Walter Smith opted for a veteran goalkeeper that was familiar to the Rangers support to provide cover for Goram. His name was David McKellar.

Born in Irvine on 22 May 1956, McKellar started out in the junior ranks, playing for Salcoats Victoria and Kilwinning Rangers before joining Ipswich Town in September 1972. He would remain in East Anglia for four years, working under Sir Bobby Robson, but although he represented Scotland at U18 level, he never made the breakthrough to the first team at Portman Road.

During his time with Ipswich, McKellar was loaned out to Colchester United and Peterborough United, but homesickness brought him back to Scotland in July 1976. A year free of first-team appearances at Dundee United followed, and after a single appearance for Forfar Athletic, McKellar dropped back down to the junior ranks when he joined Ardrossan Winton Rovers.

Taking that step back propelled him forward, though. In April 1978, Tommy Docherty offered McKellar the opportunity to sign for Derby County who were in the top flight of English Football at that time. He made his debut in a 2-0 defeat against Arsenal at Highbury on 16 December 1979 and made a total of 41 league appearances during his time at the Baseball Ground.

McKellar lost his place to Roger Jones at the start of season 1980/81 and opted to join Brentford in September 1980. They were two tiers lower than Derby, but over the next two seasons David McKellar was their number one goalkeeper. After making his league debut in a 3-0 win over Blackpool on 20 September 1980, McKellar played 84 of the next 85 Division Two matches that Brentford contested. He kept 29 clean sheets, including six in succession between 27 December 1980 and 31 January 1981.

But after a falling-out with the Brentford manager, Fred Callaghan, McKellar had a short spell in Hong Kong before he sealed a move to Carlisle United. And it was at Brunton Park that the Ayrshire man would achieve cult-hero status.

After making his league debut against Cambridge United on the opening day of season 1983/84, McKellar kept the gloves throughout the season. He would register 19 shutouts which, at the time of writing, remains a club record. McKellar also kept a clean sheet in the second round of the Milk (League) Cup against Division One Southampton. His opposite number that night was Peter Shilton.

Carlisle were in the hunt for automatic promotion until a late loss of form saw them finish seventh in Division Two. A 3-0 win over Charlton Athletic on 17 March – a match that saw McKellar and his defence keep the opposition out for the sixth successive match – moved Carlisle up to third place in Division Two. But a run of five draws and five defeats in their final ten games extinguished any notion of the likes of Liverpool, Everton or Manchester United visiting Brunton Park in season 1984/85.

A further 40 league appearances followed for McKellar in that campaign, but the heady heights of the previous campaign were never reached. Heavy defeats against Brighton, Oxford United and Wimbledon were part of a wretched start that yielded just three wins on the opening 14 Division Two matches. Form didn't improve much after that either and, on what would be McKellar's last league appearance of his first spell with Carlisle, Oldham Athletic won 5-2 at Brunton Park to consign The Blues to a 16th-place finish. The Oldham goalkeeper that day was Andy Goram.

McKellar would leave Carlisle in the summer of 1985, joining Hibernian for a fee of £8,000 as understudy to Alan Rough. But the move turned sour, with the Edinburgh side threatening legal action when McKellar returned south just three months after signing for the club. He was allegedly unhappy that the Easter Road side would not cover any of his travelling or accommodation expenses, while the Hibernian manager, John Blackley, stated in the *Glasgow Herald* that, 'It is my belief that he [McKellar] made no serious attempt to find family accommodation in the town which suggests that his heart was never in Hibs. He can go as soon as we get our money back.'

There were rumours of interest from Rochdale and Wrexham, but rather than secure a permanent move away, McKellar had spells on loan at Manchester City and Newcastle United instead. The latter yielded ten appearances between March and May 1986, but hopes of a longer stay in the North East of England were dashed when the manager, Willie McFaul, was dismissed.

Instead, when McKellar left Hibernian in the summer of 1986 he moved to Hamilton Academicals. And it was while with the Accies that Dave first came to the attention of the Rangers followers.

Hamilton, under the guidance of John Lambie, had just been promoted to the Premier Division, but they would endure a tortuous league campaign. They won just six of their 44 league games, and regular thrashings were the order of the day. McKellar, who appeared in 36 of those matches, was beaten five times by Dundee United (1-5) and eight times by Celtic (3-8), but he was spared the worst hammering of them all, a 7-0 defeat against Hearts at Tynecastle on 13 December.

A total of 93 goals were conceded in the league. The elusive first win wasn't registered until Accies defeated Goram's Hibernian 3-1 on 29 November. Only nine clean sheets were kept in the 48 matches played across the three main competitions, but one of them was at Ibrox on 31 January 1987.

When Hamilton were drawn against a reborn and rampant Rangers in the third round of the Scottish Cup, no one gave them a chance. After a sticky start, Graeme Souness had his Rangers side on the hunt for a domestic Treble. But thanks to a stellar performance from Dave McKellar, the headlines screamed 'Humiliation' as Hamilton humbled Rangers.

Adrian Sprott scored the only goal of the game, and he is the Hamilton player most will refer to when looking back on the match. But were it not for McKellar, Rangers would have advanced comfortably to the next round. He defied the home side on numerous occasions, but it was his save from Ally McCoist after 60 minutes that had Chick Young, writing in the *Evening Times*, purring. Young said McKellar's stop from McCoist's header was 'a miracle save and a miracle escape for Accies'. Sprott scored ten minutes later, and rather than Chris Woods hogging the headlines for setting a British record after going 1,196 minutes without conceding a goal, all the talk was of how McKellar had thwarted Rangers.

'He had the game of a lifetime,' said Ally McCoist. 'He was a lovely guy, an absolute diamond. That was a shock result and a lot of that has to do with how John Lambie had the Accies organised, but also the performance of Davie McKellar. He was absolutely outstanding. I can't remember who it was from, but he made a save across to his right-hand side, and I thought at that point he was going to have one of those days. When he came to Rangers, he was great to have about the place and I hope he enjoyed his time at Rangers as much as the boys did having him at the club.'

Remarkably, a year later, McKellar was shutting out Rangers again in the Scottish Cup. Having lost his place to Rikki Ferguson at Douglas Park, McKellar joined newly promoted Dunfermline Athletic, making his debut in a 3-0 home defeat against Dundee United on 13 February 1988. A week later, the Pars welcomed Rangers to East End Park for a Scottish Cup fourth-round tie. Similarly to the previous year with Hamilton, McKellar wasn't expected to come out on top. But he did, shutting out Rangers while Mark Smith and John Watson scored to give Jim Leishman's side a stunning win.

With Ian Westwater firmly established as the Dunfermline number one the following season, McKellar had a short spell on loan at Hartlepool United before joining Carlisle United once again. The side he re-joined were now in Division Four, but McKellar cemented his status as a hero with the Brunton Park fans, winning their Player of the Year award in season 1988/89.

A return to Scotland with Kilmarnock followed, but after making his sixth and final league appearance for the Ayrshire side in a 1-1 draw against Falkirk at Rugby Park on 15 September 1990, his playing days looked to be over. That was until Walter Smith stepped in.

He told the *Rangers News*, 'Jim [Fleeting, the Kilmarnock manager] gave me a call to make sure I was hanging about the house, but he wasn't going to tell me which club had come in for me. After a lot of persuasion, he told me it was Rangers. I thought he was at it, so I put the phone down, but it was only afterwards I realised he was being serious.'

A call from Walter Smith followed shortly after. With young understudy Colin Scott recuperating from a knee injury, the Rangers manager needed someone to be on standby should his new number one succumb to injury or suspension. In the end, neither happened, but for a self-confessed Rangers fan, it was a season to remember for Dave McKellar.

He made only one first-team appearance for Rangers. On 22 October 1991, Rangers took a strong XI to face Forfar Athletic in a testimonial match for Rab Morris. Joining McKellar were the likes of John Brown, Ian Durrant, Ian Ferguson and Pieter Huistra. Rangers won 5-2, with Gary McSwegan scoring four of the goals.

But Dave McKellar didn't leave Rangers empty-handed. He was an integral part of the reserve team that won the Premier Reserve League title in season 1991/92. He played in 26 of the 33 matches and was also part of the side that lost 3-2 on penalties in the final of the Reserve League Cup. In the penalty decider, he saved from Raymond McStay, but his opposite number, Pat Bonner, denied John Spencer, Sandy Robertson and David Hagen.

McKellar retired at the end of the season and moved into management. He enjoyed spells with Kilbirnie Ladeside, Largs Thistle, Saltcoats Victoria, Ardrossan Winton Rovers, Ardeer Thistle, Petershill and Irvine Meadow before moving on to a career in social services.

Since joining Rangers the previous summer, Goram hadn't missed a competitive match. But at the start of season 1992/93 – a campaign that would prove to be one of the most memorable in the history of Rangers Football Club – he started to suffer from the knee trouble that would dog him for the rest of his playing career.

Walter Smith needed another dependable deputy and the man he went for this time was Alistair Espie Maxwell.

Born on 16 February 1965, Maxwell had spent almost his entire playing career with Motherwell, save for a loan spell with Clydebank in 1987 during which he made one appearance for the Bankies and a similar stint with Bolton Wanderers in 1992.

A product of Fir Park Boys' Club, Maxwell made his first appearance for the Motherwell first team in April 1984 but spent the majority of his time initially as deputy to either John Gardiner or Cammy Duncan.

Maxwell played in the opening 15 matches of season 1984/85 – a campaign that saw Tommy McLean's side promoted to the Premier Division – but over the next three seasons he only featured in 26 league games as the Fir Park side consolidated their place in the top flight.

Ally eventually supplanted Cammy Duncan midway through season 1988/89, and for the next two seasons he didn't miss a single league game. But it would be the Scottish Cup campaign in season 1990/91 where Maxwell would carve his name into Motherwell folklore.

Wins over Aberdeen, Falkirk, Morton (after a replay and a penalty shoot-out) and Celtic (also after a replay) took Motherwell into the final where they would face a Dundee United side managed by Tommy McLean's brother, Jim. It was dubbed 'The Family Final', but it will also be remembered for the heroism of Ally Maxwell.

Motherwell led 1-0 at the interval, but early in the second half Maxwell collided with United's John Clark. It was established later that Maxwell had broken ribs, ruptured his spleen and was seeing double from time to time, yet he soldiered on throughout a second half that seesawed from end to end. A last-minute goal from Darren Jackson restored parity at 3-3 and forced extra time, wherein Stevie Kirk scored what proved to be the winner for Motherwell. But it was a late save from Maxwell that preserved that lead, the Motherwell goalkeeper flying to deny the United captain, Maurice Malpas, an equalising goal.

Remarkably, the match would be the last Maxwell would play for Motherwell. A contractual dispute saw him left out of the side in season 1991/92. He spent time on loan at Bolton Wanderers, but looked to be in limbo in the summer of 1992 until Walter Smith stepped in.

Maxwell made his Rangers debut in a 7-1 win against Queen of the South at Palmerston Park in a pre-season friendly, but his league bow came in a symbolic match in that epic campaign. With Goram sidelined with a thigh problem, Maxwell was in goal for a 4-3 defeat against Dundee at Dens Park. That was on 15 August 1992, and Rangers wouldn't taste defeat again in any competition until 20 March 1993.

Maxwell would make a further nine league appearances that season, but it was season 1993/94 when he came to the fore. With Goram recovering from knee ligament surgery, Maxwell was handed the number one jersey. But his early experiences were the proverbial mixed bag.

Although he registered clean sheets in each of his first two Old Firm games – a 0-0 draw in the league at Parkhead and a 1-0 win at 'neutral' Ibrox in the League Cup semi-final – and earned a call-up to the Scotland squad for a World Cup qualifier against Switzerland, Maxwell made some high-profile mistakes too. He was criticised for errors against Aberdeen and Levski Sofia, but it was blunders against Celtic at Ibrox that thrust him into the limelight for the wrong reasons.

A week after he had picked up a League Cup winners' medal, Rangers defeating Hibernian 2-1 in the final, Rangers faced Celtic in the league. The defending champions had made an uneven start to the season, winning just five of their opening 12 league fixtures.

But Celtic's form was indifferent too, with just three wins on the board prior to their trip to G51. In a typically tight match, Ally McCoist put Rangers in front after 67 minutes, but just three minutes later, the visitors were level. Pat McGinlay's cross looked to be a straightforward take for Maxwell, but he fumbled the ball and John Collins stepped in to equalise. A late goal from Brian O'Neill earned Celtic maximum points.

But both Maxwell and Rangers recovered from that setback. Maxwell, who had missed only one league match up until that point, due to the effects of flu, kept seven clean sheets as Rangers lost just one of their next 16 matches to propel themselves back to the top of the table. And Maxwell also shut out Kilmarnock in the Scottish Cup semi-final, a 0-0 draw at Hampden the precursor for a 2-1 win for Rangers in the replay. Alas, it would be the final of the Scottish Cup that season that would provide for many of the abiding memories of Ally Maxwell's Rangers career.

Although the Light Blues had limped across the line, winning just one of their last six league games, the Premier Division trophy sat next to the League Cup in the Ibrox Trophy Room which meant Walter Smith's side stood on the cusp of history. A victory over Dundee United at Hampden in the Scottish Cup Final would see Rangers become the first Scottish side to win back-to-back Trebles.

Understandably, Smith's side went into the match as favourites. United had finished sixth in the league, and although they had beaten Rangers 3-0 at Ibrox back in December, Rangers had comfortably won two of the other three league fixtures. But Ivan Golac's side defied the odds and claimed the trophy when they capitalised on a calamitous moment in the Rangers defence. Dave McPherson rolled a pass back to Maxwell, but as Christian Dailly converged on the Rangers goalkeeper, Maxwell's attempted clearance hit Dailly. The United forward, who would later prove to be an asset for Rangers as a utility player, seized upon the loose ball, and although his attempt on goal didn't find the net, the ball struck the post and rebounded to Craig Brewster who was left with a simple tap in.

That moment summed up what had been a rollercoaster season for Maxwell. He had made 43 appearances, keeping 13 clean sheets. He had tucked two winners' medals into his glove bag, but although he played a key role in what was a ragged season overall for Rangers and was selected for the Scotland B team against Wales, it was unfortunately a couple of the errors he made that stood out.

The 1993/94 campaign was of a similar ilk for Andy Goram too.

He had been exceptional on numerous occasions in season 1992/93, playing every minute in all bar three of the 44 games that Rangers had gone unbeaten in since losing in Dundee in August 1992. Among those outstanding displays, three stood out: Leeds United at Elland Road, Celtic at Parkhead and Aberdeen at Pittodrie.

'When it came to signing Scottish players, Walter did superbly well,' said Richard Gough. 'He brought in Goram to replace Chris Woods, and also the likes of Stuart McCall and Gordon Durie. Once Andy got his confidence back after those early mistakes, it was plain sailing. We had John Brown, Dave McPherson and me heading balls away, but we knew if we missed one then Andy was there. At that time I used to play a very high line very close to the halfway line, which meant if the defenders made a mistake, the attacker would be through on goal and onside. But one-v-one, Goram was very difficult to beat. He managed to get inside the heads of a lot of strikers and he almost instinctively knew where they were going to put the ball. His coordination was excellent. He saved my skin a few times.'

And on the Leeds game, Gough added, 'He had three or four crucial saves on the night, but by then they were saves that I expected him to make.'

'Andy enjoyed games like those ones,' added Sir David Murray. 'He thrived on the pressure and that's what made him a great goalkeeper. Some players come to Rangers and can't handle that pressure, but that certainly wasn't the case with Andy. Having a great goalkeeper like Andy wins you points and makes a huge difference to where you end up in the table at the end of the season. Another example is Allan McGregor.'

But Goram was starting to experience trouble with his knees and knee ligament surgery in the summer of 1993 would rule Goram out for a number of months. He returned to action late in January 1994, playing three times for the reserves, but it would be 12 February 1994 before he appeared for the first team. A throat infection counted Maxwell out of a 2-0 win over Hibernian, but Goram's season was ended abruptly a couple of months later. After a run of nine appearances, Goram picked up a thigh injury in a 0-0 draw against Dundee United. He then tore a muscle in his back in the Ibrox gym, and it soon emerged that there may well be a premature end to Goram's Rangers career.

Incensed by Goram's fitness levels and attitude, Walter Smith placed his number one goalkeeper on the transfer list in the summer of 1994. After a sublime season in 1992/93 where Goram cemented his status as one of the best goalkeepers in the world – breathtaking performances against Leeds United, Celtic and Aberdeen immediately spring to mind – the end appeared to be nigh for him. He had made just ten appearances in season 1993/94, but after the gauntlet was thrown down by Smith, Goram responded. He reported for training trim and ready to go and was promptly taken off the transfer list.

'Had Andy not got himself fit, I don't think Walter would have messed about,' said Sir David Murray. 'He would have given Andy a final warning, but had Andy not done what he asked him, I don't think Walter would have thought twice about deciding to sell him.

He wouldn't have wanted to do it, but had he had to, he would have done so.'

He added, 'You had a different breed of players back then. There weren't as many agents around and players would come to do the deal with you. Players were paid roughly the same amount of money, and the bond in that group is one that will be very difficult to recreate in my opinion.'

Goram was back to his brilliant best in the early weeks of season 1994/95. Although Rangers were beaten 2-0 in Greece against AEK Athens, Goram made a number of outstanding saves to keep the scoreline respectable. He would play in each of the opening 17 league games too, keeping seven clean sheets. But a calf injury called a halt to that run of games, and when his comeback match against Partick Thistle at Firhill was aborted after just 29 minutes by another injury to the same calf, Goram's season was effectively over. He went under the knife to solve the problem in February and didn't play again for the first team until he came on as a substitute in the final game of the season against, ironically, Partick Thistle.

Seeking a replacement for Goram after those opening 17 league games, one might have suspected that Ally Maxwell would have stepped back into the breach, but that wasn't the case. Instead, Walter Smith handed the gloves to Colin Scott, who despite being only 23 was one of the longest-serving players at Ibrox at that time.

Scott had first arrived at Ibrox as a 16-year-old in 1986 and had had spells on loan at Brentford and Airdrie. But his big break looked set to be on the horizon when it appeared he would be the second-choice goalkeeper at Ibrox for season 1991/92. Alas, a cruel twist of fate denied 'Scooter' that opportunity.

He had been hampered by a knee injury – he had twisted it on only the second day of pre-season training – but was declared fit to play in the second game of the Premier Reserve League campaign against Hearts at Ibrox. The match marked the first appearance in a Rangers jersey for their new signing, Alexei Mikhailichenko, and Rangers ran out comfortable winners by four goals to nil. Scott even managed to save a penalty kick. But after the match the club doctor, Donald Cruickshank, recommended that Scott travel to the USA to undergo surgery to correct cartilage damage.

However, after a period of rehabilitation, Scott was back in contention, and he would make his first-team debut in a 1-1 draw against Exeter City on 8 September 1992, coming on as a substitute for Ally Maxwell. But when a similar change was made just over a year later, Scott earned himself a place in the history books.

Clubs in Scotland had been permitted to list a reserve goalkeeper among their substitutes since the start of the season, and when Maxwell was unable to come out for the second half of a league match against Raith Rovers on 2 October 1993 due to a virus, Colin Scott became Rangers' first-ever substitute goalkeeper.

A first start came the following midweek – a late Dougie Arnott double earned Motherwell a 2-1 win at Ibrox – but Scott would have to wait until the latter part of the season to feature again. A back injury ruled Maxwell out of the final Old Firm game of the season, so Scott stepped up and dealt with most of what the Celtic attackers threw at him. He was only beaten by a well-executed free kick by John Collins that, in fairness, his more experienced colleagues would also have struggled to keep out.

Scott kept his place for the remaining three league games, including the 1-0 defeat against Hibernian at Easter Road that sealed six-in-a-row. That took his total appearances for the season to six. He would make four more in season 1994/95, but he would make what would be his last league appearance of the season when he replaced Goram in the match at Firhill in which the Rangers number one was stretchered off with his calf injury.

Ally Maxwell, seemingly out of the picture and available for transfer, was suddenly back in contention, his appearance against

Falkirk on 14 January 1995 being only his second for the first team since that fateful Scottish Cup Final. He would play a part in 11 of the last 15 league games, but his time at Rangers was coming to an end too. His last match for the club was on the final day of the season, a 1-1 draw against Partick Thistle at Ibrox.

Maxwell left Rangers in the summer of 1995, signing for Dundee United in a deal that netted Rangers a transfer fee of £250,000. He would make 55 appearances for the Tannadice side before he lost his place to Sieb Dijkstra.

In September 1998, Maxwell left United and signed for Morton. He was recruited by Billy Stark to fill the void left by the long-serving David Wylie who had joined Clyde, and over the next two seasons Maxwell made 71 appearances and kept 20 clean sheets.

But this was a Morton side on the cusp of crisis, and in December 2000 they went into administration. Maxwell, who was now coaching the goalkeepers at the club, was appointed caretaker manager at the end of the following month. Assisted by the former Celtic player Owen Archdeacon, Maxwell would be in charge for 14 matches, Morton winning five and drawing three of them. That meant that under Maxwell, Morton had accrued more points (18) than they had in the opening 22 matches (17). Alas, it wouldn't be enough to keep Morton in the First Division. They were five points adrift at the bottom of the table when Maxwell took over, and although they clawed back the deficit, Morton couldn't gather enough points to survive. They finished ninth, three points adrift of eighth-placed Airdrie, and were relegated to the Second Division along with Alloa Athletic.

In that run of games, Maxwell played twice, the last of which was as an outfield substitute in the final game of the season against Alloa Athletic. But before the month of May was out, Maxwell was made redundant by the administrators.

Spells as goalkeeper coach with Hamilton Accies and the SFA followed before Maxwell joined Sereno Soccer Club in 2002. The club was based in Arizona, and Maxwell was their director of goalkeeping between 2002 and 2008. He currently holds a similar role with SC del Sol in Phoenix.

As for Colin Scott, he had one more season at Rangers, playing three league matches in season 1995/96, the last of which was a 3-2 win over Falkirk in March 1996. He joined Hamilton Accies and spent time with Raith Rovers and Clydebank before he enjoyed the most successful spell of his career when he signed for Queen of the South in 2000. He stayed at Palmerston Park until 2007 when injury forced him to retire.

* * *

Goram, Maxwell and Scott were three of the four goalkeepers who played for the Rangers first team in season 1994/95. The other was Billy Thomson.

William Marshall Thomson was born on 10 February 1958 in Linwood. After some impressive displays with Glasgow United, Thomson signed for Partick Thistle in February 1975. He made his debut as a 17-year-old in a friendly against Vejle Boldklub, one of eight appearances he made for the Jags. One of those was in a Glasgow Cup semi-final against Rangers in March 1976.

The St Mirren manager, Jim Clunie, liked what he saw in Thomson and duly submitted an offer of £50,000 for his services in August 1978. This was accepted and for the next six seasons Thomson hardly missed a game for the Saints, making over 300 appearances before he was sold to Dundee United for £75,000 in June 1984.

He joined a United side that had just missed out on a place in the European Cup Final – Jim McLean's side had lost to AS Roma in the semi-finals – and after spending time as understudy to Hamish McAlpine, Billy established himself as the number one goalkeeper.

In season 1986/87, United played 70 matches in all competitions. Those included wins at home and away against Barcelona in the UEFA Cup, a two-legged UEFA Cup Final, a League Cup semi-final and a Scottish Cup Final. Thomson was the last line of defence in 61 of the 70 games, but he ended the season empty-handed. IFK Gothenburg won the UEFA Cup – Thomson was superb in the first leg despite having to have five stitches inserted behind his ear early in the game after bravely thwarting a Gothenburg attack – and a goal from future team-mate Ian Ferguson saw the Scottish Cup draped in black and white ribbons rather than black and tangerine.

Thomson would remain a fixture in the United side until he lost his place to Alan Main in 1989. He eventually left the club in 1991, signing for Motherwell who were on the lookout for a replacement for Ally Maxwell.

Thomson missed only one league match in season 1991/92, his ten clean sheets including one against Celtic at Fir Park and two at Easter Road. But after playing in the opening eight league matches the following season, Thomson lost his place to Sieb Dijkstra, and by the summer of 1994, at the age of 36, Thomson looked set to sign a new contract with Motherwell, until Walter Smith made him an offer to sign a two-year deal.

'It was actually Bomber [John Brown] that called me and said that Rangers were interested in signing me,' recalled Thomson. '[Motherwell manager] Alex McLeish had offered me a new contract, but once I knew the move to Rangers was on the cards that was it for me.'

With Goram still battling back to full fitness, Maxwell troubled by an issue with his shoulder and Colin Scott nursing a dislocated thumb, Smith faced going into the early matches of the campaign with only the untried Neil Inglis to call upon. In the end, Thomson wasn't required, but he would have a role to play as the season progressed.

'I knew when I spoke to Walter that I was being brought in as cover for the other goalkeepers,' said Thomson. 'I was fine with that. I loved training with the likes of Andy, although he would do most of his work on the bike in the gym before we did a double session with [goalkeeping coach] Alan Hodgkinson on a Thursday.'

He added, 'Andy was an exceptional goalkeeper and a really nice guy. I had played against him when he was at Hibernian and he would always make time to have a chat with me after games. I worked with Stefan Klos when I came back to the club as goalkeeper coach in 2001 and I don't think you can split the two of them in terms of ability.'

After making his debut in a pre-season friendly against Ikast FS on a pre-season tour of Denmark, Thomson made his first competitive appearance in a 2-0 win over the Dundee United side he had served with such distinction. On April Fool's Day 1995 at Tannadice, Gordon Durie opened the scoring after just 12 seconds in what was Thomson's first Premier Division match since November 1992.

Billy kept his place for the next two league fixtures, wins over Aberdeen and Hibernian, the latter being the match that secured the points required to clinch the league title. He also made his Old Firm debut, although it was one to forget, with Celtic winning comfortably at Hampden and Thomson ordered off with six minutes to go. Having already shipped three goals, Thomson was given his marching orders by referee Les Mottram after he wiped out the diminutive Brian McLaughlin as the Celtic winger looked to add a fourth goal.

'I was at fault for the first goal,' recalled Thomson. 'I was trying to anticipate a cross coming in, but Rudi Vata beat me at my near post. Craig Moore scored an own goal too. I have no complaints about the red card either. I came out and wiped McLaughlin out. It was the first and only time I was sent off in my career.'

Thomson made a further two first-team appearances for Rangers in season 1995/96. One of them came in the Champions League.

'I was on the bench in Turin, and we got an absolute doing,' said Thomson. 'At half-time in the game at Ibrox, Andy couldn't continue so I went on. Juventus were an exceptional side, but I thoroughly enjoyed the match even though we were beaten 4-0. To play in the Champions League at 38 was a great experience, although it doesn't top the UEFA Cup run that I was part of with Dundee United. We played something like 70 games and the games against Barcelona and Borussia Monchengladbach were fantastic occasions.'

He joined Dundee in August 1996 and made 33 appearances for the Dens Park team. Although his time with Dundee was brief, Thomson endeared himself to their fans thanks to a magnificent performance in a League Cup tie against Dundee United at Tannadice. After producing a series of saves during the match, Thomson then saved penalty kicks from Gary McSwegan and Owen Coyle in the shoot-out. The Dens Park side reached the semi-finals of the competition where they lost out to Hearts.

But in the summer of 1997, it was time to call it a day and after retiring, Thomson embarked on a career coaching goalkeepers. His first role was with Dundee.

'I picked up a back injury that meant I couldn't train much,' recalled Thomson. 'If I had played on the Saturday then it would most likely be Thursday or Friday before I trained. That was hard for me as I loved training. I had a year left of my contract, but the manager, John McCormack, brought me in pre-season and offered me the coaching role.'

He continued, 'John had been looking to bring in Robert Douglas who was with Livingston at the time. He asked me to go and have a look at him in a pre-season tournament and I was impressed so recommended that John sign him. Rab was a part-time fireman and a part-time bricklayer, and after negotiating with Jim Leishman, John got him for £100,000. John was concerned with the size of the fee, but I assured him it was well worth it.'

Thomson was proven correct, with Douglas establishing himself in the Dundee first team before moving to Celtic in 2000. During his time at Parkhead, he would play in a UEFA Cup Final and win three league titles and three Scottish Cups and also earn recognition at international level.

In addition to Douglas, Thomson also worked with Jamie Langfield and Derek Soutar, but after five years at Dens Park, a change in manager proved to be the catalyst for a return to Rangers.

'John McCormack left and was replaced by Jocky Scott before the Bonetti brothers came in,' said Thomson. 'Initially, everything was fine, but I soon heard that they were recruiting an Italian goalkeeping coach. The first one that came in lasted about five weeks, but the second took over from me. But not long after that, John Brown called me and told me that Dick Advocaat wanted to bring me in as goalkeeping coach at Ibrox. I met with Dick and agreed to move, and I spent the next six years working with the club.'

Advocaat's plan was for Thomson to work with the first-team goalkeepers, but Billy soon recognised the potential in a couple of young goalkeepers on the books and reckoned they would benefit from training with the senior goalies.

'Greegsy [Allan McGregor] and Buzz [Graeme Smith] were both of a similar age and both excellent prospects,' said Thomson. 'Dick wanted me to work solely with the first-team goalkeepers like Stefan Klos and Jesper Christiansen, which was fine, but I arranged to do some sessions with Allan and Graeme before the first-team lads reported for training. Eventually I managed to convince Dick to let Allan and Graeme join Stefan and the rest of the first-team keepers, and Allan in particular elevated himself as a result of working with players of that calibre.'

He continued, 'There were times when Greegsy would come to me frustrated at the lack of opportunities to play in the first team at Rangers. He went out on loan a couple of times and there were occasions when he told me he was thinking about leaving. But I encouraged him to persevere as he would get a chance eventually and it worked out pretty well for him.'

Thomson left his role at Ibrox in August 2007 and moved to Kilmarnock with whom he stayed until he was appointed goalkeeping coach at Stranraer in June 2021.

Capped seven times for Scotland, Billy Thomson made 13 appearances for Rangers if you include non-competitive matches such as friendlies and testimonials. He conceded 19 goals and kept two clean sheets.

He concluded, 'I've often thought about what would have happened if I had gone to Rangers earlier in my career. When I was with St Mirren, I heard they were interested in signing me, but back then the players didn't have the same power as they have now. The club would simply refuse an offer and you had to stay put. Malcolm Allison, who was manager of Crystal Palace, also came in for me but he was knocked back too. But even though I was 36 when I signed for Rangers, it was just tremendous to get the opportunity. At one point I think I was one of the oldest players ever to play in the Champions League. I thoroughly enjoyed my time at the club both as a player and as a coach.'

Sadly, Billy passed away on 5 February 2023 following a short illness. He was 64.

* * *

The title win in season 1994/95 was Rangers' seventh in succession. But they faced a new challenge for the top honours in season

1995/96 as the quest for the coveted nine-in-a-row started to gather pace.

Old Firm rivals Celtic hadn't contested the race for the title for some time. Since winning the league in their centenary season, 1987/88, they had finished third four times, fourth twice and as low as fifth in season 1989/90. But the appointment of Tommy Burns was about to change that.

The former Celtic midfielder had guided his side to their first domestic honour for five years when they defeated Airdrie in the 1995 Scottish Cup Final. And in what was his first full season in charge at Parkhead, he was hoping to assemble his troops to outgun Rangers and win the Premier Division championship. The fact they didn't was down in no small part to the brilliance of Andy Goram.

Bouncing back from injury, Goram enjoyed his most consistent run of games for a number of years, playing in 47 of the 53 competitive matches Rangers played. He excelled at all levels, but it was in the games against Celtic that he really came to the fore.

Rangers faced their Old Firm rivals on six occasions that season and posted a record of three wins and three draws. Only five goals were conceded, with three of them coming in an epic 3-3 draw at Ibrox in November. Goram kept three clean sheets and made countless saves to deny Burns and his team. But it is a save in that six-goal thriller at Ibrox that stood out more than most.

The match had ebbed and flowed, Celtic taking the lead through Andreas Thom before Rangers thought they had equalised through David Robertson. The full-back's goal was ruled out – TV pictures would reveal that it should have stood as he was onside – but Brian Laudrup did eventually restore parity before half-time. A John Collins penalty six minutes after the restart edged the visitors ahead again before Ally McCoist did what Ally McCoist did on a regular basis: rescued Rangers with a vital goal.

But just three minutes after McCoist's header had nestled in the net, Goram ensured that the game remained level. Jackie McNamara crossed from the right, and Pierre van Hooijdonk met it on the volley from no more than six yards' range. A goal seemed certain until Goram raised his right arm and diverted the ball wide for a corner. It was a remarkable save, but for Goram that kind of thing was becoming the norm rather than the expectation.

'That was a remarkable, an incredible moment,' said Ally McCoist. 'It was probably his best save, but for me, in terms of level of performance throughout the game, Andy's performance against Leeds at Elland Road was second to none. We played well and deserved our victory, but Andy was superb that day.'

'We trained the way we played back then,' said Richard Gough. 'Barry Ferguson was a young kid at the club at that time, and he used to come and watch us train. He couldn't believe how intense and aggressive it was. But at times our training was tougher than the games we would play on a Saturday. Even in training, Andy didn't want to lose goals. That save was incredible. It's been shown a lot since Andy left us and rightly so.'

Of the six league games Goram missed, Colin Scott stepped in for three of them, the last of which, a 3-2 win over Falkirk at Ibrox in March 1996, proved to be his last appearance for the club. Billy Thomson also made one league appearance – a 2-0 win over Falkirk at Ibrox – and Thomson also came on as sub for Goram in the 4-0 Champions League defeat against Juventus at Ibrox after Goram had to be withdrawn at the interval with a hip injury.

The last two games missed by Goram were covered by a new signing from Aberdeen, Theo Snelders.

Theodorus Antonius Gerardus Snelders had first come up against Rangers during the early part of his career when his FC Twente Enschede side had come to Ibrox for a pre-season friendly in August 1985. But he would become much more familiar to the Rangers supporters after he joined Aberdeen in the summer of 1988.

Signed to replace Jim Leighton who was heading south to join Manchester United, Snelders soon established himself as one of the best goalkeepers in the country. In season 1989/90 he was part of the Aberdeen side that won both domestic cup competitions, the Dons beating Rangers 2-1 in the League Cup and Celtic 9-8 on penalties in the Scottish Cup. In the latter match, Snelders plunged to his left to save Anton Rogan's spot kick, which allowed Brian Irvine to net the decisive penalty.

Snelders was rewarded for his performances throughout the season when he was named the Scottish PFA Players' Player of the Year, but he suffered disappointment in season 1990/91. In October he fractured his cheekbone following a collision with Ally McCoist at a rain-soaked Pittodrie. He returned after missing nine matches, only for another injury to rule him out of the final-day decider against Rangers at Ibrox.

Aberdeen finished a disappointing sixth in the league in season 1991/92, but they emerged again the following season as the principal challengers to Rangers. Alas, they would end up as runners-up in all three major tournaments, with Snelders getting caught out by a new ruling in the League Cup Final.

The 'pass back' rule had just been introduced which meant that a goalkeeper was no longer allowed to use his hands when dealing with a back pass from one of his own players. With the score at 0-0, Ian Durrant tried to play a pass forward, but David Winnie jabbed out his foot and diverted the ball back towards Snelders. Caught in two minds as to whether or not he could pick the ball up, Snelders tried to control it on his chest, but it rebounded to Stuart McCall who slotted the ball into the net.

Aberdeen came second once again to Rangers in the league in season 1993/94, but the following season they almost suffered the ignominy of relegation for the first time in their history. They finished second bottom and needed a play-off against Dunfermline Athletic to preserve their top-flight status.

By March 1996, Snelders was playing second fiddle to Michael Watt, but Walter Smith offered him a lifeline when he made a £300,000 bid for his services.

And he was thrust straight into action, making his debut against Raith Rovers at Stark's Park within 24 hours of putting pen to paper in what would prove to be one of the most significant matches in the nine-in-a-row run. Snelders was beaten twice, and with two minutes to go, Rangers were 2-1 down. But two late goals from Ally McCoist and a penalty from Gordon Durie eked out a vital 4-2 win.

With Goram rested for the upcoming Scottish Cup Final, Snelders kept his first clean sheet on the final day of the season when Rangers won 3-0 against Kilmarnock at Rugby Park, but he would be used sparingly in what would be an historic season 1996/97 for Rangers. He made seven appearances, including two against Ajax in the Champions League. But when Goram was ruled out of the crucial final Old Firm league match of the season at Parkhead, Snelders was also unavailable. His place was taken by the recently recruited Andy Dibble.

In what would be his last season as a Rangers player, 1997/98, Snelders made a further 13 appearances for the club. With the Finnish international Antti Niemi recruited in the summer of 1997, competition for the number one jersey was fierce, and the Dutchman made his final bow when he came on as a substitute for Niemi in Ian Durrant's testimonial on 28 April 1998.

Snelders was eventually released after making 27 appearances for Rangers. He had a couple of seasons with MVV in Holland before retiring.

* * *

The 1995/96 season ended with two virtuoso performances. Paul Gascoigne scored a stunning hat-trick in the penultimate league game against Aberdeen to seal eight-in-a-row, and 20 days later, Brian Laudrup broke Hearts with a devastating display that produced two goals and three assists in the Scottish Cup Final.

Goram had thus added another two medals to his collection, but sights were now set firmly on gaining arguably the most important one of them all, a record-equalling ninth successive league title for Rangers.

The Goalie started the first eight league matches before injury counted him out for three league games, a League Cup semi-final, and a Champions League double header against Ajax. But he was back in between the posts when Rangers travelled to Parkhead to face Celtic. And it would be yet another occasion when he would break the opposition's heart.

Rangers took the lead after seven minutes thanks to a long-range effort from Brian Laudrup, and when he was fouled in the box after 69 minutes, an opportunity presented itself to double the lead. Paul Gascoigne spurned it when his tame penalty was saved by Stewart Kerr. Another gilt-edged chance was passed up with seven minutes remaining when Peter van Vossen somehow managed to spoon the ball over a gaping goal. And Rangers would have been left to rue those missed opportunities were it not for Andy Goram. Celtic were awarded a penalty late in the game, Pierre van Hooijdonk took it, but Goram plunged to his right to parry the ball to safety.

'I told him to dive to his left,' recalled Richard Gough with a chuckle. 'But he said to me "I've got this", and he was right. He went the right way, saved it and we went on to win the game.'

Goram would play in all but one of the next 17 league games, a virus counting him out of a 2-1 win at Easter Road in January. Rangers dropped just three points in that run, losing 1-0 at

Tannadice in December, and the victory over Hibernian came two days after a couple of Erik Bo Andersen goals and a thumping free kick from Jorg Albertz had chalked up three wins out of three against Celtic in the league. That meant it was now nine Old Firm games undefeated for Rangers, but ten-in-a-row would prove elusive.

Wins over St Johnstone and East Fife had earned the Light Blues a place in the last eight of the Scottish Cup. They were drawn against Celtic but chose this match to turn in their worst performance of the season. Goram was beaten inside the opening 20 minutes by Malky Mackay and a Paolo Di Canio penalty, and Rangers offered little in response. The Treble dream had been shattered.

There was a suggestion that Celtic, trailing leaders Rangers by five points, were well-placed to derail what looked like a relentless run to nine-in-a-row. The final Old Firm league match was just ten days away, but Rangers would go into it without their talismanic goalkeeper. Goram twisted his knee in a midweek league defeat against Dundee United at Ibrox and was ruled out of the showdown in Glasgow's East End. It was time to play the emergency loan card, and on the double Rangers were able to call upon Andrew Gerald Dibble.

The 'Three Cup' team from season 1896/97 that won the Scottish Cup, Glasgow Cup and Charity Cup. Goalkeeper Matthew Dickie is fifth from the left in the back row

The first player signed by Rangers from an English club, Herbert Lock provided a resolute last line of defence in a Rangers career that spanned World War I

Aided and abetted by some of the finest players to ever play for Rangers, Willie Robb was one of the most consistent goalkeepers ever to play for the club

Tom Hamilton was a fine goalkeeper and was the custodian when Rangers defeated Celtic 4-0 in the 1928 Scottish Cup Final, ending a 25-year wait to win the trophy

Pictured here alongside Alex Venters, Jerry Dawson (right) was nicknamed 'The Prince of Goalkeepers'

Bobby Brown was the last line of the famous 'Iron Curtain' defence that kept forwards at bay in the years that followed World War II

George Niven, fourth from the right at the aircraft door, with his team-mates prior to another European adventure. Niven was the first goalkeeper to play for Rangers in European competition.

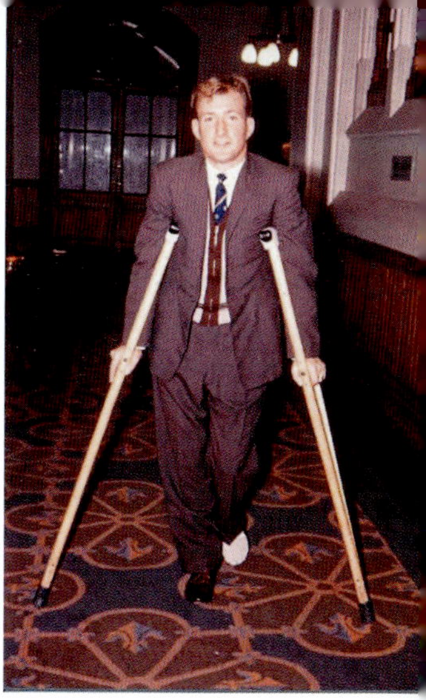

Billy Ritchie on crutches after injuring his ankle in 1960. Ritchie would play a key role in the revered Rangers team of the early-to-mid 1960s

Eric Sorensen (left) and Norrie Martin pictured at Ibrox ahead of season 1968/69

Rangers goalkeepers through the generations (L-R): Jerry Dawson, Bobby Brown, George Niven, Billy Ritchie, Norrie Martin, Peter McCloy and Stewart Kennedy

Dubbed the 'Girvan Lighthouse', Peter McCloy was at Rangers for 16 years. He holds the record for the most appearances made by a goalkeeper for the club in the post-war era.

Stewart Kennedy and Jock Wallace at Hampden in August 1974. Kennedy would be an ever present in the league that season as Rangers won the title for the first time in 11 years

Jim Stewart makes a diving save in the 1981 Scottish Cup Final at Hampden. After a 0-0 draw, Rangers won the replay 4-1.

Nicky Walker shouts instructions during the 1987 League Cup Final against Aberdeen. Rangers won 5-3 on penalties after an enthralling 3-3 draw

Two cornerstones of the Graeme Souness revolution, Terry Butcher and Chris Woods. Woods was the most expensive goalkeeper in Britain when he joined Rangers in 1986

(Far left) Simply known as 'The Goalie', the late Andy Goram is arguably the greatest-ever Rangers goalkeeper

(Left) Although in the twilight of his career when he joined Rangers in 1994, Billy Thomson was an able deputy for Andy Goram and later served the club as a goalkeeping coach

Lionel Charbonnier's Rangers career was badly compromised by a knee injury, but he remains a cult hero with the Ibrox followers

Cool, calm, collected and consistent, Stefan Klos – Der Goalie – is another goalkeeper held in high regard by the Rangers supporters

Neil Alexander provided stiff competition for Allan McGregor between 2007 and 2012. He also stayed with Rangers when they were demoted to the lower leagues in 2012.

Signed from Kilmarnock in July 2013, Cammy Bell was part of the team that won the League One title, but his time at Rangers was blighted by injury

Wes Foderingham played a key role in the last stage of the journey through the leagues then served the club well once Rangers returned to the Scottish Premiership

(Above and left) Allan McGregor enjoyed two spells with Rangers, making over 500 appearances for the club and establishing himself as one of the greatest goalkeepers to don the gloves. (Right) Following in the footsteps of his dad, Jim, Colin Stewart is the man tasked with getting the first team goalkeepers ready for action.

Chapter 9

On the Double

DURING THE nine-in-a-row era, 348 league matches were played. Over the course of those matches, Rangers somewhat ironically called upon only NINE goalkeepers. As we have seen, the mainstays of that epic era were Chris Woods and Andy Goram, but when they couldn't be called upon, several dependable deputies stepped into the breach. We have already read about and heard from a couple of them, so it is appropriate to round off this part of the goalkeeper story with the last of those deputies, the man nicknamed 'Officer Dibble', Andrew Gerald Dibble.

In the opening 29 league games of season 1996/97, Andy Goram had played 25 times and when he was unavailable Theo Snelders stepped in. Rangers had won all but eight of those matches. But Celtic were clinging to their coat-tails, albeit by their fingertips, and looked to have secured a psychological edge when they won that feisty Scottish Cup quarter-final tie by two goals to nil in early March. With another Old Firm clash looming, Rangers appeared to have been rocked as, six days after the Cup exit, they lost 2-0 at home to Dundee United.

The United loss would prove to be Goram's final appearance of the season. In addition to the ongoing issues with his knees, he had injured his ribs in training ahead of the Scottish Cup clash at

Parkhead. It later transpired that Goram had cracked his ribs, but a painkilling injection helped him pass a fitness test 75 minutes ahead of kick-off. He took another injection to face United too but continuing to do so wasn't sustainable.

Walter Smith was now on the horns of a dilemma. Theo Snelders had been in the squad for the Celtic match and had taken part in the warm-up only to be replaced at the last minute by Peter van Vossen. An injury appeared to have been the reason for the Dutchman's omission, so Smith had to decide whether to pitch young Michael Rae into the white-hot Parkhead cauldron or bring in someone on loan. He chose the latter, and that put in motion a series of events that brought Andy Dibble to Ibrox.

Born in Cwmbran on 8 May 1965, Dibble had started his career with his boyhood heroes, Cardiff City. He was a left-back until the age of eight – 'I was horrendous' was his humble assessment of his time in that position – but decided to have a go playing in goal when he was ten. Within a year he had signed as a schoolboy at Ninian Park, and six years later he was in the first XI.

Dibble actually made his Cardiff debut on his 17th birthday, against Crystal Palace when he replaced the injured Ron Healey. Just over an hour prior to kick-off Dibble was actually cleaning Healey's boots as part of the veteran's pre-match preparations, but a troublesome hernia that would effectively end his career ruled Healey out.

Cardiff lost 1-0 to Palace, and a couple of weeks later young Dibble was playing in the Welsh Cup Final against Swansea City. Cardiff lost 2-1 over two legs, but Andy had done enough to convince the manager, Len Ashurst, that he had what it took. In season 1982/83 the Bluebirds soared up the Third Division table. They finished as runners-up to Portsmouth to earn promotion to the second tier.

Steve Humphries started the season in goal before handing the gloves to Martin Thomas. But Dibble got his opportunity after a

2-1 defeat away at Lincoln City on 13 November. That defeat was City's fifth in their opening 16 league matches, but young Dibble enjoyed a run of 14 matches before Jim Brown and Eric Steele were drafted in. But Len Ashurst turned to his young starlet for the final six matches. Cardiff won four and drew two of them, and Dibble has fond memories of that campaign.

'We had a great team,' recalled Dibble. 'Although I was very young, the manager showed a lot of faith in me. The club had a couple of goalkeepers on loan, like Martin Thomas. Once I got in, I felt privileged to keep my place in a great side that had the likes of Jeff Hemmerman scoring goals, Gary Bennett and Jimmy Mullen at the back, and Dave Bennett, who won the FA Cup with Coventry City, in midfield.'

Cardiff enjoyed a season of consolidation in the second tier in season 1983/84, finishing 15th. Dibble missed only one league match – a 1-0 defeat at home against Blackburn Rovers in December – and he must have done enough to catch the eye, as in the close season he was off to London for the princely sum of £125,000. His destination in the capital was Luton Town, and while Dibble admits he was sad to leave Cardiff, he was tempted by the lure of top-flight football.

Luton had won promotion to Division One a couple of seasons earlier, and after a dramatic last-day escape from relegation at the end of season 1982/83, David Pleat's side had finished a respectable 16th the season before Dibble arrived. They had also reached the last four of the FA Cup, losing to eventual winners Everton.

'I had been training a couple of times a month at Watford, so everyone thought I was going to go there,' admitted Dibble. 'But David Pleat came in at the last minute and I ended up signing for Luton Town. Luton was a smashing football club, and David Pleat would be great in the modern game. He favoured all-out attack and would rather win a game 5-4 than 1-0.'

Dibble's first season at Kenilworth Road ended with Luton finishing a couple of places below mid-table, but the Welshman's season ended on 13 November at Old Trafford. He had played in 13 of the opening 15 league games and three times in the League Cup, but it would be the following season before he would don the gloves for the first team again.

'I was 19 when I went there, but David Pleat put me in at the start of the season,' recalled Dibble. 'But then I tore my medial ligaments when I twisted awkwardly against Manchester United.'

While Dibble was trying to regain fitness, there were big changes afoot in the close season in 1985. The grass on the pitch was replaced by the now infamous 'artificial' surface, and Dibble admits he wasn't its biggest fan.

'We were hard to beat at home and not many teams came and got a result, but I picked up some nasty injuries as a result of the pitch,' said Dibble. 'It wasn't like the modern 5G surfaces the players are used to now. It was very hard and not good for goalkeepers. I damaged my elbow and my knee and that meant I missed out on playing football matches.'

Dibble was up against the late Les Sealey for a place in the Luton team. He came in after Dibble's injury at Old Trafford and was a mainstay for the next two seasons. Andy only played eight times over the course of 1985/86 and 1986/87, and to get game time had spells on loan at Sunderland and Huddersfield Town. But towards the end of season 1987/88, Dibble was recalled to the Luton starting XI.

When Dibble had been on the periphery of the team, there had been a change in manager, with Pleat initially replaced by John Moore before Ray Harford took over. And Harford presided over a momentous campaign that saw the Hatters reach the FA Cup semi-finals and claim a major domestic honour. Andy didn't feature until April, although his first appearance of the season was an FA Cup semi-final against Wimbledon's 'Crazy Gang' at White Hart Lane.

'Les was "Mr Consistency", so it took me a while to get my place back in the team,' said Dibble. 'In the semi-final against Wimbledon I had had a very good match until I brought down Terry Gibson to concede the penalty that let them back into the game.'

Mick Harford put Luton ahead, but after Dibble fouled Gibson, John Fashanu levelled the scores at 1-1 before Dennis Wise slid in to net the winner for the Dons. Dibble kept his place in the team, though, and 15 days later he was stepping out at Wembley in a national cup final. And this time he would emerge as the hero of the hour, saving Nigel Winterburn's late penalty kick.

'The elation of winning the League Cup more than made up for the horrible feeling of losing to Wimbledon,' said Dibble. 'When it comes to saving penalties there is always an element of luck, and it was on my side that day.'

Luton trailed 2-1 against Arsenal when Winterburn stepped up, but within minutes of Dibble's save, Brian Stein levelled the scores at 2-2 before Danny Wilson scored the winning goal. But despite carving a niche in Luton's history, Dibble elected to move on in 1988. He joined Manchester City for a fee of £240,000.

'Manchester City are a fantastic club and are still close to my heart,' recalled Dibble fondly. 'The fans were fantastic, and Maine Road was full more often than not back then. That generated a terrific atmosphere, and it was just a great place to play football.'

Andy made his Manchester City debut against Hull City at Boothferry Park and made 45 appearances during season 1988/89. City finished as runners-up to Chelsea to secure promotion, and Dibble was a mainstay again on their return to the top table of English Football. He made a total of 37 appearances, and all seemed to be going well until one fateful day in March 1990.

City travelled to Nottingham to face Forest at the City Ground. They lost the game 1-0, the only goal coming in controversial circumstances. Garry Parker's cross from the right wing was grasped by Dibble. As the Welshman cupped the ball in his right hand and readied himself to clear, Forest midfielder Gary Crosby came from behind him, headed the ball out of his grasp and stroked it into the empty net with his right foot. In today's game, the goal would almost certainly have been ruled out, but referee Rodger Gifford allowed it to stand, and Andy Dibble's City career suffered as a result.

'My first season there was really special as we got promoted from Division Two,' said Dibble. 'I got on really well with [City manager] Howard Kendall, but the next season he brought in Tony Coton. After being the number one for two years, that was difficult to take.'

Over the next three seasons, Dibble made only seven appearances for City. During that time, he had spells on loan at Aberdeen, Middlesbrough, Bolton Wanderers and West Bromwich Albion.

'As you didn't have substitute goalies back then, the only way to keep my first-team appearances up was to go out on loan,' said Dibble. 'The move to Aberdeen was one that went really well for me [Dibble kept four clean sheets in the five games he played, including one in a 3-0 win over Celtic], and I was disappointed I couldn't stay longer. Unfortunately, there were rules in place that meant I couldn't play in European matches, so that opened the door for Michael Watt to come into the team.'

Dibble eventually edged himself back into the Manchester City team – he made 23 appearances in season 1994/95 – but it was a false dawn. On 1 December 1996, Andy made his 140th and last appearance for City in a 3-0 defeat against Wolves at Molineux.

'Frank Clark came in as manager at City and it soon became apparent there was no future for me at the club,' recalled Dibble.

'But then I got a phone call from Walter Smith offering me the chance to go to Rangers. It took me less than two minutes to say yes to him, I was up there like a shot!'

He added, 'I thought I was moving from one big club to another, but I don't think I appreciated how big Rangers were until I went out onto the pitch for my debut. And after that, being in and around the city of Glasgow reinforced that I had joined one of the biggest clubs in European football.'

The Celtic match was the proverbial powder keg. A Rangers win would to all intents and purposes secure that coveted ninth league title in a row. Defeat could have given Celtic a lifeline.

'I had a good idea of how significant nine-in-a-row was,' said Dibble. 'But it's only once I arrived in Glasgow that I realised just how much it meant. And that wasn't just the supporters, you could sense how much it meant to the players and the football club too.'

Rangers edged the game 1-0. Mark Hateley, whose return was another Walter Smith masterstroke, was ordered off, and at the end of the game Ian Ferguson and Paolo Di Canio went toe-to-toe. And added into the mix was the Rangers players mocking Celtic's 'huddle' as part of the post-match celebrations. But Dibble's abiding memory from the game isn't any of those incidents, it was the reaction of the players in the dressing room. That drove home to him how significant the match was.

'The lads, many of them top, international players, were ecstatic,' said Dibble. 'A number of them were in tears too, crying because they were so happy.'

A 2-1 defeat at home to Kilmarnock was an unexpected bump in the road, but Dibble kept another clean sheet when Raith Rovers were hammered 6-0 at Stark's Park. The finishing line was now in sight. All Rangers had to do to clinch nine-in-a-row was beat bottom of the table Motherwell at Ibrox. The champagne was on ice, but it was to fall flat when Smith's side lost the game 2-0.

'I think I gave away a penalty in that game, so not a good memory,' recalled Dibble. 'But you get games like that in football. Sometimes, against all odds, the underdogs win. We didn't take Motherwell lightly – our attitude for that game was the same as it was for the Celtic game – but there are some days when things just don't go right for you and that was one of them.'

Tension was now mounting. Rangers had two games to play, difficult fixtures at Tannadice and Tynecastle. Celtic were breathing down their neck, waiting for another slip-up. But it wasn't forthcoming. While Dibble dealt admirably with whatever Dundee United threw at him, Brian Laudrup leapt and met an exquisite cross from Charlie Miller flush on his forehead. The net bulged and history was made.

'I remember the final whistle and the celebrations that followed,' recalled Dibble. 'I can still picture it now. It had been a long season for the lads, and we celebrated in style.'

The campaign drew to a close three days later when Rangers lost 3-1 against Hearts at Tynecastle. The result mattered little, though, and the match is memorable only because it marked Barry Ferguson's first-team debut.

For Andy Dibble, it was the last of his seven appearances for Rangers.

'I'm really proud and privileged to have played a part in nine-in-a-row,' said Dibble. 'I had played at Wembley with Luton and been capped by Wales, but that game at Parkhead, keeping a clean sheet on my debut in a pressure-pot game, will live with me forever.'

There are a couple of other moments from that season that are indelibly inked in Dibble's memory too: a helicopter ride back to Ibrox and a tattoo.

'Flying back to Ibrox from Tynecastle was my first-ever time in a helicopter,' laughed Dibble. 'We were doing it in style, but the crowd when we got back to Ibrox was unbelievable. It was pouring with rain, yet the Rangers fans still filled the stadium. Moments like that made me want the season to keep going for longer. I wanted to stay with Rangers longer too, but it wasn't to be.'

And the tattoo?

'The lads and I were in Canada after the season finished, and after a few beers, they convinced me to get the tattoo as something to remember them by. When I got home, my wife wasn't best pleased when she saw it!'

He added, 'That trip was a great way to end my time at Rangers. The staff, players and fans had looked after me from the minute I came through the front door. They made me feel so welcome right up to the end. No doubt about it, Rangers is a special football club.'

The sum total of Andy Dibble's Rangers career is seven matches, the final seven of the 348 that made up that historic nine-in-a-row era. But in that short period of time, Dibble became a cult hero among the Rangers supporters, and those feelings are reciprocated.

After leaving Rangers, Dibble became something of a nomad. He had short stints at ten clubs, including a return to Luton and a three-year stay at Wrexham. He also suffered chemical burns while playing for Barry Town in the League of Wales, and during his spell at Wrexham he broke his arm and severed tendons in his finger.

After making almost 400 league appearances, Dibble retired as a player in 2006 and moved into coaching. He has since had spells coaching goalkeepers at Accrington Stanley, Coventry City, Peterborough United, Rotherham United and Cardiff City. He returned to Scotland to take on the role of Head of Goalkeeping at Motherwell at the start of season 2022/23 but now holds a similar role with Accrington Stanley.

Capped three times for Wales, Andy Dibble made seven appearances for Rangers. He conceded seven goals and registered four shutouts.

* * *

What would be Andy Goram's final season as a Rangers player, 1997/98, was once again blighted by injury. He played in 25 of the 36 league games as the bid for ten-in-a-row eventually foundered and, like so many others, Goram made his last Rangers appearance, in the 2-1 defeat against Hearts, in the Scottish Cup Final.

It wasn't the way the career of arguably the greatest-ever Rangers goalkeeper should have ended. Since signing for the club, Goram had won six league titles, three Scottish Cups and two League Cups. Looking at league, Scottish Cup, Scottish League Cup and European matches, he conceded an average of a goal every 1.817 games and his shutout record stands at 108. Taking into account friendly matches and testimonials, Goram totalled 282 appearances in a Rangers jersey.

His Old Firm record is impressive too. Goram faced Celtic 26 times in a Rangers jersey. Fifteen of the matches were won and he tasted defeat on only five occasions, recording 11 shutouts and conceding 22 goals.

Departing on a free transfer in the summer of 1998, Goram played one league game for Notts County before he joined Sheffield United. He was brought in to provide cover for Alan Kelly and Simon Tracey and made a total of nine appearances for the Blades.

A return to Scotland was on the horizon, though, and Andy signed for Motherwell in January 1999. A series of impressive displays followed and he was appointed captain by manager Billy Davies. After making 69 appearances for Motherwell, Goram left in March 2001. His destination? Old Trafford!

Manchester United were pushing for the Premiership title and in the latter stages of the Champions League, but injuries to Fabien Barthez and Raimond van der Gouw meant Sir Alex Ferguson was in desperate need of goalkeeping cover. His brother, Martin, who was chief scout at Old Trafford recommended going for Goram on a short-term loan deal.

Ferguson is said to have scoffed at the idea initially, but after some further thought he contacted Goram. But when Ferguson called, Goram thought that it was a prank call and told the caller in no uncertain terms where to go. Ferguson called back and an unlikely deal was done.

Goram, who penned a deal to the end of the season, made two appearances for United. His debut was a 4-2 win over Coventry City at Old Trafford. He was substituted by Van der Gouw after 66 minutes and the same thing happened in his only other Red Devils match, a 2-1 defeat against Southampton at The Dell.

Despite his limited game time, Ferguson ensured that Goram received a league medal, and The Goalie returned to Motherwell in the summer of 2001. But his contract was not extended at Fir Park, and after making guest appearances for Blackpool and Boreham Wood and playing a trial match for Hamilton Accies, Goram had a short spell with Coventry City for whom he made seven appearances.

At the age of 38, Goram's next move took him to Queen of the South where he balanced playing with his coaching commitments with Motherwell. In his single season at Palmerston Park, Goram was part of the Doonhamers side that won the Scottish Challenge Cup in October 2002 – goals from John O'Neill and Derek Lyle secured a 2-0 win over Brechin City at Broadwood – and he ended his career after short spells with Oldham and Elgin City.

After hanging up his gloves, Goram took on the role of goalkeeping coach at numerous clubs, including Clyde, Hamilton Accies, Ayr United and Cambuslang Rangers.

Sadly, the greatest-ever Rangers goalkeeper is no longer with us. It was announced on 30 May 2022 that Goram had terminal cancer. He passed away at the age of 58 on 2 July 2022.

'The Goalie was one of the first to phone me when I got my Stage 4 cancer diagnosis,' recalled Scott Nisbet. 'After that he would call and text me regularly to ask me how I was getting on. When he got diagnosed, I was devasted. He texted me to let me know, and when I asked him if he had got his results, he told me that the doctor had asked if he wanted to have his family round about him. I knew then that it was serious, and he didn't have long left to live. He was given six months but was gone within weeks. I cried when I found out he had passed away.'

Nisbet concluded, 'Andy was my pal, a boy's boy, and the life and soul of the party. He was by far the best goalkeeper I played with. We all had each other's backs in that dressing room, but it didn't matter what stature of player you were; Andy wouldn't hold back in telling you if you did something wrong in a game. But it would all be forgotten about after he had said his piece. He loved his time with Rangers and the best way to sum him up is to say that he was simply the best.'

Richard Gough was fortunate to play in a defensive unit with some exceptional goalkeepers in his career – the likes of Ray Clemence, Jim Leighton and Chris Woods – but he rates Goram as the best.

'I played with Chris Woods from 1987 to 1990 and I thought we would be hard pushed to replace him,' said the nine-in-a-row captain. 'But Andy proved me wrong. You don't know how good a goalkeeper is until you lose him, and when he didn't play, Andy was a big loss to the team even though we had good backup goalkeepers at the time. Other than one goal that Roy Aitken scored for Aberdeen, I can't remember many occasions when Andy was beaten by a shot from outside the box.'

Gough added, 'I said recently that when I was captain, I had very good players round about me. In that squad there were three or four other players who could have been captain, and Andy was one of them. He was a leader. He hated to lose games and didn't suffer fools gladly. I loved him because we were very close. We would talk before games and then get together to reflect afterwards and talk about what we maybe could have done better. I always felt safe when Andy was behind me.'

Sir David Murray offered similar thoughts.

'It's only once someone has gone that you look back and realise how good they were,' said Sir David. 'That's the case with Andy, and he merits being recognised as the greatest Rangers goalkeeper ever.'

The last word on Goram from the inner sanctum at Ibrox goes to Ally McCoist who was at Goram's bedside when he passed away.

'He had all the attributes you need to be a goalkeeper,' said McCoist. 'He was mad, but he was brave too and worked very hard. And he had a desire to win, even if it was five-a-side in training. I've never met anyone with a desire to keep the ball out the net like Andy had. I used to do commentaries on the five-a-side games, and he would go mental if I scored. He would chase me, punch me, but thankfully he wasn't the fastest, so I used to get away with it.'

McCoist concluded, 'He's the best I've played with. We used to warm up together. I would hit the ball into him, but over the course of time there was something that I had forgotten. When Andy was in the hospice, we were sitting talking about old times. Back then, when we were warming up, I always had to put the last shot into the net, something that used to annoy him. He looked at me at that point and smiled and asked me if I remembered what happened after that. I couldn't, so he told me that I used to take out my chewing gum and throw it onto the penalty spot. And I did, after every warm-up, I did that. I couldn't believe he remembered that, and I got up and gave him a big cuddle.'

Andrew Lewis Goram, Rangers Football Club's greatest-ever goalkeeper.

Chapter 10

A Different Perspective on The Goalie

JIM FOX met Andy Goram by chance around 1995.

'Ally McCoist and Ian Durrant used to play in the Ken MacLeod golf tournament that was held in Largs,' said Fox. 'One Sunday afternoon The Goalie appeared. The next day Ally and I were scheduled to go to the races at Newcastle, and The Goalie asked if he could join us. When we landed in Newcastle, Ally went to visit his father-in-law at the time who wasn't well, and The Goalie and I spent some time together in Newcastle. We didn't get back to Largs until late at night, so he asked if he could come and stay with me. I had a house on the shore front where I lived by myself, so I said it wasn't a problem. I had a new housemate, as about two-and-a-half years later, he was still there!'

Living in Largs rather than in the goldfish bowl of Glasgow was certainly beneficial for Goram, and he and Jim had many memorable moments together as Rangers completed the final stages of an historic sequence of nine successive league titles.

'Andy was a lot of fun,' said Fox. 'He was good company, and we had a lot of laughs. We never had a cross word in all the time we lived together. But Andy was also very articulate and clever. He had beautiful handwriting, and he would spend a lot of time sitting with a glass of wine at the front of the house writing messages for the Rangers fans. He enjoyed doing things for the fans, especially the good-looking ones! He definitely had an eye for the girls.'

He added, 'We would go out in Largs a lot too. We would go into a pub called 'Charlie Smith's' where everyone knew everyone. But we would have our own wee corner where we would sit and Andy never got any hassle.'

In addition to working his way through Jim's wine collection, Goram also made use of some of the garb in Fox's wardrobe too.

Jim recalled, 'I would usually still be in bed when Andy got up in the morning to go into training. He would always leave me a note in the kitchen that said, "first up, best dressed", as he'd be away out the door wearing my Versace clothing.'

He added, 'That was a great time for Andy and Rangers. They were winning all the time, but the moment that sticks out for me was when The Goalie saved the penalty from Van Hooijdonk. He was really chuffed to win man of the match that night, and he gave me the magnum of champagne that he was presented with.'

This was a special time for Goram, and although he moved away from Largs when he left Rangers in 1998, he and Fox remained close until the end.

'He knew it was coming, but he faced it head on,' said Fox. 'It was unbelievable how brave he was. I would go up and see him twice a week, and his ex-wife, Miriam, his son, Danny, Ally, and Bomber [John Brown] would be there too. We would sit and have a laugh and tell stories and take a wee trip down memory lane. During one of those visits, Andy told me he would be honoured if I would carry his coffin. On the Saturday he died, Ally phoned me from Andy's bedside to tell me that he had slipped away. Although it was expected it was still terribly sad.'

Jim Fox remembers his friend as the life and soul of the party, someone who loved a laugh. And that is perhaps summed up by the invitation Goram sent to his friends for his Rangers leaving do in May 1998. It read:

The Goalie (ex R.F.C)
Requests the pleasure of
………………..
At
'The Goalies Leaving Do & Pre World Cup Bash'
(venue to be announced: Top Secret)
On Sunday 17th May 98
(meet at 1.00pm…16 Newhaven Grove, Largs)
1pm – Champagne Reception
2pm Transport to Venue
7pm Karaoke. 12 Midnight STOMACH PUMP (optional)

RULES & REGULATIONS

1. BUS LEAVES 2pm PRONTO (Italiano) FROM 'FOX/GORAM' CASTLE
2. NOBODY TO BE SOBER UNDER ANY CIRCUMSTANCES
3. BRING YOUR OWN 'DRINKING HEAD'
4. BRING AN OVERNIGHT BAG WITH (TRUNKS/BIKINI)
5. PREPARE YOURSELF FOR A 'RIGHT GOOD SOIREE' (that is French for Blooter)

FOR THOSE WHO REQUIRE AN ALIBI TOUGH SHIT YOU SHOULDN'T BE COMING

God bless you, Andrew Lewis Goram.
May you rest in peace.

Chapter 11

The Dawn of a New Era

DICK ADVOCAAT'S arrival was the catalyst for the departure of players who had been the bedrock of the team under Walter Smith. Ally McCoist and Ian Durrant joined Kilmarnock, Stuart McCall went to Bradford City, while Richard Gough returned to the United States. And with Andy Goram also departing, one of the first tasks for Advocaat was to select a goalkeeper. The natural progression could have seen Antti Niemi become the new number one, but the Little General decided to go out and recruit a flamboyant French international to provide competition. His name was Lionel Charbonnier.

Charbonnier, an amiable Frenchman who has never hidden his love for Rangers and their supporters, must be one of the unluckiest goalkeepers in Rangers' history. Part of a World Cup-winning squad and rated in the top ten goalkeepers in the world by FIFA, he arrived in Glasgow in July 1998 and, after getting into the team, he looked set to take over the gloves from the late, great Goram. But an injury sustained in a UEFA Cup tie against Bayer Leverkusen would be the beginning of the end of the enigmatic Frenchman's Rangers career.

Born in Poitiers on 25 October 1966, Charbonnier was around three or four years old when his older brother, Thierry, took him under his wing and helped his younger sibling develop his talent.

'Thierry was a very good goalkeeper, better than me,' smiled Charbonnier. 'He didn't want to become a professional footballer, so he became my first coach. I started to play in games when I was five years old. That was younger than you should have been to play in tournaments, so we had to get permission from the opponents for me to play. I think they said "yes" as I was quite small, but when I played against them and did well, very soon they started to say that I couldn't play. That meant I couldn't play in tournaments for a couple of years until I reached the required age. I thought that was very cruel as all I wanted to do was play. I didn't care if we won or not.'

It was clear at that early stage that Charbonnier had the potential to do well in football. And when he was 17 years old, he was signed by AJ Auxerre, playing in the same youth team as Basile Boli and Eric Cantona. That side won the French National Junior Cup, and Lionel, Basile and Eric would all eventually make the step up to the first XI. But for Charbonnier the wait would be longer than the others.

'The goalkeeper at the time I came to Auxerre was Joel Bats who was in the French national team,' recalled Charbonnier. 'Bruno Martini was also at the club, but he was on loan at Nancy, and there was another young goalkeeper called Eric Durand too.'

Bats would join PSG in 1985 at which point Bruno Martini became the number one goalkeeper. Martini would go on to make over 300 Ligue 1 appearances for Auxerre, and as he rarely missed games, Charbonnier, now the second choice following Durand's departure to FC Gueugnon, remained with the B team.

Lionel would make his Ligue 1 debut in a 2-1 win over Laval on 23 July 1988, but it wasn't until the start of season 1991/92 that he started to stake a claim for the gloves. He appeared sporadically, but finally got his opportunity to play more regularly after Martini sustained a knee injury late in season 1993/94.

'In my opinion, Martini was the best goalkeeper in Europe at that time,' said Charbonnier. 'But when I came into the team I did well and after a short time, Gerard Houllier asked me to join up with the national team. And that season I was in the team that won the Coupe de France too. This was the first time an Auxerre team had ever won that competition.'

But Charbonnier would also succumb to a knee injury himself. He played in the opening 24 Ligue 1 matches in season 1994/95 and the opening rounds of the European Cup Winners' Cup. But by the time Auxerre faced Arsenal in the quarter-finals, Charbonnier was on the sidelines.

'I got injured in training,' he admitted. 'We were practising corner kicks, and three players ended up on my back. My foot got stuck in the turf, and my body turned due to the weight of the players. The result was that I ruptured the cruciate ligament in my left knee.'

That was February 1995. It would be 4 November that year before he played for the first team again.

When Lionel came back into the team, Auxerre were fourth in Ligue 1. But at the end of the season, he became a champion. He kept 14 clean sheets in a run of games that saw Auxerre win 13, draw five and lose four matches. That was enough to secure the club's first-ever Ligue 1 title, Guy Roux's side finishing four points better off than runners-up Paris Saint-Germain. And Charbonnier added another Coupe de France medal to his collection too when Auxerre defeated Nimes 2-1 in the final.

The wily Roux had been in charge of Auxerre since 1964. He had been instrumental in the development of a state-of-the-art youth academy which was opened in 1980, and he and Daniel Rolland were key figures in Charbonnier's career.

'When you have a career that lasted as long as mine you must have good luck,' said Charbonnier. 'I worked with lots of good coaches, starting with Daniel Rolland who was the coach at the Centre de Formation [youth academy]. The academy was the best in France at that time and probably one of the best in the world. Daniel helped with the development of Eric Cantona and Basile Boli, and we won many titles with him.'

He added, 'Guy Roux was in many ways like a second father for me and my team-mates. We came from all over France and were alone without our families. Auxerre was a family club, and Guy Roux was the father of that family. He was strict at times, but he taught me so much not just about football but also rules of life too.'

Charbonnier played 31 of the 38 Ligue 1 matches in season 1996/97 and all but one of Auxerre's eight Champions League matches. And the latter saw him experience the atmosphere at Ibrox for the first time.

After hammering Alania Vladikavkaz 10-3 on aggregate, Rangers were drawn alongside Auxerre, Grasshopper Zurich and Ajax in a mouthwatering group. Walter Smith's side were heavily beaten in their first game in Zurich – the fact that Andy Goram was man of the match illustrates that Rangers were fortunate to only lose 3-0 – and welcomed Lionel and Auxerre to Glasgow for the second round of fixtures.

'I thought it would be very easy for us to beat Rangers until I heard the noise inside Ibrox,' recalled Charbonnier. 'It was unbelievable, and I knew at that moment that it would be a difficult match for Auxerre.

'As a player you want to play in stadiums like Ibrox and experience that kind of atmosphere. It gave me extra motivation to win, but it also made me want to play for these supporters one day too.'

He added, 'The atmosphere in Auxerre was unbelievable too, but the stadium was much smaller. When we played against

Borussia Dortmund in the UEFA Cup semi-final, the Auxerre fans were incredible. But when I came to Rangers, I was on the bench for the game against Parma. After the game I spoke to their goalkeeper, Gigi Buffon. I said to him that Parma had won the UEFA Cup, but I couldn't recognise the team. When I asked him what had happened, he reckoned that the atmosphere in Ibrox had played a part. He said it was the best he had played in up to that point in his career. And even when he signed for PSG late in his career, he still said that Ibrox was in the top three in terms of atmosphere that he had experienced. The Bears should be very proud about that.'

Charbonnier would get his wish. Season 1997/98 would be Lionel's last as an Auxerre player. He missed out as his side won the Intertoto Cup, beating MSV Duisburg 2-0 on aggregate in the final, but managed 24 Ligue 1 appearances. He was also in the side that lost 5-3 on penalties to Bordeaux in the Coupe de Ligue Final. But when the opportunity came to sign for Rangers in the summer of 1998, Lionel seized it.

'I didn't hesitate,' he recalled. 'Mr Murray phoned me during the World Cup. I don't know how he got my phone number as the French national team had given each of us a phone that I thought only my family knew the number for. It took me by surprise when Mr Murray said that he wanted me to sign for Rangers. But we had a good conversation, and although my agent said other teams wanted to sign me, I didn't want to know. I wanted to sign for Rangers.'

Charbonnier would have big gloves to fill. Arguably the club's finest-ever goalkeeper, Andy Goram, had left the club at the end of the previous season. He would be a tough act to follow.

'I knew that it would be difficult as Andy was such a famous goalkeeper,' said Charbonnier. 'All the fans I spoke to in the streets of Glasgow would talk about Andy Goram. I didn't want the Bears to forget about Andy, all I wanted to do was try and get to the same level as him in the hearts of the Rangers fans.'

Lionel made his Rangers debut in a pre-season friendly against Falkirk on 17 July 1998. But when the competitive action got underway five days later in a UEFA Cup tie against Shelbourne at Prenton Park in Tranmere, Advocaat selected Antti Niemi. The Finnish keeper would play in the opening three UEFA Cup matches and the opening league fixture against Hearts too.

Charbonnier was unavailable as he had been struggling with a thigh injury, but he recovered to make his Scottish League debut against Motherwell on 15 August 1998. In front of him, Colin Hendry also made his debut that afternoon, and he was one of only two Scots in a cosmopolitan starting XI. Lorenzo Amoruso, Sergio Porrini and Arthur Numan joined Hendry in the back four, while Giovanni van Bronckhorst, Ian Ferguson, Jorg Albertz and Andrei Kanchelskis made up the midfield. An Englishman, Rod Wallace, and an Argentinian, Gabriel Amato, formed the front two.

A late Albertz penalty earned the first league win of the Advocaat era against Motherwell, and Lionel played in each of the 13 league and League Cup matches that followed. That run included his first taste of the Old Firm derby.

'The one game I knew you had to perform well in was the Old Firm,' said Charbonnier. 'I was always motivated to play in every game, but I felt that more than any other, the game against Celtic was the one in which I had to be very good.'

He continued, 'Everyone remembers my save from Larsson's header. I knew that Andy Goram had made a lot of big saves against Celtic, and I knew that a save like that was almost as important as any save I would make in a cup final.'

Charbonnier's save was crucial in a match that ended in a 0-0 draw, and it secured the place in the hearts of the Rangers fans that Lionel had sought since he signed for the club.

'It wasn't long after that that I felt that the fans had adopted me,' said Charbonnier. 'I used to live in Bath Street, and when I met the fans, everyone was always very kind. When they started to sing my name to the tune of "La Marseillaise", it was unbelievable. That kind of thing doesn't happen in France. The fans were now close to me, and I was very close with the fans.'

In addition to featuring in domestic games, Lionel was number one in the UEFA Cup too. He kept a clean sheet in a superb 0-0 draw against PAOK Salonika and was part of the XI that defeated Beitar Jerusalem 5-3 on aggregate. But those results were all topped by a 2-1 win over Bayer Leverkusen in Germany. Barry Ferguson was immense in midfield, and current Rangers manager, Gio van Bronckhorst, netted one of the goals.

A goal from Jonatan Johansson earned a 1-1 draw in the second leg at Ibrox on Guy Fawkes night, but the Charbonnier bonfire that had burned so brightly was cruelly extinguished. After 65 minutes and with Rangers 1-0 ahead, Charbonnier came to his near post to deal with a corner kick. He landed awkwardly and within minutes his first season as a Rangers player was over.

'I told Advocaat I was tired after the World Cup, but he didn't listen' was Charbonnier's reflection on what led up to him sustaining a similar injury to his right knee to the one he had sustained to his left while at Auxerre. 'He said that I couldn't be tired as I hadn't played in any of the games. But he didn't know that I was the number two goalkeeper to Barthez which meant that even though I didn't play, you had to train more.'

This was the first sign of friction in the relationship between manager and player.

* * *

With Charbonnier out of action, Antti Niemi took over in goal initially, and the Finn was in the starting XI when the first leg of the domestic Treble was secured in the League Cup Final against St Johnstone.

Born in Oulu, Finland on 31 May 1972, Antti Mikko Niemi arrived at Ibrox from FC Copenhagen. After starting his career with short spells at Oulun Luistinseura and Rauman Pallo, Niemi signed for HJK Helsinki, making his debut when he came on as a substitute for Juha Karjalainen in an 8-2 win over FC Reipas Lahiti. Jari Litmanen scored a hat-trick for HJK.

Niemi eventually became the HJK number one early in season 1992/93 and by the time he left to join FC Copenhagen, he had made 107 appearances for HJK, keeping 45 clean sheets. He chalked up a further 47 league appearances while in Denmark and was in the side that beat Ikast FS 2-0 in the final of the Danish Cup. A few weeks later, though, Niemi was bound for Scotland as Walter Smith tempted him to join Rangers.

Niemi, who seemed set to join Coventry City until Smith stepped in, joined a Rangers squad that were pursuing a tenth successive league title, but he came in under the radar as the spotlight was on the significant financial investment in Lorenzo Amoruso, Sergio Porrini and Marco Negri. Nonetheless, Niemi's signing undoubtedly gave the player pool more depth, with the Finn and Theo Snelders competing with Andy Goram for the number one jersey.

Opportunities to play would, however, be rare in season 1997/98. Niemi played in a couple of low-key bounce games against Ayr United and Morton – Rangers won both 9-0 – and he also featured against Everton at Goodison Park in a testimonial match for Dave Watson in July 1998. And seven days later he was handed his competitive debut in a Champions League qualifier in the Faroe Islands against GI Gotu Itrottarfelag.

Goram had picked up a groin injury in training, so the Finn was thrust into action. And if some rumours were to be believed, then

Niemi looked set for an extended run in the team. The *Glasgow Herald* reported that Goram was set to be transfer-listed after failing to turn up on a couple of occasions for treatment. The report even suggested that Goram had body swerved a session to attend the Open Golf that was taking place at Royal Troon.

In the end, Goram got himself back to full fitness, but in the meantime, in the Faroes, doubles from Durie and McCoist and a goal from Negri secured a comfortable 5-0 win. The goals scored by the irrepressible McCoist earned him the distinction of scoring the most goals in European competition for a Scottish team.

Niemi kept his place for the second leg where Rangers racked up a further six goals without reply, but Goram was back in position for the opening two league matches and the ill-fated double header against IFK Gothenburg. A 3-0 thrashing in Sweden – the fact Goram was man of the match sums up how inept Rangers were on the night – effectively ended hopes of qualifying for the Champions League group stages. But when the Rangers number one missed out through injury again, it was Snelders who stepped into the breach.

Niemi's only game time had been 90 minutes for the reserves in a 1-1 draw against Celtic and another full match for Finland against Switzerland. But he broke an index finger in the latter match and that counted him out when the opportunity arose to get back into the first team following a recurrence of Goram's groin complaint.

The initial diagnosis was six weeks of inactivity for Niemi, but an operation was eventually required, and the Finn wouldn't play again until he featured in a 2-0 win over Dundee United reserves shortly before the end of 1997. He had actually been pencilled in to play before that against Kilmarnock reserves but missed out. Young Michael Rae played instead, but after he was injured in the first half, the redoubtable John Brown had to take over the gloves. Rangers won the game 4-1.

Niemi continued his comeback in a 4-1 defeat for the reserves at Pittodrie in January 1998, and also played for the second XI when they defeated Celtic 3-1 in the last four of the Reserve League Cup. That set the Finn up for a first-team return, and when Goram was struck down with bronchitis, Niemi deputised against Dunfermline Athletic in February 1998. Remarkably, seven months after arriving at the club, this would be his league debut. Alas, a late equaliser from Harry Curran spoiled the occasion somewhat, and the two points dropped would prove vital come the end of the season.

Goram came back into the side the following week, but when he was afflicted by injury again, Niemi featured in four of the last six league games as the tilt for ten ended in failure. But although Niemi missed the Scottish Cup Final, with the legendary Goram set to be released in the summer the Finn looked set to become the number one goalkeeper at the club.

Niemi began Dick Advocaat's first season in possession of the gloves. He started the opening friendly of pre-season against Molde FK – he was replaced by Knut Dorum Lillebakk who made a guest appearance for Rangers – and also the UEFA Cup qualifying matches against Shelbourne, conceding three goals in the first leg at Prenton Park in Tranmere before keeping a clean sheet in the return leg at Ibrox. And when the curtain was raised for the new league campaign, the Finn was beaten twice when Hearts defeated Rangers 2-1 at Tynecastle.

The initial return to fitness of Charbonnier meant he had to cool his heels on the sidelines after that, but Charbonnier's misfortune against Bayer Leverkusen seemed to have opened the door for a return to the starting XI. Niemi would play six successive league games, but one of them would be a chastening experience, Rangers losing 5-1 to Celtic at Parkhead.

Nonetheless, Niemi was part of a side that won four of those six matches, but his time in the first team came to an end when, in December 1998, Advocaat dipped into the transfer market and persuaded Stefan Klos to come to Glasgow.

The German played a key role as the league title was regained and shut out Celtic as the domestic Treble was completed with a 1-0 win in the Scottish Cup Final. It looked as if both Niemi and Charbonnier would have their work cut out to get back into the team, but on reflection, the Frenchman knew fairly quickly after Klos arrived that that would be the case.

'When Mr Advocaat signed Stefan Klos, I spoke to a few players and their opinion was that it would be difficult for me to play,' recalled Charbonnier. 'I tried my best and had a very good relationship with the fans, but I knew that even if I was doing better than Stefan, he would play as he was Advocaat's guy. I had no problem with Stefan – he was a very good goalkeeper – my problem was with Advocaat. He knew I was in the hearts of the Rangers fans, and he tried many times to make trouble for me.'

Charbonnier made his first-team comeback in a 2-1 defeat against St Mirren in a pre-season friendly in Paisley in July 1999. But significantly, Klos was selected for the other six friendly matches that were played, and the German also kept goal in the opening two league matches and the first three qualifying matches for the Champions League.

Lionel was then offered an opportunity to return to the team when Klos sustained a knee injury. He came back for a 4-1 win over Dundee United, and then played well as Rangers saw off a spirited Parma side in the final qualifying round for the Champions League. And when Rangers kicked off their Group F campaign with matches against Valencia, Bayern Munich and PSV Eindhoven, Charbonnier was still in possession of the gloves. But when Klos regained fitness, he came straight back into the team at Charbonnier's expense.

The sum total of Charbonnier's first-team appearances in season 1999/2000 was 11. In those 11 matches, he kept four clean sheets, but over the course of the campaign, Advocaat also selected Mark Brown and Thomas Myhre when Klos was injured again. The latter came in as an emergency loan from Everton for a UEFA Cup tie against Borussia Dortmund.

By that stage, Antti Niemi had moved on to pastures new. In December 1999, Rangers accepted an offer of £400,000 from Hearts, and during his time in Edinburgh the Finnish goalkeeper showed the attributes that had attracted the attention of Walter Smith back in the summer of 1997.

Niemi, who had had a loan spell with Charlton Athletic prior to moving to Tynecastle, made 114 appearances for Hearts. And as time moved on, potential suitors were becoming more frequent at Hearts games. Eventually, Southampton, managed by Gordon Strachan, made the Edinburgh side an offer they couldn't refuse for the services of Niemi. The Saints paid £2,000,000 for him in the summer of 2002, and Niemi would enjoy four years on the south coast. During that time, he made 123 appearances and made history too.

Southampton reached the final of the FA Cup in May 2003. Niemi had played in every round bar the semi-final as the Saints defeated Tottenham Hotspur, Millwall (after a replay), Norwich City, Wolverhampton Wanderers and Watford on the road to the Millennium Stadium in Cardiff. But in the final against Arsenal, he tore his calf muscle after 67 minutes and had to be replaced by Paul Jones. It was the first time ever that a goalkeeper had been substituted in an FA Cup Final.

Southampton were relegated at the end of season 2004/05, but although Niemi stayed to try and help them bounce straight back, the Saints failed to do so. In January 2006, Niemi left Southampton and signed for Fulham, and he would go on to make 63 appearances during his time at Craven Cottage. He conceded 95 goals and kept 13 clean sheets, notably against Liverpool in May 2007.

But season 2007/08 would be Niemi's last as a professional footballer, and a 3-0 defeat against Manchester United at Craven Cottage on 1 March 2008 would prove to be his last match. An injury to his Achilles was swiftly followed by an issue with his wrist which forced Niemi to call it a day.

Capped 68 times by Finland, Antti Niemi's Rangers story is another of those that fit rather neatly into the 'what might have been' category.

* * *

Mark Brown, who would later become one of only a handful of players to play for both Rangers and Celtic, had been with Rangers since 1997. He made his competitive debut at the age of 19 against Dunfermline Athletic in the League Cup, although he had played in a couple of friendly matches in Norway in July 1998.

The cup tie against Dunfermline 15 months later would be one of only five further appearances he made for the first team. His last came on 22 October 2000 in a 2-1 defeat against St Johnstone at McDiarmid Park.

Brown joined Motherwell in 2001 but was one of 19 players released by the club in May 2002 when the club entered administration. He subsequently joined Inverness Caledonian Thistle where he excelled, earning a Scotland B cap and shutting out Celtic in the quarter-finals of the 2003 Scottish Cup.

That performance probably helped him secure a move to Parkhead where he was ostensibly backup for Artur Boruc. In his three seasons with Celtic, Brown made just 13 appearances and had a spell on loan with Kilmarnock before he was released in January 2010.

At that point Brown joined Hibernian for whom he made his debut on 22 August 2010 against Rangers. He was beaten three times in that game by Kenny Miller. However, a couple of months later, he kept a clean sheet at Ibrox when Hibernian reversed that scoreline.

A change in manager meant a change in goalkeeper in January 2011. Colin Calderwood brought in another goalkeeper with a Rangers connection, Graeme Smith, and for the rest of Brown's time at Easter Road, he vied with Smith and Graham Stack for the gloves.

Stack was the man in possession when Hibernian reached the Scottish Cup semi-final in 2012, but he had to be withdrawn with 17 minutes to go after picking up a thigh injury. Brown took his place and was also selected for the final against Hearts. Alas, that match would prove to be one to forget as the sunshine most certainly didn't shine on the side from Leith, Hearts winning by five goals to one.

Brown joined Ross County in the summer of 2012, and after making 71 appearances for the Dingwall side, he finished his playing career with Dumbarton. The last of his 31 appearances for the Sons came in January 2017, and a couple of months later it was announced that he had left the club to pursue a career in the police force.

Thomas Myhre only spent a month as a Rangers player. With Klos and Charbonnier unavailable for a UEFA Cup tie against Borussia Dortmund at Ibrox, Dick Advocaat was reluctant to pitch Mark Brown into action. Instead, he was granted permission to make an emergency loan signing, and Everton manager, Walter Smith, answered the SOS from his former club by offering them the services of Myhre.

Myhre, born in Sarpsborg, a city that is 59 miles from the Norwegian capital, Oslo, had joined Everton for £800,000 in November 1997. He had big gloves to fill at Goodison Park as he took over from the legendary Neville Southall, but Myhre acquitted himself well before sustaining a couple of injuries that saw him lose his place to Paul Gerrard. He broke his ankle while on international duty with Norway, but his comeback had to be put on hold when he slipped getting out of the bath and cracked a small bone in his foot.

Just 48 hours after signing, Myhre kept a clean sheet as Rangers defeated Dortmund 2-0, but goals from Victor Ikpeba and Fredi Bobic in the return leg forced a penalty decider. But although Myhre saved the penalty taken by Christian Nerlinger, his opposite number, Jens Lehmann, did likewise, stopping efforts from Giovanni van Bronckhorst, Arthur Numan and Claudio Reyna.

Myhre made a further three appearances for Rangers: league wins over Motherwell and Kilmarnock and a 2-1 defeat at home against Dundee. The latter was one of just two league losses Rangers suffered all season.

After five appearances, two clean sheets and five goals conceded, Myhre returned to Merseyside once Charbonnier had regained fitness. The Frenchman played in a 1-0 win over Hearts at Ibrox – a match at which the 100th anniversary of Ibrox Stadium was recognised – before he made his last appearance of season 1999/2000 on 27 December 1999, a 1-1 draw against Celtic at Parkhead. Klos had broken his hand, but he came back into the team in the new year and very soon was defying Celtic and earning the nickname Der Goalie.

Charbonnier remained at Ibrox, but he would make just three more appearances for the first team, all in friendlies ahead of season 2000/01. His final appearance for Rangers came as a substitute for Klos in a 3-0 win over Glentoran at Ibrox on 29 August 2000. By then the Danish goalkeeper Jesper Christiansen had been brought to the club. It was apparent that Lionel had no future at Rangers.

'I'm not sure that Advocaat liked that I was in the hearts of the Rangers fans,' recalled Charbonnier. 'He tried to get me in trouble a few times with the other players in the dressing room too. Advocaat tried to break the relationship I had with my team-mates, but we were all very close because of the success that we had.'

He added, 'There was a story in one of the newspapers that said I was speaking badly about Rangers. That was awful for me, and totally wrong. But Advocaat asked me to prove that I never said that. This made me very upset. I had played for him a number of times when I had to take painkillers – Voltaren, I think – and that had given me problems with my stomach. Yet he still put me in the middle of the dressing room and asked me to prove to my team-mates that what was written in the papers wasn't true. But guys like Craig Moore and The Hammer (Jorg Albertz) told me they knew I hadn't said these things. I didn't have to prove anything.'

The whole situation left a bitter taste in Charbonnier's mouth, and it made his mind up that he had no future at Ibrox as long as Advocaat was the manager. This was a difficult decision for the Frenchman given the strong bond he had with the dressing room and the Rangers supporters, but his relationship with Advocaat was broken beyond repair.

At the end of season 2000/01, Charbonnier joined Lausanne in Switzerland. The club were in some financial trouble and were relegated at the end of Charbonnier's only season there. To try and help with the predicament the Lausanne chairman found himself in, Charbonnier went without pay. He has to this day never asked for a penny of that back. 'I never wanted to put the chairman in more trouble,' he said.

The Frenchman retired from playing thereafter, and moved back to his home town, taking on the role of General Manager at Stade Poitevin. He also had a spell as manager of FC Sens before leading the Tahiti U20 side to the FIFA U20 World Cup in Egypt in 2009. Charbonnier's side topped a group including New Zealand, New Caledonia and Fiji to qualify for the finals where they were bracketed with Spain, Venezuela and Nigeria in Group B.

It was the first time Tahiti had made it through to the finals, but future Rangers player, Aaron Niguez, scored twice as Spain thrashed Tahiti 8-0, and Salomon Rondon, who has played for West Bromwich Albion and Everton, scored a hat-trick as the Venezuelans racked up a similar scoreline in Tahiti's second match. A 5-0 defeat against Nigeria saw Charbonnier's side eliminated at the group stage.

Since then, Charbonnier has had managerial roles in Indonesia, France and Congo, and he cites Dick Advocaat as having an influence on his coaching philosophy.

'When I finished playing, the French national team encouraged myself, Laurent Blanc and Didier Deschamps to do our coaching diploma,' said Charbonnier. 'Even though it was awful at times with Mr Advocaat, I learned a lot of things that I was able to use when I became a coach too. That was important. He was a very good tactical coach, but his man-management and the way he was with some players was not so good.'

Charbonnier, who holds a FIFA Pro Licence, spends his time these days working with FIFA as an instructor and also does some media work for RMC Radio. But no matter where he finds himself in the world, Rangers are never far from his thoughts. And when Rangers returned to Auxerre to play a UEFA Cup tie in 2006, it was apparent that the Rangers fans hadn't forgotten their former goalkeeper either.

'I will never regret joining Rangers,' said Charbonnier. 'I love the fans, and when Rangers came to play Auxerre lots of them came to watch the match. I was out in the city centre with my wife, and there were thousands of Rangers fans there. One of the fans spotted me, and all of a sudden, the fans started to sing my name to the tune of "La Marseillaise", just like they had done when I lived in Glasgow. It was very noisy, and people were coming out of shops and restaurants to see what was going on. I was very emotional – I think I was crying – and it just showed that the Rangers fans never forget you. I love the Bears, and they make me very happy. It is just a shame that my relationship with one guy meant that I couldn't play more times for those fans.'

If you include friendly matches, Lionel Charbonnier made 35 appearances for Rangers. He conceded 23 goals and kept 14 clean sheets. He is a cult hero among Rangers fans from that generation, but his Rangers career will always be a case of what might have been.

Chapter 12

Der Goalie

ONE AREA of the team where Rangers have always seemed to recruit well is the goalkeeping department. And when it comes to great Rangers goalkeepers, there are few better than the man signed from Borussia Dortmund on Christmas Eve 1998, Stefan Klos.

Born in Dortmund on 16 August 1971, Klos started his career with TSC Eintracht Dortmund before joining Borussia Dortmund in 1990. He would start what would be an eight-year association with BVB, playing with their second XI in the Fußball-Oberliga Westfalen, the fifth division in the football pyramid in Germany.

Klos made his Dortmund II debut on 5 August 1990 in a 3-2 win over Paderborn, but seven days later he was ordered off with 20 minutes remaining of a match against VfL Bochum II. That setback didn't deter the young goalkeeper, though, and he would miss only three of the 30 league matches played that season. Dortmund II finished fourth in the table.

Klos had obviously done enough to impress the BVB management, as he had also played twice for the first team. His debut came on 4 May 1991 in a 2-2 draw against SG Wattenscheid 09 – Klos replaced Wolfgang de Beer – but he came into a side that were in the throes of a slump. BVB hadn't won in the league since mid-December, their winless run comprising five draws and five defeats. The last four of those defeats had been in succession, while the first had been a 7-0 thrashing at the hands of VfB Stuttgart.

De Beer came back into the side a couple of weeks later for a 3-2 home defeat against Bayern Munich – a certain Brian Laudrup was among the goals for the visitors – and would keep his place for the last four league games and also the opening seven of season 1991/92. But when Klos took the gloves for a 3-1 win over 1FC Koln on 6 September 1991, he became BVB's number one. Remarkably, the next Bundesliga game Klos missed was on 18 May 1996, and that would be the only league encounter he was absent from before he left to join Rangers.

Consistency of selection was becoming a hallmark for Klos. After making his debut, Klos missed only 16 BVB matches, chalking up 339 appearances for the club. In that time frame, he picked up Bundesliga titles in 1994/95 and 1995/96, three German Super Cups, the Champions League and the Intercontinental Cup. His record stands at 399 goals conceded and 114 clean sheets.

Rangers were therefore signing a seasoned professional. When it became apparent that he wasn't going to be offered a new deal at Dortmund, Klos had opportunities to go to either Real Zaragoza or Valencia, but after a round of positive discussions and some sage advice from his countryman, Jorg Albertz, he was Glasgow-bound. Aged 27, it looked like he was going to spend the peak years of his career at Ibrox.

Klos made his debut on Boxing Day 1998 – Sergio Porrini scored the only goal of the game – and kept goal for the 17 league matches that followed. In that time frame, Rangers rattled off 12 wins and four draws on the road to the league title, memorably sealing it with an emphatic 3-0 win at Parkhead on 2 May.

By the end of that month Klos was gripping another trophy in his gloves. Wins over Stenhousemuir, Hamilton Accies, Falkirk and

St Johnstone had propelled Rangers into the Scottish Cup Final against Celtic. And Klos kept a clean sheet at the newly revamped Hampden as Rangers secured the domestic Treble courtesy of a goal from Rod Wallace.

There would be more of the same for Rangers the following season. But for Klos, it was a stop-start campaign blighted by injury. A knee injury and broken wrist sustained stopping a close-range shot from Jorg 'The Hammer' Albertz in training counted Klos out of 12 league matches. But he was back between the posts for the last 19 fixtures, keeping 11 clean sheets and conceding a mere 12 goals as Rangers cantered to the title. Their points total of 90 was 21 better than runners-up Celtic.

There is one game from that season that stands out more than most for Stefan Klos, though, the night the phrase 'Der Goalie' was coined for the first time. Rangers went to Parkhead on 8 March and won by a goal to nil. Rod Wallace got the goal, but Klos was rightly lauded post-match for an incredible performance that defied a Celtic side that dominated for the most part. Two of the saves made by Klos – one with outstretched foot to thwart Viduka and a one-handed save from a Weghorst header from point-blank range – fell into the 'jaw-dropping' category.

The Scottish Cup was also retained, Klos playing in every round and conceding just one goal. The trophy was secured on a day Hampden turned orange as the Rangers supporters paid homage to their Dutch manager. On the pitch, Klos was largely inactive as Rangers cantered to a 4-0 win over Aberdeen.

Advocaat had now won five trophies out of a possible six domestically, and his side had impressed in the Champions League too, narrowly missing out on qualification from Group F. But the appointment of Martin O'Neill as Celtic manager would bring Rangers crashing down from the crest of the wave of success they were riding on.

Klos played in the opening eight league matches of O'Neill's first season in charge. Rangers won six of them, but they were also humbled at Parkhead, Klos conceding six goals in a humiliating 6-2 defeat. The tide was starting to turn, but as Rangers continued to flounder, Klos was once again sidelined, damaged ankle ligaments eventually ruling the German out until December.

Mark Brown deputised in the first three league matches Klos missed, but a new kid on the block claimed the gloves for the other fixtures for which Klos was absent.

Jesper Ringsborg Christiansen was born on 24 April 1978 in a city called Roskilde, which is located 19 miles west of the Danish capital, Copenhagen. After developing a liking for playing in goal, young Jesper had spells with Football Club Roskilde and Ølstykke Fodbold Club before joining Odense Boldklub in 1998.

In Christiansen's first season, Odense won promotion to the Danish Superliga as First Division champions, and when Lars Hogh retired in January 2000, Christiansen became the club's number one. But a few months later, Dick Advocaat came calling and Jesper signed for Rangers.

He was thrust in at the deep end too. His debut was against Sturm Graz in the Champions League – Rangers lost 2-0 – and three days later, Christiansen would endure a somewhat inauspicious league debut. Rangers had lost two league matches in a row when they welcomed Kilmarnock to Ibrox on 28 October 2000. Ninety minutes later it was three successive league defeats, Christiansen having to fish the ball out of the net three times as the Ayrshire side recorded their biggest-ever victory at Ibrox.

He conceded in his next two league appearances too, but at least on those occasions Rangers won. St Mirren were beaten 7-1 at Ibrox – Kenny Miller scored five of the goals – while Aberdeen were edged out 2-1 at Pittodrie. There was, however, a clean sheet for the new boy in the League Cup when Dundee United were swept aside by three goals to nil in the last eight of the competition, but he conceded another two in a 2-2 draw against AS Monaco that thwarted attempts to qualify for the knockout stages.

And that as they say was that for Jesper Christiansen. He played in a pre-season friendly match against VV Capelle ahead of season 2001/02, but with first-team opportunities limited, Christiansen joined Vejle Boldklub on loan in January 2002. His performances there earned him a place in Denmark's squad for the 2002 World Cup, but it didn't herald a new dawn in terms of his Rangers career.

With Advocaat seemingly putting his faith in a young upstart called Allan McGregor, Christiansen moved on loan to VfL Wolfsburg in July of 2002. He would eventually leave Rangers when he joined Viborg FF on a permanent deal in 2003.

And it was back in his homeland that he re-established his credentials as a goalkeeper. After 18 months with Viborg, he was transferred to FC Copenhagen in 2005. For the next three years, Christiansen was named Danish Goalkeeper of the Year, an award that had been won in the past by Peter Schmeichel. In addition, he won four Danish Superliga titles, a Danish Cup and two Royal League titles. The latter was an annual tournament featuring teams from the three Scandinavian monarchies, namely Denmark, Sweden and Norway.

Christiansen also achieved something with FC Copenhagen that he hadn't done while with Rangers. He played twice against Celtic in the 2005/06 Champions League, the Danes winning 3-1 in Copenhagen and losing 1-0 at Parkhead. The winning goal in the latter came from the penalty spot, Christiansen being beaten by former team-mate Kenny Miller.

Jesper also played in the 1-0 win over Manchester United, and that clean sheet would be one of 74 he would keep in over 200 appearances for FC Copenhagen. He joined IF Elsborg in June 2010, and after making 32 appearances he turned into a journeyman, winding down his playing career with Odense, Vendsyssel, Akademisk Boldklub Gladsaxe and Viborg.

Capped 11 times by Denmark, Christiansen is now a goalkeeping coach with Nykøbing FC. He only made seven appearances for Rangers, keeping one clean sheet.

* * *

Stefan Klos returned to action on 18 November 2000 in a drab 0-0 draw against Dunfermline Athletic. From then he would miss only EIGHT of the next 225 competitive matches Rangers would play. The extraordinary run of consistency during which Rangers won the League Cup, Scottish Cup and the domestic Treble was only ended when Klos suffered knee ligament damage in training in January 2005.

Klos's stats in that run of games were phenomenal. In season 2001/02, he only conceded 26 goals in 36 league appearances (equivalent to a goal every 1.385 games), but he bettered that in season 2002/03 when Rangers won what to date is the last of their seven domestic Trebles. Klos was only beaten 28 times in the 38-game league campaign, and he kept 18 clean sheets, including six in succession between 25 August and 28 September.

The title race went down to the wire. Rangers eventually edged out Celtic by one goal, but while many will reflect on the attacking display that saw the Light Blues score six times against Dunfermline Athletic, few may recall the important intervention from Stefan Klos. With Rangers leading 3-1, the German threw himself across his goal to claw away an effort from Craig Brewster that was destined for the top corner. Had that gone in then the Premier Division trophy could well have been bedecked in green and white ribbons rather than red, white and blue.

All three trophies were surrendered in a doleful season 2003/04. It was one of those moments in Rangers' history where things went from the sublime to the ridiculous. Rangers won 12 of their first 15 league matches, but over the course of the season lost five times against Celtic. Martin O'Neill's side were champions by a margin of 17 points. Klos did his best to stem the tide. He featured in 34 of the 38 league matches, keeping 15 clean sheets.

Alex McLeish was under pressure at the start of season 2004/05. With Craig Moore stripped of the captaincy, the Rangers manager appointed Klos in his place saying that the German 'fitted the bill perfectly' given his 'experience and knowledge of what the club is all about'. But the skipper endured an uncomfortable baptism. Rangers lost out to CSKA Moscow in the Champions League qualifiers and won only two of their opening five league matches.

Rangers were in dire straits, but a 2-0 win over Aberdeen in the League Cup at Pittodrie was vital as was a penalty shoot-out success against CS Maritimo in the UEFA Cup. The ship was steadied, and buoyed by two wins in November over Celtic; Rangers were in fine fettle.

Klos was in excellent form too. He was an ever-present who provided a steady hand as always. In the opening 23 league matches, he had kept 12 clean sheets and conceded only 11 goals. Rangers only lost one of those matches and won 17 of the other 22.

But a training-ground injury threatened to upset the applecart. Attempting to thwart one of his team-mates in a one-v-one situation in training, Klos tried to change direction but caught his studs in the turf. A ruptured cruciate ligament was the result. Surgery beckoned and the Rangers captain's season was over.

Klos's knee injury left manager Alex McLeish with a big decision to make at a pivotal point in the season. Did he pitch Allan McGregor into action, or instead seek an experienced replacement for Klos? He opted for the latter.

Ronald Katarina Martinus Waterreus was 35 years old when he joined Rangers from Manchester City. Born in Lemiers, a village located just over 60 miles from Eindhoven, Waterreus started his career with Roda JC, making his league debut against the team that he would later spend a decade with, PSV Eindhoven, on 15 August 1992. The likes of Ronald Koeman and Romario were in the PSV team that day.

For the next two seasons, Waterreus was a mainstay in a Roda side. He missed only three league matches, and although Roda finished in 11th place in season 1992/93, they only missed out on a place in the top five the following season by one point, thereby qualifying for the UEFA Cup.

Waterreus emerged as a dependable last line of defence, keeping 19 clean sheets in 65 league appearances. Two of them came against PSV Eindhoven, the latter being a stunning 4-0 win in March 1994. Arthur Numan was part of the vanquished Eindhoven side that day.

Perhaps those performances sealed the next move in Ronald's career, for in the summer of 1994 he signed for PSV. He competed with Stanley Menzo for the number one jersey and had to wait until November to make his Eredivisie debut, keeping a clean sheet in a 0-0 draw against FC Volendam.

The PSV line-up included the likes of Boudewijn Zenden, Luc Nilis and Ronaldo, but the season would end without a trophy. Although Ronaldo netted 30 goals, PSV finished third behind Ajax and, ironically, Roda JC.

There would be a silver lining the following season, though. PSV won the KNVB Cup (their equivalent of the Scottish Cup), beating Sparta Rotterdam 5-2 in Feyenoord, and that would be the first of 11 pieces of silverware Waterreus would pick up during his time with PSV. In addition to four league titles, the goalkeeper, who was instantly recognisable thanks to his bubble permed mullet, also played his part in six successes in the Dutch Super Cup.

During his stay at the Phillips Stadion, Waterreus established himself as one of the best goalkeepers in the country. By the time he played his last Eredivisie match on 9 May 2004 against ADO Den Haag, Ronald had kept goal 285 times for PSV in the league, conceding an average of a goal every 1.118 games and registering 122 shutouts. On the rare occasions he missed matches, it was usually through injury, although he did have to sit out through suspension too, notably after the four red cards picked up during his time with PSV.

Making an impression at club level earned Waterreus international recognition too. He won the first of seven caps for Holland when he replaced Edwin van der Sar at half-time in a 2-0 win over England at Wembley in August 2001. He was on the bench for the play-off matches against Scotland for Euro 2004, and his last cap also came when he replaced Van der Sar at half-time in a friendly, this time against the Faroe Islands.

That was on 1 June 2004 and, by that point, Waterreus had decided to leave PSV. He made the last of his 385 appearances for the club just under a month earlier, and he elected to join Manchester City. But with David James firmly established as the club's number one, Waterreus would only make two appearances for City. Both came in the League Cup, a 7-1 win over Barnsley and a 2-1 defeat at the hands of Arsenal.

Ronald was therefore the perfect fit for McLeish, and he plugged the gap Klos left superbly. After making his debut against Dundee United in the League Cup semi-final at Hampden, Waterreus played in 13 of the last 15 league games and also the League Cup Final. By the end of May he had two winners' medals in his glove bag, Rangers winning 5-1 against Motherwell at Hampden and securing the league title in dramatic fashion in the dying minutes of the season.

Rangers travelled to Easter Road knowing that they had to win and hope Celtic lost at Motherwell. Going into the final moments, both sides led 1-0. But Scott McDonald scored twice for Motherwell, and the helicopter carrying the league trophy had to change direction and head for Edinburgh.

The clean sheet kept on that fantastic final day was one of five Waterreus kept in those 13 league games, and he had done everything Alex McLeish had asked of him. But ahead of season 2005/06, with Klos back to full fitness, the Rangers manager had a decision to make. Should he reinstate Klos, or stick with Waterreus? McLeish opted for the latter, and the Dutchman missed only three matches in what would be a doleful season 2005/06.

At one point Rangers went nine games without a win and that pretty much ended any notion that the league title would be retained. Celtic eliminated Rangers from the League Cup, and Waterreus didn't complete the set of major domestic honours either. He kept a clean sheet as debutant Kris Boyd scored a hat-trick against Peterhead in the third round of the Scottish Cup, but the road to Hampden was blocked emphatically by Hibernian who won 3-0 at Ibrox in round four.

The sole highlight from the season was a history-making achievement. After battling past Anorthosis Famagusta from Cyprus to make the Champions League group stages, Rangers finished second in Group H to become the first Scottish club to qualify for the knockout stages. At that point, McLeish's side were desperately unlucky to lose to Villarreal on the away goals ruling. Waterreus played in both qualifiers, the six group stages games, and home and away against the Spaniards. His record was two shutouts and 11 goals conceded.

Ronald Waterreus played what would be the last game of his Rangers career on the final day of season 2005/06 against Hearts at Ibrox. He was replaced by Lee Robinson after 78 minutes after he appeared to have torn his hamstring. But all was not as it seemed.

An article had been published in the Dutch football magazine, *Voetbal International*, ahead of a home game against Motherwell in April 2006. In it, Waterreus is said to have suggested the club and his team-mates had let down Alex McLeish, who was set to step down as manager at the end of the season. As a result, he was roundly booed by sections of the Rangers supporters in the 1-0 win over Motherwell.

It was later confirmed that the translation was 'an unfair representation of his opinions', but Waterreus was clearly irked. He would later confirm that he faked the injury against Hearts to see if the fans were still going to boo him. Instead, he received a standing ovation.

Paul Le Guen would be the new man in charge after McLeish departed, and his arrival elicited excitement among the Rangers supporters. After starting his managerial career with Stade Rennes in 1998, Le Guen had replaced Jacques Santini as the Olympique Lyonnais manager in 2002. He would guide his side to 86 wins in the 156 matches they played in addition to three successive Ligue 1 titles and three French Super Cups. The club had made inroads in the Champions League too, reaching the quarter-finals in seasons 2003/04 and 2004/05.

It would appear the incoming manager was keen to keep his two experienced goalkeepers at the club, but while Klos would stay at Ibrox, Ronald Waterreus departed when contract negotiations reached an impasse. After dropping his demand for a two-year deal, Waterreus is said to have asked for a 25 per cent pay rise to stay at Ibrox for another season. Le Guen refused and turned his attention to Lionel Letizi instead.

But in an interview published in February 2018, Waterreus suggested that it was actually a couple of typographical errors that stopped him signing on the dotted line. He received his copy of the contract by fax, but his name was spelt wrongly. He asked for the error to be corrected and another copy to be sent. But on the revised copy, his agent, Kees Ploegsma, allegedly had his name incorrectly spelt. Enough was enough as far as Waterreus was concerned.

Waterreus moved to AZ Alkmaar for whom he made six appearances before moving to the USA to sign for New York Red Bulls. After 18 MLS appearances, he decided to retire.

During his 18-month spell at Rangers, Ronald Waterreus made 64 appearances. He conceded 65 goals, kept 19 clean sheets, and won a league title and a League Cup.

* * *

Although fit again, Stefan Klos only made three appearances for Rangers in season 2005/06. They came in a League Cup tie against Celtic in which he conceded a late own goal, and league matches against Aberdeen in November and Dunfermline in March. And just as it looked like he had an opportunity to be reinstated as the Rangers number one under Le Guen's leadership, the German was ruled out for four months after damaging shoulder ligaments in a cycling accident in Switzerland.

Allan McGregor looked set to be offered an opportunity to impress, but Le Guen elected to go back to France to recruit the experienced Lionel Letizi. On reflection, that would be the first of a number of mistakes the Frenchman made during his ill-fated spell as the Rangers manager.

Chapter 13

Revolt Rather than Revolution

BORN IN Nice on 28 May 1973, Lionel Letizi had started his playing career with OGC Nice, the team that Rangers had played in their first-ever European Cup match back in 1956. Following in the footsteps of his father, Alain, who played in goal for AS Cannes, Letizi would be part of the Nice side that won the Ligue 2 title in season 1993/94, and after a series of fine displays in the top flight, he earned a transfer to FC Metz in the summer of 1996.

Letizi would stay with Metz for four seasons. He made 169 appearances and kept 63 clean sheets, and in that time frame, *Le Grenats (*The Maroons) finished as runners-up in Ligue 1 in season 1997/98 and reached the final of the Coupe de la Ligue in May 1999, losing out to Lens by one goal to nil at the Stade de France.

By then, Letizi had been recognised at international level. After playing in the French side that reached the quarter-finals of the 1996 Olympic Games in Atlanta and winning caps at U21 level, Lionel won the first of four caps for France on 11 October 1997 in a friendly against South Africa. But such was the competition for the number one jersey at that time, opportunities to win further caps were limited. Although named alongside Fabien Barthez and Lionel Charbonnier in France's provisional squad for the 1998 World Cup, Letizi didn't make the final 22 and had to be content with a watching brief as his country went on to defeat Brazil 3-0 in the final.

But the exclusion didn't deter Letizi. A move to Paris Saint-Germain followed in 2000, and over six seasons Letizi established himself as the number one goalkeeper at the club, playing in the Champions League and winning a couple of Coupe de France medals. He had also played against Rangers in the UEFA Cup, keeping clean sheets in Glasgow and Paris before Rangers eliminated PSG on penalties.

It looked therefore as if Rangers had secured the services of a seasoned pro, although Letizi wasn't the only veteran French goalkeeper to be linked with the club in the summer of 2006. The former Manchester United and Marseille goalkeeper Fabien Barthez was on the lookout for a new club, and Ibrox was a possible destination. But although Le Guen spoke with Barthez's agent, Jean-Marie Cantona, brother of Eric, it appears that the salary demands of Barthez were in excess of what Le Guen wished to pay.

Letizi made his Rangers debut on the opening day of season 2006/07, making a winning start as goals from Libor Sionko and Dado Prso were enough to see off Motherwell at Fir Park. A 2-2 draw against Dundee United followed before Letizi made the first of a number of errors that would cost Rangers points. Rangers were leading Dunfermline Athletic 1-0 at East End Park when their French goalkeeper came off his line to catch a cross. But instead of clutching the ball, he fumbled it and Owen Morrison capitalised.

Despite the mistake, Letizi kept his place the following week when Rangers defeated Hearts 2-0 before injury sidelined him. In his absence, Allan McGregor came in and acquitted himself superbly which is why Le Guen's decision to drop him to accommodate the return of Letizi for a league match against Inverness Caledonian

Thistle at Ibrox was met with condemnation by the Rangers supporters. And their ire was raised further when the returning Letizi fumbled once again, spilling a shot from Craig Dargo into the path of Graham Bayne who netted the only goal of the game.

Letizi would make just three more appearances for Rangers, league matches against St Mirren and Motherwell and an historic 3-2 win over AS Livorno in the UEFA Cup. The latter was the first time Rangers had recorded a victory on Italian soil in a European competition.

By the time Le Guen ended his short stint as Rangers manager early in 2007, Letizi was already out of favour. Allan McGregor was the man in possession, and with Stefan Klos back in contention, Letizi was third choice and surplus to requirements when Walter Smith came back to rescue Rangers. It came as no surprise then when Letizi was released from his contract towards the end of January 2007.

After leaving Rangers, Lionel went back to his first club, OGC Nice. Initially, he signed a six-month deal, he was recruited as cover for a young Hugo Lloris, and he made only one Ligue 1 appearance before the end of the season, conceding three goals in a draw against Le Mans in May.

Despite limited game time, Letizi was retained by Nice, and when Lloris left to join Olympique Lyonnais in the summer of 2008, Letizi came back into the team. But his return would be brief, with David Ospina, who would go on to play for Arsenal, taking over in goal for the majority of the games played.

After making 44 appearances in his second spell with Nice, Letizi decided to retire in the summer of 2011. He has remained with the club since then, taking on the role of goalkeeping coach under Claude Puel, Lucien Favre and Patrick Vieira. His current title is Entraîneur Général des gardiens du centre de formation, or Head Coach of the goalkeepers at the training centre.

In his eight appearances for Rangers, Lionel Letizi kept only one clean sheet – a 2-0 win over Hearts at Ibrox – and conceded ten goals.

* * *

With Allan McGregor making the goalkeeping position his own at Ibrox, opportunities for Stefan Klos were limited. He made only two further first-team appearances for Rangers, both of which came in the UEFA Cup. He came on for Nacho Novo 15 minutes from the end of a 4-0 win over Hapoel Tel Aviv at Ibrox – McGregor had been ordered off – and made what would be his final appearance for the club when CA Osasuna came to Glasgow in the last 16 of the competition. The match ended 1-1.

Although some may have called into question his ability with the ball at his feet and pointed out that Klos wasn't particularly comfortable dealing with cross balls, his shot stopping was outstanding. His professionalism and the way he conducted himself also set an example to up-and-coming youngsters like Allan McGregor.

Stefan Klos should be regarded as one of the finest goalkeepers ever to serve Rangers Football Club. He made 297 appearances, conceded 225 goals and kept 142 clean sheets. He won four league titles, four Scottish Cups and two League Cups and was inducted into the Rangers Hall of Fame in 2009.

Remarkably, given his consistency at both Dortmund and Rangers, Klos was never capped as a full international by his country. He played against Scotland at U21 level – the Scots winning 5-4 on aggregate in the last eight of the 1992 European U21 Championship – but with Oliver Kahn and Jens Lehmann as his contemporaries, an opportunity to win a full cap was not forthcoming.

A quiet, private man, Klos is currently based in Switzerland.

Our journey through time to look at the history of the Rangers goalkeeper has now arrived at the summer of 2007. After a turbulent couple of seasons, the steady hand of Walter Smith was now on the tiller. And donning the gloves was a man that would go on to be regarded as one of the finest purveyors of the art of goalkeeping ever to play for Rangers, Allan James McGregor.

Chapter 14

Greegsy

ON 31 January 2022, Allan McGregor celebrated his 40th birthday. Now of a vintage when most footballers had hung up their gloves or boots, McGregor was still going strong and was firmly established as the number one goalkeeper at Rangers. By the end of the season, he would have played a key role in a side that made it through to a major European final and won the Scottish Cup for the first time in 12 years. And over that period, he also cemented his status as one of the finest goalkeepers ever to play for the club.

Born in Edinburgh, McGregor started his journey with Hutchison Vale.

'I was playing one day with one of my mates that was older than me,' said McGregor. 'We were kicking a ball around and he suggested I go along to training with Hutchy. I wore a goalie top, but had they told me to play outfield then I would have done. But ever since that moment, I've always been a goalkeeper.'

He added, 'My idols were Andy Goram and Peter Schmeichel, two totally different goalkeepers, but both brilliant at what they did.'

The seeds had been planted, a career as a goalkeeper beckoned. And that career would start at Rangers, although McGregor's career was almost over before it started.

'I used to come through and train with Rangers during school holidays,' recalled McGregor. 'I was 13 or 14 at the time, and that was some experience. Hutchy used to train at Crammond on a Friday night, and the Edinburgh-based Rangers youngsters trained there too. A guy called Jim Daubney looked after them, and I think he asked the guys at Hutchy to send a couple of players up to train with Rangers after our session, and I eventually signed for the club as an "S" form.'

He continued, 'We used to train at various places like Jordanhill and Partick, and I remember they used to make us move the goals and they weighed a ton! It was hard and I was really nervous, but it was great experience. I remember being on the bus and I always felt that if one of the players didn't have a seat then I had to get up and give it to him. And there was one day when Gazza, sitting up the back of the bus with a wet top on, pulled out a bacon roll from his pocket and ate it before we trained.

'There was a lot more respect back then too. We used to have to knock on the door before we went into the first-team changing room, but those kinds of things built your character.'

And there would be further character-building when it came to the tasks that were assigned to the youngsters.

'Our jobs included washing something like 30 balls and blowing them up,' said McGregor. 'We also had to make sure the cones, poles and bibs were on the bus. We were also responsible for getting the water onto the bus too. I remember one day in pre-season that I thought Gary Dewar had done the water, but he thought I had. The players ended up training when it was roasting with no water! I got it tight from a few of the players, and I never forgot water after that.'

He added, 'We would report at 8am in shirt and tie and sometimes we wouldn't get away until after 5pm. I stayed in digs in Bearsden initially. I would get the train to Partick then the tube in to Ibrox. Eventually, I moved in with Tiny Gallacher, who worked at Ibrox, with Stevie McLean in the second year of my apprenticeship. She stayed close to the stadium, which was handy, although one night I remember Bomber [John Brown] phoning us after 5pm and telling us to ger our arses back to Ibrox because the showers weren't clean enough!'

There would be a couple of early setbacks for the youngster – injuries to his wrist and hand restricting appearances – but McGregor eventually earned a full-time deal in 1998.

'When I was with the youth team, you would train twice a week then play in the Youth League on the Sunday,' recalled McGregor. 'But when I was 17, I broke my left wrist. I saved a shot but fractured my scaphoid. I got an operation which didn't really work, so I spoke to Doc Jackson who found a guy in Derby who carried out a different operation that involved a bone graft. All in, I reckon I was out for about two years, and it was touch and go as to whether I would actually play again. Even now I have to strap my hand up. I made a save in training with my left hand recently, and if my hand hadn't been strapped, then my wrist would probably have snapped.'

But McGregor showed the necessary fortitude to come back, and manager Alex McLeish decided he was ready for the first team. He made his debut at Station Park in Forfar on 24 February 2002, coming on as substitute for Stefan Klos.

'We were either 5-0 or 6-0 up when the manager turned to me and asked if I was ready to go on,' said McGregor. 'Obviously I was, and after a quick warm-up I was on.'

A league debut followed before the season had ended – McGregor played in the last two matches against Aberdeen (2-0) and Dunfermline Athletic (1-1) – but the consistency and brilliance of Klos meant that the opportunity for regular game time was limited. Over the course of the next two seasons, McGregor only made six competitive appearances for the first XI, and at the start of season 2004/05 he moved to St Johnstone on loan.

'I was at the age when I needed and wanted to play games,' said McGregor. 'I went to St Johnstone for the first six months of the season, and it was good to get a taste of regular first-team football. I wasn't going to get that at Rangers at that time so moving there definitely helped me.'

He added, 'I used to be on at Thommo [goalkeeping coach, Billy Thomson] a lot, asking him if I could be considered for cup ties for Rangers against lesser opposition, but it's only now that I look back and understand why that wasn't possible. At Rangers, you have to win every game, and as much as you wanted to play, I realise now why I wasn't picked as often as I would have liked.'

McGregor returned to Rangers in January 2005 after keeping 11 clean sheets in the 26 appearances he made for the Saints. And it looked like he would get the chance to establish himself in the Rangers first team when Stefan Klos injured his knee in training.

'I played against Livingston before we signed Ronnie [Ronald Wattereus] when the [transfer] window opened,' recalled McGregor. 'Before Ronnie came in there was just me and Buzz [Graeme Smith] – two young goalies – so you can understand why we went out and got another one in.'

Wattereus played in 13 of the last 14 league games and also kept goal in the semi-final and final of the League Cup. But as his deputy, McGregor was on the bench which meant he got to experience first-hand one of the most memorable occasions in the club's history, Helicopter Sunday.

'That was absolutely mental,' recalled McGregor. 'When the first roar went up with about two minutes to go, my first reaction was "surely not?", but the hairs started to stand up. Even Alex McLeish didn't know what was going on. These were the days when you needed to take a radio to the game to listen to scores from the other ones, so we were all frantically trying to find out what was happening. And then another roar went up, but it was still a case of "surely not?"'

He added, 'It was an incredible feeling. Obviously, you would much rather have played in the game, but given the circumstances and the excitement, that one is up there at the top when it comes to league titles that I have been part of with Rangers.'

But at the outset of season 2005/06, with Klos fit and McLeish deciding whether he or Wattereus would be the first-choice goalkeeper, McGregor was once again third in line. At what was a vital stage of his career, he was loaned out to Dunfermline Athletic.

'By then I was 23 and I had spoken to Thommo and told him that I needed to be playing games,' said McGregor. 'Fortunately, Dunfermline took me on, and it was another good move for me as they were in the top flight at the time. Going there also gave me a chance to prove what I could do.'

Although Dunfermline struggled in the league – in his 26 Scottish Premiership appearances, McGregor only kept five clean sheets and conceded 40 goals – they did reach the League Cup Final.

'Reaching a cup final doesn't happen that often for Dunfermline so the week leading up to the game was different to what it would be at a club like Rangers,' said McGregor. 'At Rangers you're more than likely to have a game the midweek before the final so you don't get the same time to enjoy the experience of the build-up. With Dunfermline we went away to a hotel for a few days and did some team-bonding which was really good.'

The Pars lost 3-0 against Celtic at Hampden, but overall, McGregor has fond memories of his time at East End Park.

'I got to work with Jim Leishman, and he was a funny guy,' laughed McGregor. 'He was an old-school manager and I got on really well with him. I really enjoyed being there, getting the chance to play in a competitive environment. That helped me gain experience that I needed coming back to Rangers.'

When McGregor came back to Ibrox in the summer of 2006, it was all change. Alex McLeish had vacated the manager's office, while Ronald Wattereus hadn't extended his contract. Opportunity knocked for McGregor, and it appeared he would once again have the chance to compete with Stefan Klos to be the Rangers number one. But, initially at least, that appeared unlikely.

'When the manager brought Letizi in, I went back and spoke to Thommo again,' said McGregor. 'Understandably, I thought that Letizi was coming in to play, but I wanted games too. I had been out on loan twice, and I thought about leaving Rangers. But Thommo told me to hold off and bide my time.'

McGregor was again third in the pecking order, but when Klos picked up another injury, he became backup to Letizi. And when the Frenchman got injured himself, McGregor looked to have another chance to impress and stake a claim. But despite some stellar displays and the accolade of Scottish Premier League Player of the Month for September, McGregor was relegated to the bench when Letizi was declared fit for a home match against Inverness Caledonian Thistle.

'I came in for about eight games and thought I did alright,' said McGregor. 'I understand now that usually when the first-choice goalie is fit again, he comes back into the team, but I didn't get that back then.'

Letizi would keep the gloves for the two matches that followed the defeat against Inverness.

But McGregor got himself back into the team for the 2-1 defeat against Dundee United at Tannadice, and he was rarely out of it for the 18 months that followed. Between 5 November 2006 and 16 April 2008, McGregor played in 52 successive league matches, but early on in that run of games he found himself working under a new manager when Walter Smith came back to resurrect Rangers.

'I never really thought that I was now the Rangers number one,' recalled McGregor. 'You just focus on playing, taking it one game at a time, and trying to do your best.'

And on working under Walter Smith, McGregor said, 'I always remember he used to say that he hated goalies. It was tongue-in-cheek, though, and I loved working under him. He had a great backroom team with Coisty, Durranty, Kenny McDowall and Jim Stewart, and they created a fun and enjoyable working environment. It was a great time to be at Rangers.'

Before Smith came back home in January 2007, McGregor had made his European debut for Rangers earlier in the season in a 0-0 draw against Molde FK in Norway. McGregor would go on to represent Rangers in another 108 matches in European competition, keeping 41 clean sheets and conceding 124 goals. In the process, he became the first Rangers player to play in 100 European ties, but when Rangers made it to the UEFA Cup Final in Manchester in 2008, McGregor was absent through injury.

McGregor played in the first 31 league games and also starred as the club came close to qualifying for the knockout stages of the Champions League. Lyon were humbled 3-0 in their own backyard, but a 3-0 hammering in the reverse fixture saw the Light Blues parachute into the UEFA Cup.

'We had seven points after three games in the Champions League, so obviously it was disappointing to go out,' recalled McGregor. 'But looking back, we had to go to Barcelona and Stuttgart then had Lyon at home. That was tricky, but it was great to compete at that level.'

But at a club like Rangers, you have to overcome adversity quickly. And Smith's side did just that, keeping themselves in the hunt for the league title. After losing against Lyon, the Light Blues won 14 and drew two of their next 16 league matches. But a midweek fixture at Parkhead would prove to be season-defining, not just for Rangers but for their number one goalkeeper too.

'He was offside as well,' reflects McGregor ruefully when he looks back on the save he made from Scott McDonald that ended his campaign. 'I remember that something didn't feel right with my ankle, but I tried to stay on. I couldn't kick the ball as I couldn't put weight on my left ankle.'

McGregor eventually left the field and was replaced by Neil Alexander, but not before he had defied McDonald again, this time from the penalty spot.

'I pushed off my right foot to dive to my left,' said McGregor. 'Had he hit it the other way then I'm not sure I would have saved it.'

He added, 'There was never any chance I would be fit to play in Manchester. I was struggling with my knee as well, and I remember going to the UEFA Cup Final and struggling to walk up the stairs. I ended up getting a clean-up operation on my knee in the close season and was back for the Champions League qualifiers against FBK Kaunas. On reflection, I probably came back too quick.'

One might have thought McGregor's haste to return was due to the fact that Neil Alexander had proved such an able deputy in his absence, but on the contrary, McGregor continued to train and play as he had done since he was a youngster.

He said, 'When I was young, training with the first team was my game, my chance to impress and show everyone what I could do. And I've been like that ever since then. Even when Neil came in, I just wanted to enjoy training and show the manager that I was doing well.'

By that stage, McGregor and the other goalkeepers at the club were working under a new goalkeeping coach, Jim Stewart having taken over from Billy Thomson. Both would play an influential role in McGregor's career.

'At different stages, yes,' admitted McGregor. 'Thommo was a brilliant coach. I would sometimes stay back, and it would just be me and him training. I must have been about 19 or 20. My mindset at that time was "Tell me what to do and I'll do it." And ultimately, Billy was influential back in 2006 when he convinced me to stay at Rangers.'

But there was a dark cloud looming on the horizon. On 21 March 2009, McGregor was beaten by Christos Karypidis and Rubén Palazuelos as Hearts came from 2-0 down to draw 2-2 at Ibrox. It would be the last time McGregor would play for Rangers until August.

Seven days after the draw against Hearts, McGregor was selected for Scotland against Holland for a World Cup qualifier in Amsterdam. Goals from Klaas-Jan Huntelaar, Robin van Persie and Dirk Kuyt earned the Dutch a comfortable 3-0 win, but when the Scotland squad returned home to their base at Loch Lomond ahead of a midweek match against Iceland at Hampden, McGregor and Barry Ferguson found themselves in trouble. A late-night breach of discipline raised the ire of manager George Burley, and both were dropped to the bench for the Iceland match. But further indiscipline followed, which resulted in an international ban and a suspension at club level too.

'There was no excuse for doing what I did [the gesture while sitting on the bench], although I think the first bit [the late-night breach of discipline] could have been dealt with better,' admitted McGregor.

It was a hard lesson to learn for McGregor as he missed out on the action as Rangers clinched the league title at Tannadice and defeated Falkirk 1-0 to win the Scottish Cup. His Scotland career looked to be over too, with the SFA stating that he would not be considered for selection. His appearance in Amsterdam looked to be the fourth and last for his country, but his ban was overturned when

Craig Levein became Scotland manager. McGregor turned in a fine display in his comeback match too, making several outstanding saves when Sweden hammered the Scots 3-0 in August 2009, and he vied with Craig Gordon for the number one jersey in the years that followed. And when he announced his retirement from the international arena in March 2019, McGregor had amassed 42 caps, just eight short of the coveted 50 that earns a player a place in the SFA's International Roll of Honour.

'I don't regret it [not getting to 50 caps],' admitted McGregor. 'Had I been younger then I might have, but back in 2009, I wasn't even going to go back and play for Scotland. But when Craig Levein took over, Walter pulled me in, gave me the eyes and told me in no uncertain terms to go back.'

Meanwhile, at Ibrox, Walter Smith also made it clear what his position was with regards to goalkeeping ahead of season 2009/10.

'He pulled Neil and me in at that start of the season and said I would play in the league games, and Neil would play in the cup ties,' said McGregor, who would miss only four league matches as Rangers retained the title.

And in season 2010/11, the Light Blues made it three-in-a-row, the now talismanic McGregor making 37 league appearances and recording 18 shutouts. He was only beaten on 28 occasions, but the standout moment in that season was without question his stunning save from a Georgios Samaras penalty late in the final Old Firm match at Ibrox.

Celtic came into the game a point behind leaders Rangers but with a game in hand. McGregor's intervention was therefore a title-defining moment.

'People forget that I saved a penalty against Hamilton a few weeks earlier,' laughed McGregor. 'But because we were so close to the end of the season and it was against Celtic, that one gets spoken about more often.'

McGregor actually has a very good penalty record, particularly against Celtic. At the time of writing, he had saved 19 of the 62 penalties he had faced (not including shoot-outs), and four out of seven against Celtic. So, what's the secret?

'A good guess' is McGregor's answer. 'You can study where someone is going to put a penalty, and maybe nine times out of ten he puts it to the right, but there's not a formula to it. If you do a maths question then the answer is the answer, but when it comes to saving a penalty, the answer isn't always so obvious.'

Allan McGregor was now at the peak of his powers, and he was front and centre again as Rangers, under the guidance of Ally McCoist, who had taken over from the retiring Walter Smith in the summer of 2011, looked set to dominate. A scintillating start to season 2011/12 threatened to leave Celtic trailing – in November, McCoist's side were 15 points clear at the top of the table – but all was not well.

The darkest of days were coming. Staring into the abyss, Rangers were soon to plummet to the depths of despair.

* * *

Although McGregor was the undisputed number one when Walter Smith took over in 2007, the wily old fox wanted another goalkeeper on the books that he could rely on in the event that McGregor picked up an injury or suspension. In the summer of 2007, he opted for experience, recruiting the former Manchester United stopper Roy Carroll.

Born in Enniskillen on 30 September 1977 and raised in a village called Tamlaght, Carroll followed in the footsteps of his father by becoming a goalkeeper.

'I started playing outfield as I was quite small as a youngster, but I started growing around the age of 14 or 15,' said Carroll. 'My dad was a goalkeeper and I used to go and watch him play on a Saturday, and after I went in goal for the first time, I really enjoyed it. I started taking it more seriously then and I started playing men's football for Fivemiletown United when I was 15.'

Carroll also made an impression when he joined Ballinamallard United, and he kick-started his senior career with Hull City in 1995. Initially understudy to Alan Fettis, Carroll made his first-team debut on 20 January 1996 against Swindon Town and would go on to make 50 appearances for a struggling Tigers side.

'I was spotted by a scout in Belfast and went to Hull on trial when I was 16,' recalled Carroll. 'I later signed on a two-year contract as part of the YTS scheme.'

Voted Hull's Player of the Year in 1996, Carroll started to carve a reputation due to his commanding penalty-area presence and shot-stopping ability. Those skills earned him a move to Wigan Athletic for what was then a club-record fee of £350,000, and he spent four seasons with the Latics, establishing himself as their first-choice goalkeeper and a favourite of the fans.

Wigan reached the play-offs in three of Carroll's four seasons with the club, and Carroll was voted best goalkeeper in the league in season 1999/2000. Despite Carroll's heroics, including a penalty save in the 2001 play-off semi-final against Reading, Wigan didn't make it to the top flight, but their goalkeeper was soon off to Premiership pastures. In July 2001, he signed for Manchester United.

'I played against Manchester United when they came to Wigan to open our new stadium in August 1999,' said Carroll. 'And when I first spoke to Sir Alex Ferguson, he told me that United had been keeping an eye on me since then. It was a great move for me, but I have to admit I was very nervous as they were such a massive club.'

Carroll would make his United debut on 26 August against Aston Villa at Villa Park. He was beaten after four minutes by Darius Vassell, and that would be the first of 46 goals he conceded in 72 United appearances. But it's a goal he didn't concede that his time at Old Trafford is best remembered for.

United hosted Tottenham Hotspur on 4 January 2005. Carroll had played in the previous 16 league matches and he walked up the tunnel at the end of the Spurs match having kept a clean sheet for the 11th time that season in the Premiership. The fact he did was due to a glaring error from the match officials.

Caught out of position when Pedro Mendes shot towards goal from the halfway line, Carroll hastily retreated to his line. When he got there, he looked to have claimed the ball, but it squirmed over his shoulder forcing Carroll to dive and paw the ball away. When he did so the ball had clearly crossed the line, but the concept of a Video Assistant Referee was still some years away. With assistant referee Rob Lewis not up with play and referee Mark Clattenburg unsighted, no goal was awarded.

Despite the error, Carroll kept his place in the team for the next five league fixtures, but when he made another mistake in a Champions League match against AC Milan in the San Siro, he was dropped and replaced by Tim Howard.

Sir Alex Ferguson reinstated Carroll for the last four league games and he would make what would be his last Red Devil's appearance in the FA Cup Final against Arsenal at the Millennium Stadium in Cardiff.

This was a second successive FA Cup Final for United. The previous season's showpiece had seen them defeat Millwall 3-0, but despite playing well around that time, Sir Alex selected Tim Howard instead of Carroll for the match. But the Northern Irishman got the nod this time around, and the match went to a penalty shoot-out wherein a miss from Paul Scholes proved costly, Arsenal winning 5-4. The following month, Carroll signed for newly promoted West Ham United, but that was after he had turned down the opportunity to stay at Old Trafford.

Carroll recalled, 'Sir Alex brought me in and offered me a four-year contract. But like the man he is, he was honest enough to say that I wouldn't be playing week in, week out as he was bringing another goalkeeper [Edwin van der Sar] in. I took a couple of days to think about it and eventually went back to Sir Alex and told him that I wanted to play football.'

Unfortunately, Carroll didn't get much chance to play football as his time with the Hammers was blighted by a back injury and off-the-field problems and he made the last of his 35 appearances for the Hammers on 3 February 2007. John Carew scored the only goal of the game for hosts, Aston Villa, and in the summer, Carroll was heading north of the border to sign for Rangers.

'I knew Walter Smith as he had been assistant manager when I was at Manchester United,' said Carroll. 'When he phoned me up and offered me the chance to sign for Rangers, I didn't hesitate as I had been a supporter of the club since I was growing up in Northern Ireland.'

Carroll penned a one-year deal with the remit of providing competition for Allan McGregor. But McGregor played to such a high standard that Carroll only played once for the Rangers first team in a competitive match. He was selected in a much-changed Rangers side that defeated East Fife 4-0 in a League Cup tie.

'When I signed, Walter was honest with me,' said Carroll. 'He said I would get games, but Allan was number one – rightly so as he was a top-class goalkeeper – and it was up to me to compete for the jersey. But I felt the writing was on the wall when we played Motherwell in the League Cup. After playing in the previous round, I thought I'd get a chance again, but Allan came back in.'

He added, 'I could have stayed at Rangers and fought for my place, but in January 2008 I got an opportunity to move back down south with Derby County. My family were still in England, so it made sense for me to move at that time. I kept watching Rangers after I left, though, and they ended up playing a lot of games that season when they reached thc UEFA Cup Final. Allan McGregor also got injured a few weeks after I left so, had I stayed, I would probably have been part of that run of games. But that's football. Things happen for a reason, and I don't have any regrets over anything I did in my football career.'

Derby were struggling when Carroll signed for the club. The Rams had won only one league game prior to the arrival of the Northern Irishman – a 1-0 win over Newcastle United thanks to a Kenny Miller goal in September – and were rooted to the foot of the table. And Carroll couldn't help stem the tide, with Derby drawing three and losing 11 of the 14 Premiership matches he played in. There were some drubbings in that run too, with County losing six goals against Chelsea, Aston Villa and Arsenal.

'We ended up getting relegated with the lowest-ever points total in the history of the Premier League,' recalled Carroll. 'I had hoped I could help out when I got into the team, but as often happens in football, it didn't work out that way. But I enjoyed my time with Derby before I left to go to Denmark.'

Carroll would be at Pride Park for 18 months, and the new season started with him as the number one. But after an ordering off against Norwich City in October, he would only make a further six league appearances. He did, however, play in Derby's run to the semi-finals of the League Cup.

'We beat United 1-0 in the first leg of the semis but ended up losing out when we went to Old Trafford,' said Carroll. 'It was good to play against some of my old team-mates and be back playing at Old Trafford, but I don't like losing. It doesn't matter who you support or what team you play against you want to win, so it was disappointing to lose the game that night.'

The second leg of the semi-final at Old Trafford would mark the last time Carroll played a first-team game for Derby. The arrival of Nigel Clough as manager hastened Carroll's departure from the club, and his next stop was Denmark.

Carroll joined Odense and excelled. He kept a clean sheet on his debut against FC Midtjylland, did likewise in a Europa League qualifying match against Motherwell at Fir Park, and ended up being voted the Danish Superliga's Goalkeeper of the Year.

'It was a privilege to win that award,' said a proud Carroll. 'I didn't realise how good the league was out there, and I enjoyed being out there. Odense was a nice place to be with good people and different culture, but I had been going through a bad time off the pitch for a while and I was out there on my own. I was coming home to see my family maybe once a month, and that was really difficult.'

When Carroll came back to the UK, he took some time out of football. He had fallen out of love with the game and felt he needed a bit of a hiatus to see if he could rediscover his zest for playing once again.

'I didn't have a club for nine months,' admitted Carroll. 'I had a trial at Sheffield United that didn't work out, and Martin Allen brought me in at Barnet for a while as a goalkeeping coach. I really enjoyed that, and that helped me get back on track off the pitch and also encouraged me to get back playing again.'

He added, 'I took a call from my agent in August 2011 during which he told me there was interest in me from clubs in Greece. Since I was a young boy I had always wanted to be a footballer, but I lost that desire for about five years. Moving to Greece with OFI Crete let me rediscover that love for the game again.'

Similarly to his spell in Denmark, Carroll was ranked among the best goalkeepers in Greece, and in January 2012 he left Crete and joined the reigning Greek Super League champions, Olympiacos.

'I was in Greece for three years and my family and I loved it,' said Carroll. 'It was a different lifestyle, and the weather was great. I was enjoying my football and got the opportunity to play in the Champions League and Europa League again.'

Carroll actually saved a penalty on his debut for Olympiacos, denying Bibras Natcho of Rubin Kazan minutes after he had come on following the dismissal of Balázs Megyeri. And after making his league debut on 18 April 2012 against PAS Giannina, Carroll played in the next 17 successive Super League matches. Olympiacos won 15 and drew three of those 18 fixtures, with Carroll shutting out the opposition on nine occasions. In addition, Carroll was also in goal when Olympiakos defeated Atromitos Athens 2-1 after extra time to win the Kypello Elladas (Greek Cup).

But Megyeri would eventually win back his place in the team, and Carroll made the last of his 34 appearances for the club when he was between the sticks for a second successive Greek Cup Final. Extra time was required again, but Olympiakos defeated Asteras Tripoli 3-1.

While in Greece, Carroll had been brought back into the Northern Ireland squad, and he would win the last of his 45 caps in a friendly against New Zealand on 2 June 2017.

A return to the UK followed his departure from Olympiakos, with Carroll joining Notts County in 2014. Spells at Linfield and Dungannon Swifts followed before he hung up his gloves in 2021.

'I had a couple of years with Notts County and was also in the Northern Ireland squad for Euro 2016,' recalled Carroll. 'David Healey brought me to Linfield, and I was there for three seasons. But I picked up a serious knee injury and not long after that I decided my body was telling me enough was enough.'

After announcing his retirement, Carroll continued to work with the goalkeeping school he had opened. He is working with the IFA at the moment, heading up Goalkeeping Development. He is also working towards his B Licence and then hopes to move on and complete his A Licence by which time he would be a fully qualified goalkeeping coach.

Although he only had short spell at Rangers, Roy Carroll looks back on it with a great deal of fondness.

He concluded, 'I was a Rangers supporter growing up and I still follow the club today. I may only have been there for six months, but I am proud to have had the opportunity to wear that famous jersey.'

* * *

Roy Carroll wasn't the only new goalkeeper on the Ibrox books in the summer of 2007. Walter Smith signed Graeme Smith on a free transfer from Kilmarnock, but he too would have limited game time.

Born in Bellshill on 3 October 1982, Smith had loan spells with Queen's Park and Stenhousemuir before he made his first-team debut for Kilmarnock in March 2004. He replaced Colin Meldrum after 47 minutes of a 1-1 draw against Hearts at Rugby Park, but the presence of Meldrum, Gordon Marshall and Alan Combe limited Smith to under 50 appearances for the club. But at the age of 24, Walter Smith reckoned Smith would provide good competition for Allan McGregor.

'I had a great upbringing at Kilmarnock,' said Smith. 'The loans were really beneficial, and I don't think I would have had the career I had if it wasn't for that. Any time I came into the team at Kilmarnock, I felt I did reasonably well, but as soon as the more experienced goalkeeper was fit, they seemed to go straight back into the team. I thought at that point that I would try my luck somewhere else, and there were a couple of clubs interested.'

It transpired that one of the interested clubs was Rangers.

'I was on holiday and on the first day, I got a call from Ian Durrant,' recalled Smith. 'He asked to be put in touch with my agent and things just snowballed from there. After I came home, I went to Ibrox and did my medical, but I had to keep things to myself for a couple of weeks. I come from a massive Rangers family, so I told my dad and my brother. But it was only when I was unveiled with Jean-Claude Darcheville that the move became public knowledge.'

He added, 'I knew I was in a battle at Rangers. Allan had started to establish himself and Roy Carroll was a Premier League goalkeeper. But for me, coming in and working with those guys every day made me a better goalkeeper. I think we all raised our own standards as we knew that if one of us slipped up, then one of us would take the position.'

Smith made his Rangers debut against SV Lippstadt 08 on 15 July 2007. Rangers won 4-2. However, he didn't feature again until he was picked for the fourth round of the Scottish Cup against East Stirlingshire at Ibrox. Smith's former Kilmarnock team-mate Kris Boyd scored a hat-trick in a routine 6-0 win.

'Roy had come in for the League Cup match against East Fife and equipped himself well, and I did the same against East Stirlingshire,' said Smith. 'But when you look now at the longevity that Allan has had at the club and the success he has enjoyed, you can understand why it was so difficult to break through.'

He added, 'At that stage, I just had to make sure that I was fit and healthy and keeping myself in the thoughts of the management team. Quite often after training they would come up to me and compliment me on how well I had done. But I had gone from Kilmarnock where a six or seven out of ten keeps you in the team to competing against full international goalkeepers. The depth of that squad was one of the reasons why we were so successful.'

And the squad got deeper when Walter Smith brought in Neil Alexander to vie for the gloves.

'As a goalkeeper, luck plays a huge role,' admitted Smith. 'I had been on the bench for the League Cup semi-final against Hearts, but Neil was the substitute goalkeeper for the Scottish Cup tie at Easter Road a few days later. Allan was sent off in that game, and that gave Neil a chance to play. But had that happened in the Hearts game then I would have got an opportunity to play and stay in the team. However, from my perspective, we had just signed another international goalkeeper, so I was going to take the opportunity of working with him to make me a better goalkeeper.'

Fast forward a couple of months and McGregor gets injured. Walter Smith now had to decide whether Alexander or Smith stepped into the breach.

'Jim Stewart, who was coaching us, was very good,' admitted Smith. 'I had worked with him at Kilmarnock, and he was very big on the goalkeeper's union. Whoever played got the backing of the others, but we would push the man in possession to ensure that he was looking over his shoulder. My mindset on a daily basis was asking myself how I could contribute better to the group. From a selfish point of view, you want to play, but everything I did at that time was my 3pm on a Saturday. I wanted to show what I could do at the highest level. And the highest level for me at that time was Rangers.'

Alexander got the nod, but Smith was on the bench for the UEFA Cup Final in Manchester in 2008 and took up the same position for the Scottish Cup Final a few days later against Queen of the South. The 3-2 win over the Doonhamers saw Smith pick up what would be the only winners' medal from his spell at Ibrox.

'If a player in your position goes down injured, you usually wait for a couple of minutes to see if he's okay before you go for a warm-up,' said Smith. 'But I wasn't like that. If our goalkeeper went down, I was out like a shot! If there was a chance to go on, I wanted to be ready. I had to be patient and wait for an opportunity.'

He added, 'We had a very close-knit changing room at that time, and that was one of the reasons why we were so successful. We had a great management team too. We were all in it together, you never felt that it was the starting XI and the rest. And a lot of that was to do with how the manager utilised the squad.'

Smith left Rangers in July 2009 and had spells with St Johnstone, St Mirren, Peterhead and Raith Rovers before hanging up his gloves. He returned to Ibrox in 2016 as a coach in the club's youth academy, and he is still with the club today, having taken on the role of Head of Academy Goalkeeping in 2018.

'In my second season [2008/09] there were a couple of chances to go out on loan, but I decided to stay at Rangers,' revealed Smith. 'If I wasn't in the first-team squad, I had no issues playing for the reserves if Tommy Wilson or Jim Stewart asked me. I just wanted to play. Ideally, that would have been in the first team, but any opportunity I got to put on a Rangers jersey, I took it.'

He added, 'By the end of that second season, I had been two years without playing first-team football. I was at a crossroads. I could have stayed for another year, but I felt that by that point I would need to reinvent myself and show folk what I could do again. I spoke to the manager and Jim Stewart during pre-season, and they told me that St Johnstone had come in for me. Initially it looked like it would be a loan deal, but I didn't want that. I didn't want to leave Rangers as I love the club, but I felt that the two seasons I had had training with Allan and Neil could have been put to good use. At that point, I decided to sign for St Johnstone on a permanent deal.'

Although Smith only made three appearances for the Rangers first team – his third came in a 3-1 win over VfL Sportfreunde Lotte in July 2008 – he has no regrets.

'You live and die by your own decisions,' said Smith. 'If I knew then what I know now then I might have gone down a different pathway. But I've been very lucky. I started out at the age of 16, played for 19 seasons and made over 400 appearances. I've been involved in squads that won League Championships, Scottish Cups and League Cups. And then I got the chance to come back to Rangers and work as a coach, so I can't complain. There are not many people who grow up as Rangers supporters and get to play for, coach or manage the club they love. I am very happy to have played for Rangers and now be part of the coaching staff, and I am thankful that I achieved those things in my career.'

He concluded, 'To be a Rangers goalkeeper you need to have a drive and determination to keep the ball out of the goal however pretty or unpretty that may look. And there is no better example of that than Allan McGregor. He has that desire not to get beaten, to get something in the way to make big saves at big moments. Andy Goram, Chris Woods and Stefan Klos were unbelievable goalkeepers and deserve their legendary status, but I think Allan just pips them when it comes to our greatest ever. The fact he won Player of the Year in season 2020/21 when we won 55 speaks volumes. There were so many games that season when we were 1-0 up or level at 0-0 and Allan would make a wonder save, one that he had no right to get to. Only the top goalkeepers make those saves. Rangers would then go on and win the game comfortably and Allan's save would get forgotten about. In terms of his numbers – shutouts, games played – and the influence he has had over his two spells, Allan is one of the greatest, if not the greatest, goalkeeper the club has ever had.'

Incidentally, Graeme Smith wasn't the only Graeme Smith to represent Rangers as a goalkeeper. The other Graeme Smith, who was known as Buzz, didn't make a competitive appearance for the club, but did play a part in a win over Feyenoord on penalties in the Newcastle Gateshead Cup in 2004. Over the course of his career, Graeme Meldrum Smith played for Motherwell, Brighton and Hove Albion, Hibernian, Gabala (in Azerbaijan), Partick Thistle, Ayr United, Brechin City and Stenhousemuir.

* * *

The position of second in command to Allan McGregor was becoming something of a conundrum for Walter Smith. But the

Rangers manager found the solution in January 2008 when he secured the services of a goalkeeper he had worked with during his time as Scotland manager, James Neil Alexander.

Chapter 15

Alexander in Adversity

BORN IN Edinburgh in March 1978, Neil Alexander was recruited by Rangers towards the end of the January transfer window in 2008. With Roy Carroll departing for Derby County, Walter Smith was on the lookout for an experienced goalkeeper to act as the understudy to Allan McGregor, and Alexander fitted the bill. Over the next five and a half years he would endear himself to the Rangers fans in a successful spell that saw Neil play a part in title triumphs, domestic cup successes and a major European final.

'I grew up supporting Hearts even though my dad was a Hibee,' said Alexander. 'I followed Hearts largely because most of the kids in my primary school class were Hearts fans. Usually, you follow in your dad's footsteps, but I actually enjoyed the household rivalry on derby day.'

He continued, 'My hero was John Robertson. He was the main man that scored all the goals and got all the headlines. Every Hearts top I got had "Robertson 11" on the back, and when I was in the school playground, I pretended to be him. I was fortunate to play with Robbo when I was at Livingston. He was player-coach, and I got to know him and his family very well outside football. It was great to have that relationship with the guy that was your idol growing up.'

Alexander was soon making a name for himself on the football pitch. In addition to playing for the school team, Alexander also represented Salvesen Boys Club, but unlike John Robertson he was carving out his reputation by stopping goals rather than scoring them.

'With the exception of my sixth year at school, I was always a goalkeeper,' said Alexander. 'In that last year at Balerno High School I played centre midfield as I was getting bored as it was too easy playing in goals. I captained the team and ended up top goalscorer.'

Alexander's time in the engine room was well spent. With an increasing emphasis on playing out from the back, it honed a side to his goalkeeping that has become essential in the modern game.

'I've always been good with the ball at my feet, composed and confident,' admitted Alexander. 'My distribution was one of the main strengths of my game and playing in midfield for the school significantly helped that side of my game.'

He continued, 'My goalkeeping heroes were Andy Goram and Peter Schmeichel. Manchester United were my English team as a youngster. I used to get goalie tops with Schmeichel on the back. It was his size and his presence and the way he commanded his penalty area that got me. For me he was everything a goalkeeper should be. When I went down to the park with my dad I would try and copy what he did. And as for Andy, he was just phenomenal, an unbelievable shot stopper.'

Alexander's dad was a huge influence on his career. He recognised very early that his son had all the necessary attributes to be a top-class goalkeeper.

'Playing in the park with my dad was how I got into goalkeeping,' recalled Neil. 'I loved diving around and getting dirty, but my dad also recognised I had great hand-eye coordination and he played a massive part in pushing me towards being a goalkeeper. Had he not seen something in me at that stage, I wouldn't have had the career I had.'

And that career started to gain momentum as Alexander matured into a young adult. Neil had a couple of years with Edina Hibs before clubs started to show an interest in him.

'I was floating around a few clubs at that time,' said Alexander. 'I was training with the likes of Hibs, Dundee United and Meadowbank Thistle, and pretty much throughout my childhood, I was out every night training. I also had a spell with Arbroath before the Stenhousemuir manager, Terry Christie, took a shine to me when he saw me play for Edina Hibs. He spoke to my parents and before I knew it, I had signed for Stenhousemuir.'

Alexander joined up at Ochilview in 1996. Formed in 1884 by a group that broke away from a junior side called Heather Rangers, Stenhousemuir was the ideal club for a young pro like Neil to start out. Although they had raised one or two eyebrows in October 1972 when they had beaten the European Cup Winners' Cup holders Rangers at Ibrox in a League Cup tie, they weren't one of the country's big hitters. However, Alexander did arrive at what was probably the most successful part of their history.

They had reached the last eight of the Scottish Cup in season 1994/95, eliminating St Johnstone and Aberdeen before losing to Hibernian. And the following season they claimed silverware when they beat Dundee United on penalties to win the Challenge Cup.

The environment was the perfect place to start for young Alexander, and he was soon vying with Steven Ellison for a place in the first team.

'Elli started the first season in goal, but I got in and played most of the games over the next two seasons,' recalled Alexander. 'Unfortunately, we got relegated in my second season, but it was a great learning curve for me. I had only just turned 18 and playing for the Stenny first team was great grounding for me. It taught me a lot.'

The Warriors finished sixth in Neil's first season at Ochilview, 33 points adrift of champions Ayr United. But although Ian Little was among the top scorers in the Second Division in season 1997/98 – he ended the season with 15 goals, just one less than the league's top marksman, Iain Stewart – Stenhousemuir eventually finished ninth, eight points better off than bottom club Brechin City but two points adrift of eighth-placed Clyde. Life in the Third Division beckoned for The Warriors, but not for their young goalkeeper.

'I didn't leave Stenhousemuir because we got relegated,' said Alexander. 'It was more of a case of me wanting to push on. I had got international recognition for the Scotland U21s towards the end of my second season when I went to the Toulon tournament. My contract was up with Stenhousemuir and that was when Livingston stepped in.'

Livingston had previously operated under the guises of Ferranti Thistle and Meadowbank Thistle and were in the Second Division when Alexander joined, having won the Third Division title a couple of seasons earlier. They had finished third in season 1997/98, missing out on promotion by just a single point, but they took the step up in Alexander's first season with Livi as they won promotion after winning the Second Division championship.

A fourth-placed finish followed in season 1999/2000 before the Livingston Lions roared to the top flight in Alexander's third and final season with them. By that point they were under new management, the effervescent Jim Leishman having taken over from the manager that signed Neil for the club, Ray Stewart.

'Jim was a big character and a great motivator, you would run through a brick wall for him,' said Alexander. 'He was fantastic in the dressing room, a great man-manager, and I really enjoyed that period of my career. I didn't really get on with Ray Stewart, but when Jim and Davie Hay took over when Ray got sacked, my career really started to progress.'

It had been a meteoric rise for Livingston, but when they eventually made it into Scottish Football's top tier, Alexander wasn't part of the squad. His rise had after all been meteoric too.

'My final year at Livingston was really good,' recalled Alexander. 'We won the First Division which got us promoted to the Premier League, reached the Challenge Cup Final, and the last four of the Scottish Cup. During that Scottish Cup run we beat Aberdeen at Pittodrie. Robbo [John Robertson] scored the only goal of the game, but I made a couple of good saves and ended up getting man of the match.'

He added, 'I was named Player of the Year even though I broke my hand a few games from the end of the season. But what I didn't know at the time was that I had caught the eye of the former Scotland international George Wood. George was goalkeeping coach at Cardiff City, and he had been coming to games to watch me for about six months. He recommended that Cardiff sign me, but I was keen to stay with Livingston and have a crack at the Premier League. But Cardiff made Livingston an offer they couldn't refuse, and I was off to Wales.'

Under the ownership of Sam Hammam and aided and abetted by the goals of Robert Earnshaw, Cardiff had finished as runners-up to Brighton and Hove Albion in the English Third Division in season 2000/01. That earned them promotion to the third tier of English Football for what would be Alexander's first taste of club football outside of Scotland.

'I had six great years with Cardiff, and I loved every minute of it,' said Alexander. 'We had great success during that time. In my first year we beat Leeds United in the FA Cup, virtually the same Leeds team that would make the semi-finals of the Champions League. They were top of the Premier League at that time, and had Nigel Martyn in goal, Rio Ferdinand in defence, and Alan Smith, Robbie Fowler and Mark Viduka up front.'

Viduka opened the scoring in the third-round tie at Ninian Park, but Graham Kavanagh equalised before Scott Young netted the winner with three minutes left. Cardiff lost 3-1 away to Tranmere Rovers in the next round, but there were other FA Cup experiences from his time with Cardiff that Alexander recalls fondly too, notably taking Spurs to a replay at White Hart Lane in season 2006/07.

'I used to watch the FA Cup matches on TV when I was a kid and I loved to see the top division teams taking on the lower league teams,' said Alexander. 'That was one of the attractions of going to Cardiff, getting the opportunity to play a part in those games against the big boys from the Premiership on their own ground.'

Alexander's FA Cup appearance against Leeds was one of 53 he made in season 2001/02. Forty-eight of those came in the league, as Cardiff came close to winning promotion. They finished fourth in Division Two, a point adrift of Reading who were runners-up behind Brighton and Hove Albion and missed out in the play-offs too. Despite winning the first leg of their semi-final away from home against Stoke City, a late James O'Connor goal in the return leg at Ninian Park forced the tie to extra time. And Alexander was then beaten by Souleymane Oulare five minutes from the end to consign the Bluebirds to another season in the third tier.

Cardiff would enjoy better fortune the following season, though. After finishing sixth, they beat Bristol City in the play-off semis before overcoming QPR by one goal to nil after extra time in the final.

Alexander was loving his time in the Welsh capital, but a change in manager looked to have cost him his place in the team. Bobby Gould sold the club to him when he signed originally, but Alan Cork was at the helm at the start of his first season. Cork was subsequently followed by Lenny Lawrence and Dave Jones.

'I was number one for the first four years,' said Alexander. 'But when Dave Jones arrived, I think he wanted a bigger goalkeeper, so he brought Tony Warner in. Martyn Margetson came in too, but I always felt I was better than both of them. I eventually managed to work my way back into the team, and when I got back in, I managed to help us avoid relegation.'

This was season 2004/05. Neil played twice in the League Cup early in the campaign, saving a penalty in a penalty shoot-out victory over AFC Bournemouth, but he had to wait until 22 January for his first league appearance. He kept a clean sheet in a 2-0 win over Burnley and kept the gloves for the 16 league games that remained after that. Cardiff eventually finished in 16th place; four points better off than Gillingham who occupied the last of the three relegation spots.

Neil played in all 46 league games the following season, and in 2006/07 missed just one of the first 40. He rates the latter as his best as a Cardiff City player, but after a 1-0 home defeat against Sunderland on 31 March 2007, he never played for the club again.

'I had been in discussions with Cardiff over a new contract but that didn't pan out the way I would have liked,' recalled Alexander. 'When it became apparent that I wasn't going to sign a new deal, I was left out of the team. I ended up signing a three-year deal to go to Ipswich Town, but knew fairly quickly it was the wrong move. Ipswich are a good club, with a great stadium and good training facilities, but it just didn't feel right for me. However, if I hadn't gone to Ipswich then I may not have got the chance to sign for Rangers.'

Incidentally, of the 29 league games Neil played during his six months with the Tractor Boys, he never tasted defeat at Portman Road or enjoyed victory on the road. The 15 home matches comprised 11 wins and four draws, while away from home, nine of the 14 matches were lost and the other five were drawn.

The last of those 29 league appearances came against Plymouth Argyle on 29 January 2007. Five days later, Neil Alexander made his debut for Rangers.

'I had heard rumours that Roy Carroll was leaving Rangers,' said Alexander. 'My agent then called and asked me if I'd fancy moving there. I told him "Yes", and within half an hour he called me back to say that if I wanted to go to Rangers, then I could go to Rangers. He then went off to tie up the deal. He did tell me not to let on to anyone I knew about the move and to make sure that the move didn't affect my performance against Plymouth or else Ipswich would pull out.'

He continued, 'I was buzzing. I ended up getting man of the match against Plymouth and saved a penalty too. We drew 0-0, and after the game the Ipswich manager, Jim Magilton, pulled me to one side and asked me if I wanted to go to Rangers. I wanted to tell him "Yes" straight away, but as I had to come across as if I didn't know about it, I asked Jim for his advice. He didn't want me to leave but said he wouldn't stand in my way, so I then told him that I wanted to go.'

That set the move in motion, and like a kid at Christmas Alexander excitedly set about planning to get himself up to Glasgow.

'After speaking to the manager, I went into the showers and told the lads I was leaving,' said Alexander. 'After that I went up to the Players' Lounge, met my wife and kids, picked up my man-of-the match award, said my goodbyes and left. I then went home and packed until about 2am.'

Three hours' sleep followed before Neil drove up to Glasgow to undergo his medical. He laughed when he recalled embarking on 'the best drive of his life'.

'I went to the training ground, passed my medical, then went and checked into the hotel I was staying in,' recalled Alexander. 'After checking in, I went to Ibrox where I was given a tour by Sandy Jardine. We then had dinner together in the Blue Room. As if that wasn't surreal enough, Sky Sports News was on the TV behind us, and as we were having dinner, the yellow bar that usually runs across the bottom of the screen for Breaking News flashed up with the announcement that I had signed for Rangers.'

Rangers were due to play Hearts that night in the League Cup semi-final at Hampden, so Alexander went along to the game and met the players and management team. Rangers won 2-0, and attention then turned to a battle against the other side from Edinburgh, Hibernian.

'Most of the lads that had played at Hampden got the next day off, but I went in and trained with [goalkeeping coach] Jim Stewart and the young goalkeepers,' said Neil. 'When we had finished, the late Jimmy Bell handed me a holdall which contained all my club tracksuits. Jimmy was amazing. He did so much for all of us. At the end of each season, I would take kits for my kids in, and he would go away and put "Daddy 25" on the back. When he passed away, we lost another club legend.'

He continued, 'When I got back to the hotel, I tried everything on, and I remember standing in front of the mirror taking photos of myself and sending them to my wife. Putting that tracksuit on was one of the best feelings ever. Now I felt as if I was a Rangers player.'

Alexander trained for the rest of the week ahead of a Scottish Cup tie against Hibernian at Easter Road. Allan McGregor was selected in the starting XI for that one, with Alexander on the bench. But when McGregor was somewhat harshly ordered off with two minutes to go, Alexander was handed his Rangers debut. He came on for midfielder Brahim Hemdani, and the first thing he had to do was face the free kick that referee Craig Thomson had awarded before sending McGregor off.

'I was actually shaking,' recalled Alexander. 'Had Hibs hit the target with the free kick, they would have scored as I was shaking that much. And even when the ball went over the bar I still couldn't stop. When I put the ball down to take the goal kick my arms were shaking. Fortunately, I only had one more touch of the ball after that before the game ended. Looking back now, though, making my debut then was maybe a blessing in disguise. As a second-choice goalie you can wait months for your debut which gives you time to think about it. That builds the pressure up, but I didn't have that issue.'

He continued, 'I made it obvious to Allan McGregor fairly early on that he was the number one and I was there to back him up. I've been in an environment where tensions rise when new goalies come into the group, but that didn't happen at Rangers. Allan and I knew each other from the Scotland squad and had a fantastic working relationship on and off the pitch. We regularly socialised away from the training pitch, and I think we brought out the best in each other. The standard of training was extremely high, and sometimes we would go for weeks without either of us dropping or fumbling a ball.'

The coach who had the pleasure of working with Allan, Neil and the other goalkeepers was himself a former Rangers custodian: Jim Stewart. And Jim is another who played a key role in Alexander's career.

'I first worked with Jim when I played at U21 level for Scotland,' said Alexander. 'He played a big part in getting me to Rangers too, and I'll always be grateful for that. He is a fantastic coach, and we had a great chemistry. The relationship with your goalie coach is vital, and Jim and I had a really strong connection. He was like a second father to me. In terms of goalkeeping coaches, Jim and George Wood are the two biggest influences on my career.'

Rangers and Hibernian drew 0-0 which meant that Alexander's full debut would come in the replay at Ibrox the following month. Rangers won that match 1-0 and that kick-started a monumental end to the season that saw Rangers fight for an unprecedented quadruple of league, League Cup, Scottish Cup and UEFA Cup. And when Allan McGregor sustained a season-ending ankle injury in a league match at Parkhead, Neil ended up playing a significant role at the business end of the season.

'I had started warming up when Allan went down with the injury and after what seemed like ages, I got the nod that I was going on,' said Alexander. 'At that stage the nerves kicked in and my heart started racing. But I settled down fairly quickly after I went on. Gary Caldwell pumped a free kick into the box and I came and claimed it. I didn't really have much to do after that other than conceding the goal that lost us the game. It wasn't my fault, but it was a kick in the teeth.'

There was no time to dwell on that, though. The big games were coming thick and fast and, as Alexander put it, it was either 'sink or swim'.

'To be part of those games at the end of that season was incredible,' said Neil. 'My next match was the Scottish Cup semi-final against St Johnstone at Hampden, and I saved two penalties as we won the penalty shoot-out. I think the fans took to me after that. We then played Fiorentina in the semis of the UEFA Cup and I made a decent save at the end and kept a clean sheet too.

'It had been a whirlwind couple of weeks. We had reached the Scottish Cup Final, were on the verge of the UEFA Cup Final, and I had played in an Old Firm game. A few weeks earlier I had been watching these games on TV, now I was playing in them.'

A 3-2 defeat at Parkhead followed the Fiorentina stalemate before a place in a major European final was at stake when Rangers travelled to Florence for the return leg. Alexander would once again play a pivotal part in the outcome.

'[Florence] was the best night of my career,' said Alexander. 'Any time I meet fans, whether it be at the shops or the petrol station, that game is all they talk about. Going into the penalty shoot-out, my mindset was that I had to save at least one penalty. If I did that and we scored our five, then I had done my job. But when Barry

[Ferguson] missed the first one it was like, "oh no, I'm going to have to save two now."'

He continued, 'There wasn't a lot of video analysis back then. The only one I knew about was Adrian Mutu. He was their main penalty taker. He tended to hit the ball to the goalkeeper's right, mid-height, so he was the only one that I had an idea of where he was going to put it. As a result, I was confident I could save his penalty. I don't think I got near their first two kicks, but when Liverani stepped up to hit their third, I just had a feeling I was going to save it. I knew he took corners and free kicks so liked to whip the ball with his left foot. And as he stood over the ball, I thought he was going to hit it to my left, so I dived that way and made the save.'

Parity was now restored. But Alexander was still focused on Mutu as he knew he would hit Fiorentina's fifth penalty. But in the end, the Romanian wasn't afforded the opportunity. Hemdani scored to edge Rangers 3-2 ahead before Christian Vieri ballooned his penalty over the bar. That allowed Nacho Novo to step forward and send Rangers to the UEFA Cup Final.

'For a split second after Nacho scored, I didn't think we were through,' said Alexander. 'I was still focused on Mutu who should have been up next. But when I realised we were in the final, I started chasing after Nacho who had ran to the corner where the Rangers fans were. That moment was probably the most exhilarating of my career.'

That moment may have been topped had Rangers overcome Zenit Saint Petersburg in the final, but it wasn't to be. The obdurate defence that had held firm for much of the march to Manchester was breached twice, and Alexander and his team-mates had to be content with a silver medal. But Neil is adamant that one man may have made a difference had he been available for selection.

He said, 'The sending off of Daniel Cousin in Florence had a massive influence on Manchester. I have no doubt he would have started in the final had he been available, and as he was a handful, he would have posed Zenit a lot of problems. He was a huge loss, and I feel our chances of success would have been higher had he started the match. That's not being disrespectful to Jean-Claude Darcheville, but Daniel was a different animal. And had Daniel played that might have changed the manager's mindset too. The way he set us up to frustrate teams worked in Europe. It kept us in the game, and we were always capable of nicking a goal. But this was a one-off match and maybe we should have been a bit more aggressive and attacked more. However, I can understand why Walter approached the game the way he did as it had worked so well for us in that campaign.'

The UEFA Cup Final was one of 68 games Rangers played in season 2007/08. The final furlong was a frantic one too. There was little time between games to reflect and reset and that meant the players couldn't really enjoy the build-up to such a massive occasion. But looking back now, Alexander only has fond memories of that time.

He recalled, 'We had flown down to Manchester and trained at the stadium. On the morning of the game, we took a walk before lunch before we went back to our hotel rooms. I was sharing a room with Steven Davis and when we put the TV on, all the news reports were about the number of Rangers fans that were in Manchester. It was at that point that it started to sink in how big a game this was. And that was the one game in my career that I was excited for. I used to get nervous before games and overthink, but in Manchester, I couldn't wait for kick-off, couldn't wait to get my shirt on with the special embroidery on it. A lot of that was to do with the fact that I couldn't wait to be part of Rangers' history. Obviously, I wanted to win the game, but looking back now just to be part of that experience was incredible for me. I'll always look back on that with a huge amount of pride.'

With Allan McGregor fit again at the start of season 2008/09, he was handed the gloves, but following some indiscipline while on international duty, he found himself dropped by Rangers. That meant that once again as the season was entering a critical phase, Alexander was back between the sticks for Rangers.

'Although I had come in and done well, I still felt that Allan was the number one,' said Neil. 'I had gained the trust of the fans, management team and coaching staff by showing them what I could do. It didn't matter what the occasion was, I could be called upon.'

He added, 'I remember watching the incident on TV. I didn't think Allan and Barry would get into that much trouble, but at training the following day we started to hear whispers that he had been called in to see Walter. We then heard his car drive away and news started to filter down to us that he had been suspended. I knew there and then that I needed to get myself switched on and focused and prepare right as I would be playing in our next game.'

Alexander had only made two league appearances that season – wins over Motherwell and Hibernian – but he was called upon for the last nine matches in the title race. Given that Rangers and Celtic were going toe-to-toe for the title, any dropped points could have been punished. As it was, Rangers won eight and drew one of the matches, clinching the title with an emphatic 3-0 win over Dundee United on the final day of the season. Alexander also collected another Scottish Cup winners' medal when Nacho Novo's looping volley was enough to see off the challenge of Falkirk in the final.

Once again Neil didn't let anyone down, so one may have suspected that he would have edged ahead of McGregor to become the Rangers number one. It wasn't the case, though.

'In all my time at Rangers, I think that was the one pre-season where I felt disappointed,' recalled Alexander ruefully. 'I don't think I made any mistakes in the games I played, games that were vital for the club. I had helped the team win the league and the Scottish

Cup, and although Allan and I both trained well, I thought what I had done might have been enough to at least start the season as the number one.'

He continued, 'Walter waited until just before the first game of the season before he brought Allan and I together in the physio's room. He told us that all the staff had had a chat, and there were some who felt I should play while others went for Allan. Ultimately, though, it was Walter's decision, and he decided that Allan should play.'

Although Walter's decision left Neil frustrated, he didn't let it get to him. He never moaned or went knocking on Walter's door. Alexander respected the decision and a lot of that is to do with the high regard in which he holds one of the greatest-ever Rangers managers.

'I had known Walter from my time with the Scotland squad,' recalled Alexander. 'I owe everything to him. He made my dreams come true. He gave me my first Scotland cap against Switzerland, took me to the Kirin Cup as his number one and then signed me for Rangers. I will be forever indebted to him and that's why I always tried to be a good professional and repay him when he played me. I was gutted when he passed away.'

Over the course of another title-winning season in 2009/10, Alexander only made five league appearances. He was, however, an ever-present as Rangers won the League Cup in a dramatic showdown with St Mirren.

'That League Cup campaign showed Walter's class once again as he stayed loyal to me,' said Neil. 'He could easily have picked Allan to play in the final, but the fact he didn't showed to me that he trusted me. He did the same when we played Celtic in the final a couple of seasons later.'

He added, 'Against St Mirren when Kevin [Thomson] got sent off I didn't think too much about it as I still felt we were good enough to go on and win the match. But when Danny [Wilson] got a red card, I thought it would be tough to get the result we all wanted. My initial thought was that our best chance was to hold out for penalties, but at that point we still had half an hour to play so we had to focus on defending. I thought there was no way we would win the game in normal time. But one quick breakaway was enough. Naisy [Steven Naismith] delivered a great ball from out wide, and Kenny [Miller] scored with a great header into the bottom corner. You were almost in disbelief when it happened, but it showed the character of that squad. We had a dressing room full of winners.'

Alexander saw very little action in season 2010/11 or 2011/12, but midway through the latter campaign, Rangers were in turmoil when they went into administration. They were eventually demoted to the lowest rung on the Scottish League ladder and, when they were, Neil Alexander became their number one goalkeeper.

'I don't want to go into too much detail in terms of what happened, but to have that squad ripped apart was horrific,' said Alexander. 'However, I had strived my whole career to get to a club like Rangers, so I wasn't in any hurry to leave. I made it clear I wanted to stay, and I genuinely wanted to be like Lee Wallace and remain with the club until they got back to the Premiership. I wanted to go down in history as one of the ones that stayed for each stage of the journey back.'

Alas, it didn't work out like that. Alongside the likes of Wallace and Lee McCulloch, Alexander was one of the experienced pros who helped the youngsters that were thrust into the squad in the Third Division in season 2012/13. But when Rangers kicked off stage two of the journey in League One, Neil had gone.

'There had been ongoing talks over a new contract since around November/December,' recalled Alexander. 'During the discussions with Ally McCoist, I felt we were making progress. He was keen for me to stay, I was desperate to stay, but nothing happened. It seemed to be dragging on and on, and the writing was on the wall when Rangers signed Cammy Bell on a pre-contract deal in January. That was the final nail in the coffin for me. That made my mind up. One of us would be sitting on the bench, and as much as I wanted to stay, I didn't want to be number two goalie in League One.'

He added, 'Leaving Rangers was the hardest thing I've ever done in my career, and it probably took me about two years to get over it. It hit me hard. I felt that after the service I had given to the club, I deserved better than what happened. I was let down by a lot of people, and without being disrespectful to those in charge of the club, I don't think it would have happened had Walter been there. I was loyal to the club, and I felt that loyalty should have been repaid. You're told there is no loyalty in football, but I thought there was so that was a hard lesson for me to learn.'

Alexander joined Crystal Palace in the English Premiership when he left Rangers. And although he was understudy to ex-Dundee goalkeeper Julian Speroni, being involved with an English Premiership club was another cherished dream for him.

'I had watched games on *Match of the Day* and *Sky Sports*, and I always wanted a jersey with my name and number on the back and the Premiership badges on the sleeves,' said Alexander. 'Going to Crystal Palace ticked a lot of boxes. I got to go to places like Old Trafford and Anfield, albeit on the bench, but even going out at these places and doing the warm-up was amazing. It was just unfortunate that it didn't work out the way I had hoped.'

Alexander made only one appearance for Crystal Palace, against Bristol City in the League Cup, and in 2014 he came back to Scotland to sign for Hearts. His league debut for the Edinburgh side was at Ibrox on the opening day of season 2014/15.

'The Championship was really strong that season, with Hibs and Rangers also involved,' said Neil. 'We won 2-1 in the first league game at Ibrox, but I got taken off on a stretcher after I came for a cross, collided with a team-mate and ended up with a shattered cheekbone, eye socket and broken nose!'

Alexander missed the next three league matches as a result but played every minute of all, bar four, of the league matches after that. Another fracture, his finger on this occasion, ruled Neil out of the last three of those. He only conceded 19 goals in his 29 league appearances and kept 15 clean sheets.

'We had a great season and won the league by 21 points,' recalled Alexander. 'Rangers finished third and eventually lost to Motherwell in the play-offs. If I'm being honest, I was still getting over leaving Rangers at that point and there was a bit of bitterness. I couldn't let the club go, and I struggled mentally with it too.'

He added, 'I had a good season at Hearts and there was a bit of satisfaction that I had shown folk at Rangers that they should have kept me as I still had something to offer. I didn't take any satisfaction from seeing Rangers struggle, though. Once I had been at Rangers, I was a fan for life, and the saying of "once a Ranger, always a Ranger" is true. When you get into that bubble, Rangers are everything. I might have grown up as a Hearts fan, but once you play for Rangers you become a Rangers fan through and through.'

Alexander had a season in the top flight with Hearts before joining Aberdeen as understudy to Joe Lewis. He returned to Livingston in 2017 and marked his second debut for the club by saving penalties from Christie Elliot, Blair Spittal and Kris Doolan as Livingston beat Partick Thistle 4-2 on penalties in the League Cup. And the season ended on a high against Thistle too, Alexander making his 47th appearance of the campaign as the Jags were beaten 1-0 in the second leg of the Premiership play-off final. That completed a 3-1 win on aggregate.

But Alexander resisted the temptation to have another crack at top-tier football, announcing his retirement from playing in June

2018. Since then, he has taken on roles as goalkeeping coach at Dundee United and Dunfermline Athletic.

Capped three times for Scotland, Neil Alexander made 94 appearances for Rangers. He conceded 79 goals and kept 40 clean sheets. He was part of the squad that won three successive Scottish Premier League titles and claimed two Scottish League Cup winners' medals and two Scottish Cup winners' medals. Neil also played in the 2008 UEFA Cup Final against Zenit St Petersburg in Manchester.

Summing up his time at Rangers, he said, 'I always knew that I was coming to Rangers as the number two goalkeeper. But in my time at the club, I was in goal for five of the seven cup finals we played. Not many understudies can say that. And I was only on the losing side in one of them, the UEFA Cup Final. Playing for Rangers was a dream come true.'

Chapter 16

The Journey Concludes (Eventually)

RANGERS STARTED life in League One with Scott Gallacher in goal. They should have been able to field their new number one goalkeeper, Cameron Bell, but a transfer embargo was in place at the time which meant Bell, who arrived on a four-year deal from Kilmarnock, couldn't be registered until 1 September 2013.

Born in Dumfries on 18 September 1986, Bell joined Kilmarnock in 2002, but he wasn't always a goalkeeper.

'When I was younger and playing with my friends, I played outfield,' said Bell. 'I was a midfielder, and I liked a tackle, but once things started to get serious and I started playing for teams, I moved in goal.'

He added, 'My goalkeeping heroes were Andy Goram and Peter Schmeichel. I looked up to them as they were doing what I wanted to do. I was similar to Andy in the respect that we both weren't very tall, but Andy was just phenomenal. Schmeichel had such a huge presence in goal too, and I always remember the "starfish" save that he was renowned for.'

Bell's chance to do what Goram and Schmeichel were doing eventually arrived, but he had to bide his time and battle back from a career-threatening injury before making the breakthrough into the first team at Kilmarnock.

'I was in the youth system at Annan Athletic when they were in the East of Scotland League,' said Bell. 'I was soon picked up by Queen of the South and I was there for a number of years. It was a great experience, and it was when I was playing in a tournament in Ayr that Alan Robertson, the youth-team manager at Kilmarnock, spotted me. I was still at school at that time, so I would travel up to Rugby Park for training twice a week while also training with a goalkeeping coach at Queen's called Robert McColm. He took me under his wing and trained me very hard. Due to all the travelling, I didn't really have a life other than football, but I absolutely loved it, and I eventually got a full-time contract.'

It is often the case with young footballers that they find themselves loaned out from their parent club to get some experience and game time at a lower level. Cammy Bell was no different, and the first of his loan spells came at Montrose. And it was while he was at Links Park that he suffered an injury that threatened to end his career before it had even started.

'Jim Weir was the manager at Montrose, and I remember being so excited when he first spoke to me,' said Bell. 'Although I was still developing as a player, I felt I was ready for first-team football. I had played in a lot of reserve games for Kilmarnock, and they stood me in good stead.'

He continued, 'I loved the experience at Montrose, getting used to having that winning mentality. But unfortunately, I got injured early on. I faced a penalty in a match against Queen's Park, and after moving one way, I tried to move in the other direction, but my knee collapsed. I played on for the last few minutes of the game, but a week or so later I found out the extent of the injury. I had snapped my cruciate ligament and a couple of other ligaments too.'

Bell was out of action for a year, and it was later revealed that medical staff at Kilmarnock doubted whether he would ever play again. But he did, and after a further loan spell at Queen of the

South, he was handed his first-team debut for Kilmarnock on the final day of the 2008/09 league season.

'Playing for Queen of the South was a great experience,' said Bell. 'They were in Europe that season as they had been in the Scottish Cup Final the year before and playing in the away game against Nordsjaelland was phenomenal. That night confirmed for me that I wanted to do this long term.'

He added, 'My Kilmarnock debut came against Motherwell at Fir Park. Jim Jefferies was the manager and I loved working with him. He gave me a chance and that would be the start of a great journey with Kilmarnock.'

Bell would play second fiddle to Alan Combe in the opening months of season 2009/10, but once he supplanted Combe in January 2010, he missed just 23 of the next 134 league matches Kilmarnock played. That level of consistency earned him a Scotland cap – Bell came on as substitute for Craig Gordon in a 2-0 win over the Faroe Islands at Pittodrie in November 2010 – and he also kept a clean sheet as Kilmarnock shocked Celtic to win the Scottish League Cup in 2012.

'There were lots of ups and downs at Kilmarnock, but I felt I had a real connection with the club,' said Bell. 'I loved the club, loved the people that worked at the club, and the fans were brilliant with me too. I really enjoyed that spell of my career and winning the League Cup was a special moment. I only realise now that I've retired that I played a part in Kilmarnock's history and how important that day was to so many. I still go up to games at Rugby Park and when I meet the supporters some of them tell me that that was the best day of their life. It was one of the best days of mine too and beating Celtic was an incredible achievement from the team.'

But all good things come to an end, and with his contract due to expire in the summer of 2013 rumours were rife that Cammy was set to step down a couple of rungs on the league ladder and sign for Rangers in League One.

'I knew at the time that there were clubs interested in me, one of whom was Rangers,' recalled Bell. 'I am a Rangers fan so the prospect of going there really appealed to me. I met with Jim Stewart who was the goalkeeping coach at Rangers then and ended up signing a pre-contract agreement in February.'

He added, 'The next few months at Kilmarnock were difficult. Some of the fans felt as if I was walking away from the club and going to one that was a couple of leagues below. But while I'll never shy away from the fact that it was a good deal for me and my family financially, it was also an opportunity to play for the club I had supported since I was a boy. It was a big decision, but as far as I'm concerned, I made the correct one.'

Bell was among a clutch of new additions at Ibrox in the summer of 2013. Jon Daly, Nicky Clark, Nicky Law were the others, but all four were affected by the transfer embargo. A ruling allowed the Rangers manager, Ally McCoist, to select two of that quartet as trialists ahead of their registration, but Bell was made to wait for his league debut. McCoist picked Law and Daly for the opening three league games before opting for Bell and Clark for the fourth, a 5-0 win over East Fife that took place the day before the embargo ended.

'The embargo was really frustrating, as I had worked hard in pre-season to be ready to go,' said Bell. 'I had played in some friendly matches working towards that first game of the season, but when I spoke to Ally [McCoist], he made it clear he was going to pick outfield players to begin with.'

In Bell's absence, Scott Gallacher stepped in, playing three league matches, the humiliating League Cup defeat at the hands of Forfar Athletic, and the opening two rounds of the Ramsdens Cup.

A product of the Ibrox youth policy, Gallacher had won a couple of Scottish Youth Cups while coming up through the ranks and had had loan spells with Cowdenbeath and Forfar Athletic before he was handed his first-team debut against Albion Rovers in the opening round of the Ramsdens Cup. Rangers won 4-0, and Gallacher would add another three clean sheets in the five other games he played for the club.

When Bell eventually made it into the team, Gallacher went out on loan to Airdrie, and in the summer of 2014 he signed a two-year contract with Hearts. His debut came, ironically, at Ibrox, when he came on as substitute for Neil Alexander in the opening game of season 2014/15. But he found it impossible to displace Alexander and made only two more appearances for the Jambos, the last of which was on the final day of the season against Rangers at Tynecastle.

A loan spell at Forfar followed before Gallacher joined Alloa Athletic in January 2016. Spells with St Mirren, Hibernian, Dumbarton, Airdrie and Arbroath followed, and at the time of writing, Gallacher, capped five times at U21-level for Scotland, was with East Fife.

* * *

Cammy Bell missed only three further League One matches in season 2013/14. He became a dependable last line of defence as McCoist's Rangers romped to the title, keeping 19 clean sheets, and only conceding 17 goals. But an injury sustained in training would rule him out of the Scottish Cup semi-final against Dundee United at Ibrox.

'I was devastated,' admitted Bell. 'We were playing small-sided games and I clashed heads with one of the other players. I ended up with concussion, but I was still desperate to play against United. I felt okay at the end of the week so I went to see the manager, but there was nothing he could do. It was in the hands of the doctor, and as frustrating as it was for me, they always make the correct decisions.'

Steve Simonsen took Bell's place for the games he missed, and the Englishman was also called upon for the Scottish Cup semi-final against Dundee United after Bell had been knocked out in training and suffered concussion.

Born in South Shields on 3 April 1979, Simonsen was a man of many clubs. After starting out with Tranmere Rovers, he had had spells with Everton – where he played under Walter Smith – Stoke City, Sheffield United and Preston North End before he signed a short-term deal with Dundee in March 2013. During his time at Dens Park, he served under former Rangers stalwart John Brown, but Dundee were relegated from the top flight at the end of the season.

With a new Dens Park deal not forthcoming, Simonsen was offered a trial at Rangers, and he impressed to the extent that he was handed a one-year contract. He would play second fiddle to Bell for most of the season, though, his first appearance coming against Forfar Athletic in January 2014 when Bell was given leave to attend the birth of his daughter.

He only made a further two appearances that season, a 3-0 win over Forfar at Ibrox and the 3-1 defeat against United in the Scottish Cup semi-final. Alas, it's for his mistake in the latter that his time at Rangers is best remembered for.

Playing at 'neutral' Ibrox, a goal from Steven Smith had pulled Rangers back into contention after United had shot themselves into a 2-0 lead. But with seven minutes to go, Simonsen was caught out trying to clear his lines, his attempted clearance ricocheting off Nadir Ciftci who milked the applause as he rolled the ball into an empty net. That error looked as if it would be the last thing Simonsen would do in a Rangers jersey, but he was offered a deal for another year in the summer of 2014. He accepted and went on to play in 18 of the first 20 Scottish Championship fixtures, covering for the injured Bell. But his run of games, which included an appearance against Celtic in the semi-finals of the League Cup, was brought to an abrupt halt when Simonsen was banned after he breached strict gambling rules.

Simonsen never played for Rangers again. His appearance at Hampden against Celtic was the last of the 31 he made for the club. He conceded an average of a goal a game and kept 14 clean sheets. He moved to India to play for Pune City in August 2015.

* * *

Rangers started what many believed would be the final stage of the journey back to the top flight with Cammy Bell in possession of the gloves. He played in the opening two league matches, but after keeping a clean sheet against Falkirk on 15 August 2014, he wouldn't feature again until March 2015.

'I received treatment after I took a sore one on my shoulder against Falkirk,' said Bell. 'I managed to finish the game and I reckoned I would be okay to play in our next game against Clyde. Normally the day after a game you don't do much in terms of training, but I decided I was going to do some light handling work to get my eye in for the game. But after I dived to save a shot that was close to my body, my shoulder dropped. I spoke to a surgeon who gave me some things to try so I could avert surgery, but my shoulder dislocated again. I knew then that I needed surgery, and that was a tough stretch as it can be hard for a goalkeeper to come back from surgery like that.'

In Bell's absence, Rangers stuttered. Hearts were running away with the title, and the completion of the last stage of the journey was in disarray. Rangers were ravaged further when, in December 2014, Ally McCoist resigned.

'In the dressing room we knew there was a sense of turmoil,' admitted Bell. 'There was a lot of upheaval, and the boardroom was really unsettled. That filtered down to the management, and Ally left and Kenny [McDowall] came in. Kenny made it clear from the start that he didn't want the job due to his affiliation with Ally for a number of years. It was almost as if he had been forced into the role, and that was really disruptive for the players.'

He added, 'I know it's often said that what happens in the boardroom doesn't filter down to the players, but it certainly did at that time. It was a difficult period, but we just had to try and get on with it.'

As the campaign progressed, it seemed the only hope of a return to the Premiership was via the play-offs. In the nine league fixtures Bell played a part in from March until May, Rangers won five and drew four. Hearts and Hibernian were among the sides beaten, but the Light Blues ended up in third place which meant they faced a total of six play-off matches to gain promotion.

'In that short period after I came back, I actually sustained a knee injury,' admitted Bell. 'I was really struggling, but I started to take injections so I could play as I was desperate to play after I had missed so many games with the shoulder injury. But there was no recovery time, it was game after game, and the journey through the play-offs was tough.'

Queen of the South were beaten in the quarter-finals, before Hibernian were vanquished in the last four. But Motherwell, who had finished second from bottom in the Premiership, proved a bridge too far.

'I think the effects of the season as a whole had an impact on the games against Motherwell,' said Bell. 'The players were mentally and physically exhausted and losing 3-1 at Ibrox was tough to take. The second leg didn't go our way either and we were well beaten in the end.'

That fateful day at Fir Park would in fact be the last time that Cammy Bell played in a competitive match for Rangers. By the time he had fully recovered from the knee injury he had been carrying,

Mark Warburton was the manager and Wes Foderingham was firmly established as the Rangers number one.

'I had an operation on my knee, and I was fit to play again just before Christmas,' said Bell. 'I was desperate to play football, and it was difficult going from being a number one to a number two. I felt I should have been first choice, and I spoke to Mark Warburton to see what my options were. A loan move was discussed, and Aberdeen were interested. Danny Ward had gone back to Liverpool and when I spoke to their goalkeeping coach, Gordon Marshall, it was clear I had a good chance of going to Pittodrie. That would have given me an opportunity to play in the Premiership, but disappointingly, the plug got pulled on the move.'

He continued, 'It was difficult being on the bench for the rest of the season, but Wes was performing very well, so I had no qualms over not playing. But although I had worked hard to get to Rangers, a club I loved, it was time to move on. After two major surgeries, I needed to be playing games, so I spoke to Mark towards the end of the season and we agreed that I would leave the club.'

Bell moved to Dundee United and then had spells with Kilmarnock, Hibernian, Partick Thistle, St Johnstone, Falkirk and Queen's Park.

'Dundee United was great,' admitted Bell. 'I played a lot of games, was made captain and had one of the highlights of my career when I saved three penalty kicks in the same game.'

That was in a Scottish Championship fixture against Dunfermline Athletic at East End Park. Gavin Reilly was the first to be denied, and Bell also thwarted subsequent efforts from Nicky Clark and Paul McMullan.

'That was on a par with winning the League Cup with Kilmarnock,' admitted Bell. 'I'll never forget it as it was so unique. I bounced around a few teams after that and ended up at Queen's Park where injuries eventually got the better of me. I decided it was time to step away from playing and I ended up at Annan Athletic as director of football. That helped fill the void that comes with not playing, and I'm enjoying doing some media work now too.'

Reflecting on his time with Rangers, Bell has no regrets.

'I have no regrets over anything in my career,' said Bell. 'I had some injuries when I was at Rangers, but they are part and parcel of football. There have been better players than me that have had their careers ended early due to injury. You have to make the most of your career, injuries are out of your control. I loved every single minute of my time at Ibrox, and I still have friends at the club.'

He concluded, 'Rangers is an amazing club. I was a fan, but until you actually experience being on the inside, you simply don't know how big Rangers is. It is an institution, and even when you live it and breathe it, you can't describe how huge the club is. It was an honour to play for Rangers, and I always look at some of the players that have played there and are still playing there – for me, Allan McGregor is one of the best goalkeepers of all time – and to be part of that journey to get Rangers back to where they needed to be is a source of great pride for me.'

Chapter 17

A Wise Move for Wes

WITH CAMMY Bell ruled out, the new Rangers manager, Mark Warburton, had a goalkeeper at the top of his shopping list ahead of his first season as Rangers manager. And in July 2015, he got one when he brought in Wesley Andrew Foderingham on a three-year deal.

Born in Hammersmith on 14 January 1991, Foderingham started his career in the youth academy at Fulham and had a spell on loan with Bromley before moving to Crystal Palace after his release from Fulham in July 2010. Loan spells with Histon and Swindon Town followed, and during the latter, Foderingham impressed manager Paolo Di Canio enough for the Italian to offer him a permanent deal.

Foderingham would play a key role in earning Swindon promotion from League Two as champions in season 2011/12, keeping 22 clean sheets and only conceding 14 goals in the 33 appearances he made. But his first full season as a permanent member of the Swindon squad got off to a tumultuous start.

After keeping clean sheets in each of his first four appearances, he conceded three goals in a 4-3 win over Stoke City in the League Cup, and in the league fixture that followed against Preston North End, he was substituted after 21 minutes after shipping another two goals. Enraged by the decision, Foderingham kicked over a water bottle and raised the ire of his manager, with Di Canio demanding an apology for his behaviour.

The Italian labelled his goalkeeper 'the worst professional I've ever seen' and said Foderingham was 'arrogant' and thought he was 'untouchable'. It looked like Foderingham would be dropped, and a career that had started to blossom could have withered at the moment.

Foderingham, however, would do as his manager asked and apologise for his behaviour. He was fined, but kept his place in the team, playing in all 46 of the League One matches contested by Swindon. The Robins finished sixth to make the play-offs, but their Championship ambitions were thwarted when Brentford edged them out in the semi-finals on penalties.

Foderingham was the Swindon custodian for the next two seasons too, missing only seven league games, but his time at the County Ground came to an end when he was released at the end of season 2014/15. His final match for the Robins was the League One play-off final against Preston North End. Swindon lost 4-0.

Almost two months later, Foderingham was making his Rangers debut on 25 July in a 6-2 win over Hibernian in the Challenge Cup. It would be one of 50 appearances he would make in a debut season that delivered the Championship title, the Petrofac Training Cup, and a Scottish Cup semi-final victory over Celtic at Hampden. His save from Scott Brown in the penalty shoot-out all but secured cult-hero status for him.

The journey had thus been completed; Rangers were back in the top flight. But while some may have hoped to see Warburton's side mount a challenge to Celtic's supremacy, the reality was somewhat different.

Despite tempting Joey Barton to join the party, Rangers crumbled. There was an early season drubbing at Parkhead where Foderingham shipped five goals, and the fallout from that one saw Barton leave the club. And after another Old Firm defeat on 31 December, the gap between Celtic and Rangers was a mammoth 19 points.

By February 2017, Warburton was gone in controversial circumstances. He was eventually replaced by Pedro Caixinha, but that didn't effect much of a change, and on 29 April 2017 Rangers were once again humbled by Celtic, the 5-1 thrashing on this occasion happening on their own turf.

Over the course of the campaign, Foderingham missed only one league fixture, the final one against St Johnstone. Jak Alnwick took his place that day, and in the League Cup the gloves were handed to Matt Gilks for all bar two of the seven matches played.

Gilks had joined Rangers in June 2016 after he had been released by Burnley. Aged 34, his CV included time with Rochdale, Norwich City and Blackpool, and three caps for Scotland. His five Rangers appearances all came in the League Cup, with the goal scored by Moussa Dembélé three minutes from the end of the semi-final the only one he conceded.

Gilks joined Wigan Athletic in January 2017, and thereafter had spells with Scunthorpe, Lincoln City, Fleetwood Town and Bolton Wanderers. Gilks announced his retirement at the end of season 2021/22, and at the time of writing he had assumed the role of goalkeeping coach at Bolton.

As Gilks departed, Jak Alnwick arrived. Born in Hexham on 17 June 1993, Alnwick had played for Sunderland and Newcastle United at youth level before turning professional with the latter in 2011. A spell on loan at Gateshead followed before Alnwick made his debut for the Magpies as a half-time substitute for the injured Rob Elliot in a 2-1 win over Chelsea at St James' Park on 6 December 2014. Papiss Cissé scored both goals for Newcastle, while Alnwick, who acquitted himself well, was beaten by a late strike from Didier Drogba.

That would be the first of just eight appearances in a Newcastle jersey for Alnwick, and with first-team opportunities limited following the return from injury of Tim Krul, Alnwick went to Bradford City on loan. That was ended prematurely by a wrist injury, and when Alnwick returned to Newcastle he found out that his contract was not being renewed.

Shortly after his release from Newcastle in May 2015, Alnwick signed for Port Vale who were playing in League One. Initially drafted in on a five-month deal, he impressed enough to earn a two-and-a-half-year contract and would make a total of 79 appearances and keep 23 clean sheets for the Valiants before Rangers came calling.

Alnwick would spend the remainder of the season as second in command behind Wes Foderingham, although he did make his debut for the club against St Johnstone in Perth on the last day of the season. Rangers won 2-1, their goals coming from Kenny Miller and Jon Toral.

* * *

It's fair to say that there had been some tough moments in season 2016/17, but they all paled into insignificance early in season 2017/18. Drawn against the minnows of Progres Niederkorn from Luxembourg in the first round of Europa League qualifying, Caixinha's side lost 2-1 on aggregate. If the knives were out after the Old Firm thrashing at Ibrox, they were being sharpened now.

With Foderingham the man in possession of the gloves, the Portuguese lasted until 25 October. The opening nine league matches had yielded five wins, two draws and two defeats. Only one clean sheet had been kept. A third draw of the league campaign against Kilmarnock at Ibrox signalled the end of the road for Caixinha. He was replaced by Graeme Murty, the club's youth development coach.

Under Murty, Rangers regrouped, and going into the penultimate Old Firm match of the season at Ibrox they were six points behind Celtic. A victory would have reignited their title challenge, and that looked promising when Josh Windass and Daniel Candeias gave the home side a 2-1 lead. But goals from Dembélé and Edouard swung the match in Celtic's favour. The title would once again prove to be elusive.

Foderingham had played in each of the 33 league matches prior to the top and bottom six splitting, but after keeping goal for a 4-0 Hampden hammering at the hands of Celtic his season was ended by a knee injury.

Jak Alnwick stepped into the breach, playing in the last five league matches. Included in that run of matches were a 5-0 thrashing at Celtic Park – the fact Alnwick was Rangers' best player shows how abysmal the performance was – and a bizarre 5-5 draw against Hibernian at Easter Road. Rangers, now under the stewardship of Jimmy Nicholl, trailed 3-0 at one point then led 5-3 before they were pegged back.

That would be the last time Alnwick pulled on a Rangers jersey. He joined Scunthorpe United on loan in August 2018, and there would be a further loan spell with Blackpool before Alnwick left Rangers to sign for St Mirren in June 2020. He is currently with Cardiff City.

* * *

By the time season 2017/18 had ended, Rangers knew who the next incumbent in the manager's office was going to be. In May 2018, Steven Gerrard was appointed, and his remit was simple: establish Rangers as a force at home first and foremost but also look to make a mark in Europe.

Among the first players to be signed by Gerrard was Allan McGregor. Vastly experienced and a favourite with the fans too, the arrival of McGregor seemed to suggest that Foderingham would have his work cut out retaining his place in the team. And that proved to be the case.

In what would be his last season at Rangers, Wes Foderingham made eight appearances. He kept three clean sheets, one of which came in an excellent 2-0 win over Celtic at Ibrox towards the end of the campaign. Foderingham was thrust into action to cover for the suspended McGregor but was rarely troubled as goals from James Tavernier and Scott Arfield helped end the season on a high note.

But that 90 minutes would be the last time Foderingham played for Rangers at Ibrox. He made the last of his 143 appearances at Rugby Park on the final day of the season, and in July 2019 he penned a three-year deal with Sheffield United.

And Foderingham has flourished at Bramall Lane. In season 2022/23, he helped his side reach the semi-finals of the FA Cup – Foderingham's saves in the quarter-final tie against Blackburn Rovers were decisive – and gain promotion to the promised land of the English Premiership.

Although perhaps not one of the goalkeeping greats, Wes Foderingham played a vital part in Rangers' renaissance. He was the custodian when the last leg of 'The Journey' was complete. He made 143 appearances for Rangers, conceded 144 goals and kept 56 clean sheets.

Chapter 18

Return of the Mac

SINCE MAKING his debut at Station Park in Forfar, Allan McGregor had made 278 appearances for Rangers (excluding friendly matches), conceded 224 goals and kept 128 clean sheets. But it looked as if the last of those shutouts, chalked up in a 0-0 draw against Motherwell in the last home game of the fateful season 2011/12, would be the last he would register for Rangers. With the club mired in a mess financially, McGregor joined Besiktas in July 2012.

'I fancied going out there,' admitted McGregor. 'It was something different, a different lifestyle. But not long after I signed, they changed the rule on the number of foreign players you could play.'

McGregor made his debut for Besiktas on 1 September 2012, keeping a clean sheet in a 3-0 win over Karabukspor. That would be one of only 26 appearances he made during his time in Turkey, with his last match for Besiktas being a 4-1 defeat against Akhisar Belediye on 20 April 2013.

'I didn't really play for the last couple of months of the season,' said McGregor.

'By that point my daughter was getting a couple of operations, so when I took a call from Steve Bruce asking me if I wanted to join Hull City, I decided to come back so I could be closer to home.'

In July 2013, McGregor penned a three-year deal with Hull City who had just been promoted to the Premier League after finishing as runners-up in the Championship in season 2012/13.

McGregor donned the gloves in England's top flight for the first time on 18 August 2013 against Chelsea at Stamford Bridge. He saved an early penalty kick from Frank Lampard, but Lampard and Oscar scored inside the opening half hour to earn the home side a 2-0 win.

McGregor made a further 25 league appearances as Hull consolidated their place in the Premier League. There would, however, be a couple of red cards, one against Crystal Palace in January that incurred a three-match ban and another against West Ham United that was later rescinded for wrongful dismissal. And after the latter, McGregor had a spell in a high-dependency unit after suffering kidney damage. The injury looked to have halted his first season with Hull, but he was back in the team by the time the Tigers had completed the road to Wembley to reach the FA Cup Final against Arsenal.

'I ruptured my kidney and managed to get myself sent off at the same time,' said McGregor. 'We were playing West Ham in London and I came out to deal with a bouncing ball. I managed to turn my body, and Mo Diame came in and put his knee into my back. He didn't mean it, but the referee decided to send me off and award a penalty against us. But as I was walking off with Doc Waller, I told him that something wasn't right, and I needed to get to a hospital. I got into the ambulance, and we must have driven across every cobbled street in London to get to the hospital. We were actually bouncing up and down in the back!'

He continued, 'When I got in, I went to do a pee and when I did it was as if someone was taking blood out of my arm. It turned out that I had a Grade 4 rupture. There are five Grades, and if it is a Grade 5 then the kidney gets removed. I was in hospital for 11 days, and they reckoned I could be out for up to three months. That would have ruled me out of the FA Cup Final which was only about seven weeks away. But I was determined to play, and I did, although I probably did come back too quickly.'

Current Arsenal manager Mikel Arteta captained Arsenal, while McGregor's future Rangers team-mate Aaron Ramsey scored what would prove to be the winning goal after extra time. Sone Aluko, who had been at Ibrox with McGregor in season 2011/12, came on as a substitute for Hull City with 15 minutes of normal time remaining.

Although Hull finished 16th in the league table, they qualified for the third qualifying round of the Europa League by virtue of finishing runners-up against Arsenal at Wembley. A victory over AS Trencin set up a tie with KSC Lokeren of Belgium, but despite a brave performance at home, Hull were eliminated on the away goals rule.

But those games would represent the high watermark of the season for the Tigers. Despite eight goals from the former Rangers striker Nikica Jelavić, Hull finished in the last of the relegation places and were demoted to the Championship. McGregor played in 26 of the 38 league games, missing some action in October with a shoulder injury. He was also replaced by Steve Harper for the last seven games.

'Getting relegated made you feel numb,' recalled McGregor. 'We drew 0-0 against Manchester United on the last day of the season, but Newcastle beat West Ham to stay up. But we came straight back up the following season.'

McGregor would play in 44 of the 46 games in the Championship and his 19 shut outs helped Hull into the play-offs. But a back injury ruled him out of action, and he missed the semi-final win over Derby County and the single-goal triumph over Sheffield

Wednesday in the final that sealed that immediate return to the top tier.

'I got a lot of scans on my back, but nobody could work out what the problem was,' revealed McGregor. 'I had an epidural in the January and another one in March, but the problem wouldn't go away. They eventually found that a small fracture in my back had grown, and the nerves were getting battered. I ended up getting an operation in the summer.'

By the time McGregor was fit to return, he had Eldin Jakupovic and David Marshall ahead of him at Hull. Inactive for the opening half of the season, he sought a loan move and secured one when Neil Warnock's Cardiff City came calling. And the intervention of one of the Cardiff physios would represent a key moment in McGregor's career.

'I played my first reserve game after the operation in November, but something still wasn't right,' said McGregor. 'A new manager came in at Hull – Marco Silva, the guy who is charge at Fulham now – and he brought in Marsh [David Marshall] and decided to play him even when I was fit again. I then got the chance to go to Cardiff. I think Neil Warnock knew Snoddy [Robert Snodgrass] who was at Hull at that time. Snoddy told Warnock I was flying and doing okay in training. I knew I couldn't turn the chance down to go there as I needed to play.'

He added, 'When I was at Cardiff there were days when I would wake up and couldn't get out of my bed because of my back. The physio came in around March/April time and he did some work on me that got rid of some scar tissue. By the time it came to pre-season, I felt brand new again.'

Despite his back issues, McGregor made 19 appearances for the Bluebirds, keeping a clean sheet on his debut against Burton Albion. He returned to Hull in the summer of 2017 and after Marshall got injured, McGregor was reinstated as number one, missing just two league games in season 2017/18. He was even made captain for the matches against Bristol City, Wolverhampton Wanderers and Sheffield Wednesday.

'During pre-season, Marsh and I were doing crossing drills with those mannequins you get,' said McGregor. 'They have a weight on the bottom of them, and when Marsh landed on that after he came for a cross, he did his ankle. That was probably why I started the season in goal, but I must have done alright as I played in most of the games.'

But as season 2017/18 drew to a close, a move was plotted for Allan McGregor to return to Rangers. After 147 appearances and 46 shutouts for Hull City, it was time for 'Greegsy' to come home.

'I was away with Scotland in March sitting playing cards and having a coffee when Bomber [John Brown] phoned me,' recalled McGregor. 'He asked me if I wanted to come back to Rangers and obviously I did. But I didn't hear anything for a couple of months after that. I was then out with my daughter in the shopping centre in Newton Mearns, and I met Davie Lavery, who is the masseuse at the club. I mentioned that I hadn't heard back from Bomber. Later that week, he called me, and things started to move after that. For me, coming back was a no-brainer. I was excited to work with Steven Gerrard as well.'

The first competitive match of the Steven Gerrard era was a 2-0 win over FC Shkupi. McGregor therefore recorded a clean sheet on what was his second debut for the club, and he registered four more after that as Rangers made it through to the Europa League group stages. A win, three draws and two defeats signalled the end of Rangers' interest in the competition, but the initial signs were positive.

Domestically, McGregor started 34 of the 38 league games, but the Premiership title still proved elusive. Despite beating Celtic

1-0 at Ibrox in December, Rangers came up short, finishing nine points adrift of the men from Glasgow's East End. Aberdeen also ended hopes of silverware in the two cup competitions, winning 1-0 in the last four of the League Cup, and edging a replay in the last eight of the Scottish Cup.

By the time that season ended, the goalkeeping fraternity at Ibrox had been swelled. In January 2019, McGregor and Foderingham were joined by Andy Firth, a goalkeeper who would go on to become a cult hero among the Rangers support.

Born in Ripon in North Yorkshire, Firth had been in the youth system at Liverpool, moving through the ranks from U11 to U23 level. Despite developing a reputation as a fine shot stopper, he found opportunities to break into the Liverpool first team hard to come by, and after a spell on loan with Chester City, Firth moved to Barrow in the summer of 2018. Eighteen appearances and five clean sheets in the National League followed before Gerrard, who had worked with Firth while he was in charge of the Liverpool U18s, brought Firth north of the border.

Signed on an 18-month deal, Firth made it into the squad a month after he signed, earning a place on the bench when Wes Foderingham was called upon to deputise for Allan McGregor. He made it into the squad on two further occasions that season too. After McGregor was sent off against Hibernian, Foderingham started the games against Celtic and Kilmarnock, and seven minutes from the end of the latter Firth replaced him for what would be his one and only competitive appearance for Rangers.

Although he never featured again for the first team, Firth was always present and correct on matchdays, and you could tell how much it meant to him even to be part of the squad at Rangers. He was his usual ebullient self and was front and centre when James Tavernier stepped up to raise the Premiership trophy above his head in May 2021.

Firth joined Partick Thistle on loan in February 2022 to get some game time, but such was the form of Jamie Sneddon, he spent the entire duration of his time at Firhill on the substitutes' bench.

At the end of the season after sitting among the Rangers fans at the Europa League Final in Seville, Firth parted company with Rangers. He signed for Connah's Quay Nomads, and he enjoyed an exceptional debut campaign. By early February 2023, Firth had made 29 appearances and kept 19 clean sheets. He had also taken part in the final of the Welsh League Cup, saving a penalty kick in the shoot-out against Bala Town. Unfortunately, the Nomads lost out in that shoot-out, going down 4-3.

Although his number of minutes played in a Rangers jersey is in single figures, Andy Firth will always be remembered by Rangers fans who followed the club in that era. And despite only making that single, fleeting appearance, he left the club as a Ranger for life.

* * *

Allan McGregor continued in the role of Rangers number one in season 2019/20, a season that would be brought to an abrupt conclusion by a global pandemic. Rangers' recovery under Gerrard continued – a win over Celtic at Parkhead compensated for a loss to them in the final of the League Cup – but abject form after the winter break would ultimately prove costly when the title race was declared over by the governing body.

But the holy grail was now within touching distance. As the world self-isolated, stadiums fell silent and people kept their distance, Rangers Football Club completed their journey and ascended once again to the summit of the Scottish game. Aided and abetted by the stellar performances of their veteran goalkeeper, Steven Gerrard's side strung together a sequence of results that saw them unbeaten over the course of 38 league games. A fantastic 55 had been secured.

Although a lot of emphasis will quite rightly be placed on the importance of the goals scored by Alfredo Morelos, James Tavernier and Kemar Roofe, and the creativity and craft of Ryan Kent, the contribution made by McGregor also merits a mention. Part of a defensive unit that conceded only 13 goals in the 38 league matches played, the Rangers number one kept 17 clean sheets in the 27 league fixtures he featured in. But for him, one game in particular sticks out.

'We beat Celtic 1-0 at Ibrox in January,' said McGregor. 'Before the game we were 16 points ahead, but they had three games in hand. If you assumed they would win those games, then a win for them would have made the gap four points. But us winning meant we were effectively ten points clear. Afterwards, I remember sitting with Davo [Steven Davis] in the physio room and saying to him that that result was massive. I don't usually say that that early in the season when there are so many big games still to be played, but even though Celtic had the games in hand, the pressure was on them to win them.'

An own goal from Callum McGregor was the difference between the sides, but Allan McGregor made a series of saves throughout to thwart Celtic. There was a double save early on to deny Odsonne Edouard, and another to keep out an effort from Leigh Griffiths.

However, it was a save later in the first half from the latter that could well be regarded as a title-defining moment. Griffiths bent a shot towards goal from distance with his left foot. The ball seemed destined for the top corner until McGregor stretched every sinew to get the fingertips of his right hand to it and divert the ball on to the post.

Gerrard's side wrapped things up with six games to spare. Arguably the most sought-after title in Rangers' history had been secured.

'The feeling afterwards was both elation and relief,' admitted McGregor. 'One of the biggest regrets is that the supporters weren't in the stadiums. They missed out, and we missed out on having them there too. I can only imagine what a full stadium would have been like when Tav lifted the trophy, but it wasn't to be.'

The journey was now almost complete. All that remained for this Rangers side was to be afforded an opportunity to dine once again at the top table of European Football. And within 18 months that's exactly what they did, thanks in no small part to a goalkeeper who was fast becoming the first name on people's lips when they talked about the greatest Rangers goalkeeper of all time.

Chapter 19

The Present and the Future

AT THE start of season 2022/23 the three first-team goalkeepers at Rangers were Allan McGregor, Jon McLaughlin and Robby McCrorie. With McGregor signing a one-year contract extension in the summer, debate over which of the trio would be Giovanni van Bronckhorst's number one raged for much of the close season. In the end, the Dutchman opted for McLaughlin.

Born on 9 September 1987 in Edinburgh, Jonathan Peter McLaughlin had arrived at Ibrox ahead of season 2020/21. He started out in non-league football with Harrogate Railway Athletic and Harrogate Town before he sealed a move to Bradford City in May 2008. McLaughlin had been training with the Bantams under the watchful eye of their goalkeeping coach, Nigel Martyn, and also been undertaking a degree in sports coaching at Leeds Metropolitan University.

McLaughlin was initially understudy to Rhys Evans, and he had to wait until the final game of season 2008/09 for his first-team debut. Concussion sustained in a friendly against Doncaster Rovers in February had prevented him stepping in for the injured Evans against Barnet, but he was eventually handed the gloves by manager Stuart McCall for a 2-0 win over Chesterfield at Saltergate. Former Rangers player Dean Furman opened the scoring, with the assist coming from a future Rangers player, Nicky Law.

McLaughlin played a further seven times in League Two in season 2009/10, and he signed a three-year contract in June. He then shared goalkeeping duties with Lenny Pidgeley the following season, chalking up a further 28 in all competitions.

A severe bout of food poisoning ruled McLaughlin out at the start of season 2011/12, but he established himself as the Bantams' number one from November onwards, missing only six of the 29 League Two matches that followed. Three of them were through suspension after McLaughlin was ordered off for the part he played in a post-match fracas following a 2-1 defeat against Crawley Town.

Season 2012/13 was a memorable one for Bradford City. With McLaughlin vying with Matt Duke for the number one spot, the Bantams reached the League Two play-off final and also the final of the League Cup.

McLaughlin came on as substitute in the latter when Duke was sent off after 56 minutes, but by then Bradford, the first side from the fourth tier to reach the final since Rochdale in 1962, were 3-0 down. McLaughlin's first task was to fish the ball out of the net after Jonathan de Guzman scored the penalty that Duke had conceded, and de Guzman scored again to complete a 5-0 rout for the side managed by Michael Laudrup.

But when Bradford returned to Wembley three months later to face Northampton Town in the play-off final, they emerged victorious, McLaughlin keeping a clean sheet – one of 12 in 33 appearances – as the Bantams soared to League One with a comfortable 3-0 win.

McLaughlin would play in all 46 league games for Bradford in what would be his last season with the club, 2013/14. After failing to agree a new contract, he left to join Burton Albion. His replacement at Valley Parade would be future England number one, Jordan Pickford.

Three seasons, 138 appearances and 50 clean sheets with Burton followed, with McLaughlin playing a key role in successive promotions from League Two and League One. In season 2014/15, the Brewers finished top of League Two – McLaughlin played in 45 of the 46 games and only conceded 37 goals – and in season 2015/16, he kept 22 clean sheets as Burton finished as runners-up behind Wigan Athletic.

Burton's first season in English football's second tier ended with the club staving off relegation by a single point. McLaughlin was once again Mr Consistent, missing only three matches, all of which were due to an arm injury. But to the surprise of many, he was released in the summer of 2017, with manager Nigel Clough suggesting that he wanted to 'move into a different direction with a different kind of goalkeeper'.Jon wasn't without a club for long, though, and returned to the city of his birth to play for Hearts. The highlights of his single season in Edinburgh were arguably a 4-0 win over Celtic, and a run of eight successive clean sheets. McLaughlin was held in high esteem, and his fine form earned him a first cap for Scotland, Jon playing in a 1-0 defeat against Mexico in June 2018.

But despite a new contract to stay at Hearts, McLaughlin joined Sunderland shortly after his international debut, and he would make 90 appearances on Wearside before Steven Gerrard came calling in the summer of 2020. With Wes Foderingham and Jak Alnwick departing, Gerrard was on the lookout for an experienced goalkeeper to provide competition for Allan McGregor and McLaughlin fitted the bill.

During what was an historic and landmark season for Rangers, McLaughin proved himself to be a dependable deputy. He made 14 appearances in all competitions and kept a remarkable 12 clean sheets. The only teams to breach his defences were Hibernian in a 2-2 draw at Easter Road and St Johnstone in a 1-1 draw in

Perth after the league split. By then title number 55 was secure and the Scottish Premiership trophy was bedecked in red, white and blue ribbons.

It was a similar story for McLaughlin in season 2021/22. He kept nine clean sheets in 16 appearances, although only one of those matches came in the Europa League as Rangers stormed through to the final in Seville. And the man that kept Europe's elite at bay on that glorious if unexpected run was Allan McGregor.

Steven Gerrard left to join Aston Villa in November. He was succeeded by Giovanni van Bronckhorst, and the Dutchman's first match in charge was the penultimate Europa League group match against Sparta Prague at Ibrox. Rangers won 2-0 and in so doing secured the two-goal win they needed to qualify for the knockout stages. But it took a remarkable double save from McGregor four minutes from the end to preserve the advantage. And it wouldn't be the last act of defiance from the Rangers goalkeeper either.

'[The double save] made the Lyon game a lot easier,' said McGregor before modestly admitting, 'That's goalkeeping, though. You make your move and you either save it or you don't. On that occasion I did, and it certainly made the game in Lyon more relaxed and less nervy.'

A stunning victory of Borussia Dortmund followed which set Rangers up for a clash with Red Star Belgrade. And once again their number one goalkeeper played a key role in the first leg at Ibrox. Rangers led 2-0 when Ryan Jack tugged Mirko Ivanic in the box. A penalty was awarded, and Rangers were reliant once again on their veteran custodian. Alexsandar Katai blasted the ball towards the bottom corner, but McGregor's right wrist seemed to be rock hard as he parried it to safety.

'Jacko still hasn't bought me a pint for saving that penalty,' laughed McGregor.

Challenges from SC Braga and RB Leipzig were then overcome, and suddenly, Rangers were in the Europa League Final. Eintracht Frankfurt stood between McGregor and his team-mates as they made a bid to become only the second side in Rangers' history to win a major European trophy. Alas, hope was followed by heartbreak, the Germans winning on penalty kicks. Looking back now, McGregor still has some regrets.

He admitted, 'I probably shouldn't, but I think about it [the final] quite often. I don't think I could have done anything with their last three penalties, but I think to myself that had I gone the right way for their first two, maybe I save one of them.'

There would be no crumb of comfort in the league either. Celtic overtook Rangers in February and never looked back. When Rangers had last made a European final back in 2008, many felt that cost the Light Blues the title. Was that also the case in 2022?

'I don't think it did as much as it did in 2008,' said McGregor. 'I think we played the same number of games, but we have a bigger squad now than we did back then.'

McGregor's final appearance of the campaign was the Scottish Cup Final against Hearts. Rangers were 2-0 ahead when he replaced McLaughlin a minute from the end of extra time, with many observers viewing that as being the veteran's Rangers swansong.

'Had we won in Seville I think it would have been hard not to retire,' admitted McGregor. 'But then again after you go away for a few weeks and think about it you tell yourself you want more occasions like that.'

Giovanni van Bronckhorst now had a decision to make. At his disposal he had two vastly experienced goalkeepers and a young protégé called Robby McCrorie. Who would be the Rangers number one as the Dutchman sought to lead his team to the promised land of the Champions League for the first time in 12 years?

McCrorie, who was held in high regard by the coaching staff, had acquitted himself well when McGregor and McLaughlin were sidelined by COVID-19 in September 2021. Thrown into a Europa League qualifier against Alashkert, he kept a clean sheet, and he did likewise when Celtic were defeated 1-0 at Ibrox in the Scottish Premiership.

Born on 18 March 1998 in Dailly, a small village located some 53 miles south of Glasgow, Robby was very much in the minority as a youngster; he actually wanted to be a goalkeeper.

'I was about five years old when I started to play for my local boys' club, Girvan Youth,' said McCrorie. 'It feels like a bit of a free-for-all to start with as everyone is trying every outfield position, but no one wanted to go in goal. My dad was one of the coaches, and he put me in goal. I don't know if it was because I was taller than everyone else, but even then, I had the appetite to be a goalkeeper. I didn't want to play anywhere else.'

He added, 'We had a good team, but I was only with Girvan for a couple of years. We went to tournaments in Ayr and England, and I think it was at the Land O' Burns tournament in Ayr that one of the Rangers scouts, Scott Bryson, invited me along to one of the community schools that Rangers ran at Cambusdoon. It was a two-day training camp – Saturday and Sunday, I think – and after the first day, Scott had seen enough. At the age of eight, I was signing for Rangers.'

Progression through the youth ranks followed, and by 2017, McCrorie was ready for first-team football.

'I had played at youth level for Rangers and Scotland, and when I went full-time with Rangers, I played reserve football at U20-level,' said McCrorie. 'But I was desperate to go out on loan to get first-team football. Berwick Rangers made an offer for me, and I jumped at it. I was buzzing, and I went on my phone to find out how far away Berwick was from my mum's house in Dailly. It didn't matter to me that Berwick was at the other end of Scotland, I just wanted the opportunity to play first-team football, something I had been chasing for over a year.'

McCrorie made the most of his opportunity with Berwick. He played in 33 of their 36 league matches and 40 in all competitions. Eight clean sheets were registered, and he collected no fewer than five awards at the club's end-of-season Player of the Year awards ceremony. Included in his haul were the Players' Player of the Year and the Supporters' Trust Player of the Year.

'That was a good spell for me as it was my first taste of first-team football,' admitted McCrorie. 'I trained with Rangers during the week then went down to Berwick to train on the Thursday night. Getting Player of the Year was good for my profile at that time too.'

When Robby returned to Ibrox, he was reporting to a new Rangers manager. Steven Gerrard had been appointed on 1 May 2018, and imbued by the confidence he had collected from his move to Berwick, McCrorie had his sights set on another loan move.

'I wanted to go and get more games, but at a higher level this time,' admitted McCrorie. 'But after two weeks, Steven Gerrard pulled me aside and said he wanted me to stay at Rangers and be involved with the first team. We had a lot of European games at that time, and I was on the bench for most of them.'

But as much as regular first-team involvement with Rangers was the goal for McCrorie, he wasn't going to get much in the way of game time with more experienced goalkeepers like Allan McGregor ahead of him at that time.

'By the time it got to January, I was desperate to play more games, so I went to Morton for six months under Jonatan Johansson,' said McCrorie. 'Even when I went back for pre-season, I knew that the way Allan was performing for Rangers meant the best thing for my development was to go back out on loan again.'

A third loan move was sanctioned by Gerrard, and McCrorie's destination this time was Palmerston Park, home of Queen of the South.

'I was only there for the first six months of the season, but ended up as their Player of the Year,' said McCrorie proudly. 'But by December, I had set myself a target of trying to get first-team games in the Scottish Premiership, so in January, I moved to Livingston on loan.'

He added, 'Coming through the Academy as a goalkeeper at that time, the question that was always asked was, "Who is going to be the next Allan McGregor?" Allan was someone I watched every day in training and in games, and he always made big saves in big moments. My objective was the same as it had always been – to try and follow in Allan's footsteps – and I knew from the discussions I had had with Steven Gerrard that he wanted me at Rangers. But the best thing for my career at that point was to go out on loan and play games.'

McCrorie made eight appearances for Livingston before season 2019/20 was halted by the COVID-19 pandemic. But he had done enough in those games to make an impression and when football resumed, McCrorie signed up for another temporary transfer. This time he would be with Livingston for the whole of season 2020/21.

'I was probably the youngest goalkeeper playing in the SPL at that time,' said McCrorie. 'There had been interest from other clubs, but because I had been at Livingston already and got to know the players I was working with, it was a no-brainer to go back there.'

McCrorie vied with Max Stryjek for the gloves at Livingston and made 18 appearances over the course of season 2020/21. On the back of that and some stellar reviews, he went back to Ibrox once more to map out his future with Steven Gerrard.

'That was the start of a really frustrating time for me,' admitted Robby. 'I wanted to play games, but because of our involvement in European competition, Rangers wanted me to stay where I was rather than go out on loan again. It was hard to argue with that, so it was important for me that I used every training session as my match. Even though I wasn't playing games, I had to show everyone at the club that I was ready to play if I needed to be.'

And he had to be ready, too. Rangers had lost to Malmö in the qualifying rounds of the Champions League, so had dropped into the Europa League qualifiers. They were drawn to face Alashkert from Armenia, and the squad travelled there for the second leg to defend a narrow one-goal lead without their number one and number two goalkeepers. Both Allan McGregor and Jonathan McLaughlin had tested positive for COVID-19, so the chance McCrorie had waited so patiently for had arrived.

'I was ready to play,' declared McCrorie. 'I have that mindset that you have to work hard so you are ready for any outcome. I played the two games [in addition to playing in Armenia, McCrorie was also selected for the 1-0 win over Celtic three days later] but I knew Allan and Jon were coming back. I had a bit of hope that when we came back from the international break that came after the Celtic game that I'd get more opportunities to play, but the manager had every right to bring either Allan or Jon in. It was still frustrating for me, though. I just had to try and use that in the right way so that I was ready the next time I was called upon.'

He added, 'I know it looked on paper as if I was third choice, but I didn't look at it that way. In my mind, I was thinking I was number one. That's the way it needs to be for every player at Rangers. It doesn't matter if it's in training or during games, you need to go out there and do your best. That's been my mindset since I was young and it's the way it has to be if you want to be successful at a club like Rangers.'

Three months after those games, Gerrard had left Rangers and van Bronckhorst was the next Rangers manager that McCrorie had to impress.

'Gio came in before the transfer window opened in January so I knew nothing would happen for me until then,' said Robby. 'When it got to January, I went to see him and told him I wanted to play games. But it ended up being the same scenario as it was under Steven Gerrard; if I was going out on loan then he would need to get another goalkeeper in first. He assured me that he knew I was ready to play for Rangers if I was needed, but he would rather I was at the club rather than elsewhere.'

He added, 'We were still in the Europa League at that point, and it was good to be part of the run to Seville. I still wanted to play, but I understood that the manager didn't want to leave himself short in any position. It was frustrating for me, but it kept the fire burning as I knew I was going to get there [into the Rangers team] at some point.'

It was clear therefore that McCrorie was one for the future, so the number one would be either McGregor or McLaughlin. Van Bronckhorst opted for the latter, and McLaughlin was in situ when PSV Eindhoven were defeated 3-2 on aggregate to secure a seat at the top table alongside Europe's elite in the Champions League. McLaughlin kept a clean sheet in Eindhoven, but when Rangers returned to Holland to face Ajax a few weeks later in the opening group match, McLaughlin conceded four goals. Given he had been beaten four times against Celtic at Parkhead four days earlier – the first and last of the goals resulted from errors from the Rangers goalkeeper – there was suddenly a clamour among Rangers supporters for McGregor to be reinstated.

The manager made the change, McGregor coming back in for the visit of Napoli in the Champions League. He showed his penalty prowess once again, saving a penalty then also the retake, but Rangers lost 3-0. Further defeats against Liverpool, Napoli and Ajax saw them rooted to the bottom of Group A with no points and 22 goals conceded. Having experienced playing at this level earlier in his career, McGregor could see the chasm that had developed between teams that were competing at that level. But that wasn't the only reason why he felt Rangers didn't muster any points.

He said, 'We didn't play anywhere near as well collectively as we had done the season before in the Europa League. Admittedly, it was a different competition, but you still had the likes of Dortmund and Leipzig and teams of similar quality in the tournament too. Maybe in hindsight we could have gone at teams a bit more than we did, but had we done so and still lost, we would have been criticised for that too. Now, we need to learn from our experience and hopefully do better next time.'

When the exit from the Champions League was followed by a wretched run in the league that saw points dropped and the gap between Celtic and Rangers grow to nine points, Rangers and van Bronckhorst parted company. The Dutchman hadn't been helped by the absence through injury of Connor Goldson and Ben Davies, but while McGregor felt that the loss of the pair had an impact, that wasn't the only reason why Rangers drew against Livingston and St Mirren and lost against St Johnstone in Perth.

He said, 'In those games we had chances to score and opportunities not to concede. You'll get games like that every season whether they have been good or bad, but unfortunately, in 2022/23 it left us in the position we were in.'

After van Bronckhorst departed, Michael Beale arrived and stabilised Rangers. And the former right-hand man of Steven Gerrard rotated his goalkeepers in his early matches in charge, giving game time to both McGregor and McLaughlin while hinting that there would be opportunities before the end of the season for McCrorie too.

'There are similarities between Michael Beale and Steven Gerrard, but the manager has got his own way that he wants to play,' said McGregor. 'He wants to let us off the leash to a certain degree while still being organised.'

Many believe that a new goalkeeper will be on Beale's shopping list in the summer of 2023. If that is the case and he does elect to bring in a new contender for the number one spot, then the new incumbent will have a hard act to follow. And that's not just referring to Allan McGregor. This book has reinforced the long-held opinion that Rangers Football Club has been served by some of the finest goalkeepers to have played the game. And if Michael Beale wants to restore Rangers to the summit of Scottish football, then he may well have to unearth a custodian of a similar ilk once again.

And who better to advise on what you have to have to be a Rangers goalkeeper than the current number one?'Focus, ability and concentration,' said McGregor. 'I learnt a lot from Stefan [Klos] without him actually saying anything. I'd watch him before games, and he would just sit there and get focused. As Rangers goalkeeper sometimes you only have one save to make in a game and you have to do it. You can be out of the game for 80 minutes then you have to make a vital save. You need focus and concentration to be able to do that.'

And who has been the finest exponent of the goalkeeping art McGregor has seen in a Rangers jersey?

'I don't want to miss anyone out, but I loved The Goalie. Some of the saves he made like the one from van Hooijdonk come to mind, but he was a great person too. I went up to see him in the hospital after he had been diagnosed with cancer and he was still being himself.'

Although we spoke in February 2023, even at that stage the inevitable talk of retirement was coming to the fore for McGregor. And although he admits to taking 'one day at a time', he's not sure he will go into coaching after he finally hangs the gloves up.

'I've always said "no",' admitted McGregor. 'It's the process that's involved that puts me off. A couple of the lads were going for their B licence a couple of years ago, and I saw an email they were sent with the list of things they had to do. I thought "no thanks", although I spoke to Steven Gerrard, and he said he was the same when he was out in LA. At that point he said the last thing he was thinking about was being a manager, so I suppose I should never say never.'

Allan McGregor made his 500th competitive appearance (league, Scottish Cup, Scottish League Cup and Europe) for Rangers on 1 April 2023 against Dundee United at Ibrox. Only Peter McCloy and Jerry Dawson have kept goal for Rangers more often. And with a shut-out count exceeding 220, McGregor merits more than a mention when it comes to debating who has been the safest pair of hands Rangers have ever had. However, with great modesty, McGregor won't be drawn on the matter.

'I'm the most "not about me" guy in the world,' said McGregor. 'That [whether he is the greatest ever] is a conversation for others to have in the pub when they are talking about all the goalies that played for Rangers and loved the club. I'm not one for personal achievements. I'd throw all the personal stuff away for this club to be successful and win things.'

There is, however, one personal honour that McGregor will always look back on fondly. In February 2023, he was inducted into the Rangers Hall of Fame, with his name added to the log of luminaries that sits above the majestic marble staircase at Ibrox. He admitted that it 'meant the world to him' and he was 'honoured and privileged', but it was deserved recognition for the service he has given to Rangers, a club McGregor himself describes as 'an unbelievable institution'.

Although he won't admit it himself, Allan McGregor is at the forefront of the discussion among supporters when it comes to talking about the greatest ever Rangers goalkeeper. His heroics will be talked about for years to come, and he will forever be mentioned in the same breath as the likes of Dawson, McCloy, Woods, Goram and Klos.

* * *

True to his word, Michael Beale gave Robby McCrorie his opportunity before season 2022/23 drew to a close. After that lengthy spell on the sidelines, McCrorie was handed the gloves for all bar one of the post-split fixtures. It was an opportunity for the 25-year-old to show his manager that he had what it took to be the Rangers number one, and he grasped the opportunity with two very safe hands.

'During the period when I wasn't playing for Rangers, I was getting selected for the Scotland national team,' said McCrorie. 'I have a very good relationship with Steve Clarke. He put his faith and trust in me, and I knew he wouldn't be calling me up if he didn't think I was good enough. That helped me keep going.'

He added, 'I would be lying if I said I didn't have doubts, and I did think about leaving. I felt as if I was good enough, but it was getting to the point when I didn't know when my chance was going to come.'

But when Beale took over, the vibe was different; McCrorie knew that this time his opportunity would come. However, just when it looked like it would, injury robbed him of his chance.

'I had never been out injured for a long period of time,' said McCrorie. 'I like to look after myself, but on 1 January, I had a freak accident in training that meant I was out for two months. That added to the frustration, and it felt that everything was against me at that time. I had had a good relationship with the gaffer when he had been at the club previously, and I knew this time I would get my chance. I had looked at games during the spell that I was out and felt there were opportunities there for me to play.'

He added, 'But this time I knew my chance was coming. The gaffer told me when he came in that I would play and get given an opportunity. That was enough for me to get myself back fit and make sure that I was ready.'

And McCrorie has repaid the faith his manager has shown in him with a series of confident and assured displays.

'I looked at the games after the split and knew that they were massive for me,' admitted McCrorie. 'I know there were some that said because the league was over, the games didn't matter, but regardless of that, you still need to win every game when you play for Rangers. It's about building momentum for next season. And all the games excited me as all the teams we played were desperate to beat us. I relished the challenge, and I wanted to perform as I don't want to be overlooked. It was about making the most of the chances I had and then waiting to see what happened in the summer.'

At the time of writing, speculation was rife that Michael Beale was still looking to bolster his goalkeeping options in the summer of 2023. But Robby McCrorie has certainly given his manager food for thought.

'I felt relaxed and comfortable in the games I've played,' said McCrorie. 'I actually think my family were more nervous than me! But because we're taught to prepare in the right way, you're more comfortable getting thrown into these situations, and I feel as if I have got the backing of everybody. The Rangers fans want to see young players coming through and making a name for themselves, and that's what drives me on.'

One of those who has backed Robby has been Allan McGregor.

'When I was 14, Jim Stewart was the goalkeeping coach, and he took us round to work with Allan and Neil Alexander,' said McCrorie. 'I only got a small insight into what he was like at that time, but I don't know if it's because we've been on a similar journey and have the same mentality that we both want to do well for the club, but I feel that recently, we have developed a good personal relationship too. I know there will be points in the future when I need advice, and I know that Allan is only a text or a phone call away. When I was growing up, he was the number one at Rangers, and in my eyes, there's been nobody better in my lifetime.'

It remains to be seen if Robby McCrorie will be the man charged with following on from Allan McGregor. But if he is, he is more than ready for that responsibility.

He concluded, 'I'm focused just now on staying in the moment. I know if I do that, keep everything simple and work hard, then that will get me places. I want to be the Rangers number one, hopefully sooner rather than later. I want to be walking out at Ibrox, week in, week out. I've put everything I could into every loan move that I've had and done exactly the same at Rangers. When I wear that Rangers strip it just feels right. I don't know if it's because I'm a fan, but I don't see it as pressure when I'm playing for the club. It's a privilege. The most important thing for me is to be the best version of Robby McCrorie.'

That 'best version' could well be more than enough to earn McCrorie a shot at being the goalkeeper who plays a pivotal role in the radical rebuild that many feel is coming at Ibrox. Whether Michael Beale recruits a goalkeeper or not, Robby McCrorie will be in the reckoning for Rangers when season 2023/24 kicks off in earnest.

Postscript

A View from the Training Ground

THE CURRENT coach of the first-team goalkeepers at Ibrox is Colin Stewart. Colin is the son of Jim, goalkeeper at Rangers between 1981 and 1984 and goalkeeper coach thereafter, and his route to Rangers was a circuitous one.

Born on 10 January 1980 while his dad was plying his trade with Middlesbrough, Stewart was destined to follow in his father's footsteps.

'I played for the school team at Kilwinning Academy and for Dreghorn Boys Club,' said Stewart. 'My dad was coaching the goalkeepers at Kilmarnock, and I ended up playing there. These were the days before youth academies, although in season 1995/96, I was playing at U16 level and took part in what was the first pro-youth league set-up.'

He continued, 'I played that full year, but there was never any conversation with Kilmarnock about a contract. I got the chance to go down south to Grimsby, but that went dead when their manager moved to West Bromwich Albion. I then went to Ipswich Town after doing well in a trial match.'

However, it didn't work out south of the border, so Stewart returned north. To help get some games, Kilmarnock sent him out on loan, and Stewart joined Clydebank in December 1999.

'The former Rangers goalkeeper Colin Scott injured his back, so Ian McCall brought me in for a month,' recalled Stewart. 'I then had about 16 or 17 games on loan at Alloa and was with Queen's Park for a wee while too. After that my contract was up at Kilmarnock, so I had a decision to make. I ended up signing for Ross County, but six months later I was in a hospital bed with a broken leg.'

Stewart completed his rehabilitation with Kilmarnock, spending a couple of days a week in the Highlands to keep in touch with Ross County. But during the spell on the sidelines, Stewart took the first steps along the pathway to becoming a coach.

'That injury probably ended any hopes I had of a career at the higher level of the game,' reflected Stewart. 'The leg break gave rise to issues with my knee, and I just wasn't fit enough anymore. I became a bit of a nomad trying to keep myself in a job. I always had a desire to play, and there were always opportunities to go and be a number two. But I reckon it was about five or six years after the injury, by which time I was 28, before I was back to full fitness again.'

Once he had recovered, Stewart had a year with Partick Thistle, signing for the Jags on 19 August 2005. He kept a clean sheet on his debut as Thistle defeated Forfar Athletic 1-0 on 24 September. But that would be one of only 15 appearances Stewart made for the club.

'I had had a chance to go to Bristol City before I went to Thistle, but the deal fell through,' said Stewart. 'I was up against Kenny Arthur at Firhill. He was in his testimonial year, but when I got the chance, I thought I did reasonably well. We got promoted that season too.'

A brief move to Grindavik in Iceland was next up for Stewart.

He recalled, 'David Hannah, who had been at Dundee United and Celtic, was out there and Siggi Jonsson, who had played with

Arsenal and Sheffield Wednesday, was the manager. The club had a good profile, and I ended up playing around 15 games for them which kept me fit during the summer.'

On his return to Scotland, Stewart signed for Livingston. He made his debut, ironically against Partick Thistle, on 19 August 2006, and his time with the club was bookended since the last of his 40 appearances for the Livi Lions also came against Thistle on 19 April 2008. A move to Morton followed, and Stewart proceeded to make 93 appearances for the club, including a 1-0 defeat against Celtic in the Scottish Cup. He was the club's Player of the Year in season 2009/10.

'We ran Celtic close,' recalled Stewart. 'There was a full house at Cappielow, and I felt we put on a decent enough show. We didn't take the chances we had on the night, but it was exciting and a nice break from playing the same teams week on week in the Championship.'

After leaving Morton, Stewart had a spell coaching in Qatar before winding down his playing career with spells at Stranraer, Cowdenbeath, Airdrie and Raith Rovers.

'When I started playing it was only really Rangers and Celtic that had full-time goalkeeping coaches,' said Stewart. 'But when I left Livingston, clubs were starting to bring them in on a part-time basis, while the top six teams in Scotland had a full-time goalkeeping coach. At some of the clubs I was at, if we didn't have a goalkeeping coach then, as I was one of the senior goalkeepers, I would end up taking the sessions.'

He continued, 'Around about 2008 I started to do my coaching badges. That helped me learn more about the game and made my mind up that I wanted to follow the coaching route. I had a chance to come in to Rangers to work with the Academy before I went to Qatar, but I decided to go with the latter and it was the best decision I ever made.'

Prior to going to the Middle East, Stewart was running coaching sessions after school then fighting through traffic to get to Kilmarnock to coach their young goalkeepers.

'I loved it, but you felt as if you were living out of the boot of your car,' said Stewart. 'But Qatar set me on the path to where I am now. I was appointed as Academy coach at Al Khor FC where I looked after the U16 and U18 teams. However, just as my family were about to move out, we decided to come back as there were a couple of uncertainties and I felt more secure as I knew the footballing circles in Scotland.'

He continued, 'When I came back, I played a few games for Stranraer and that gave me the bug again. I then went to Cowdenbeath, but I was also continuing my coaching education doing work with the SFA. I was working with guys like Scott Booth, Scott Gemmill, Billy Stark and Ricky Sbragia, and that gave me an insight into the elite performance level.'

With some clubs not yet in a position to employ a goalkeeping coach, Stewart continued playing before he got the opportunity to be co-manager at Kilwinning Rangers.

'My brother was the goalkeeper for Kilwinning at the time and he called me one day to tell me that the manager had left the club,' recalled Stewart. 'I had just finished my badges and was signing month-to-month contracts with clubs to keep myself involved in the game. I decided to have a crack at managing Kilwinning, although my dad thought I was mad to take the job.'

But it would prove to be a good move. Stewart's spell at Kilwinning would lay the groundwork that led the club to the West of Scotland Football League (WOSFL) and their move to Kilwinning Sports Club.

Colin added, 'Kilwinning was in a bit of a turmoil at the time, but I really enjoyed it. They were struggling for investment and sponsorship, so I got involved in that side of the game. I had also started my own coaching business, and I combined that with working with Kilwinning and working with the Scotland U17s. And while I was with the U17s, we went to Malta for the European Championships in 2014 and reached the semi-finals.'

And then came the opportunity to work with Rangers.

'I had been working as a part-time coach with the club at night since I had come back from Qatar,' admitted Stewart. 'The club were progressing back up through the divisions and I got plenty of opportunities to gain more experience. I picked up more and more hours and there was talk of a full-time job. However, it looked like I was going to St Johnstone when Tommy Wright was the manager. At that time, August 2015, Paul Mathers left St Mirren to come to Rangers to work with my dad. But within 24 hours, Paul joined St Johnstone and I ended up at Rangers!'

Stewart was appointed as Head of Academy goalkeeping at Rangers, while dad, Jim, was looking after the first-team goalkeepers. However, Jim left when Pedro Caixhinia took over as manager, the Portuguese deciding to bring in his own goalkeeping coach.

'That was a difficult moment,' admitted Stewart junior. 'My dad had guided me as a young player, as a senior player, then provided further guidance when I was a young coach. He was the first person I would call when I needed advice, and suddenly he wasn't with the club anymore.'

Caixhinia and his backroom team didn't stay in Glasgow very long. The Portuguese was sacked in October 2017 after just 229 days in charge. His goalkeeping coach, Pepe Belman, left too, which meant Colin was now catapulted from the Academy to first team.

'That was an eye-opener,' admitted Stewart. 'I had gone from developing young goalies to working with the first-team goalkeepers. They had to have that winning mentality you need at Rangers.'

Graeme Murty and then Jimmy Nicholl took charge after Caixhinia left, before Steven Gerrard was appointed as the Rangers manager in May 2018. When a new manager comes in, there is usually an expectation that he will bring in his own staff, so having not long been in the role Stewart could have found himself surplus to requirements.

'You have to have a confidence in your own ability, but ultimately these decisions are taken above your head,' admitted Stewart. 'Thankfully, it's worked out for me, and the club have been brilliant. I had worked with Graeme and Jimmy for eight months during what was a transition period, but you still wonder if you are going to get kept on. The club assured me that I would be okay, but it was a couple of days before we started pre-season before I got a call from Steven that confirmed I was part of his team.'

Stewart was therefore part of what would be an historic title win in season 2020/21, but when Gerrard left to join Aston Villa and Giovanni van Bronckhorst came in, there wasn't as much uncertainty as there had been in the past.

'When Steven moved on, the club were doing really well,' said Stewart. 'We had a really good group of goalkeepers, and there was honesty and transparency from Ross Wilson and Gio. I hadn't been particularly lucky as a player, but luck has been on my side during my coaching career.'

He added, 'When The Boss [Michael Beale] came back, although I knew him and had that familiarity, I didn't take it for granted that I would be kept on. When Gio called me when he knew he was leaving, you naturally go through all the emotions. In the same way you would be if a friend or family member lost their job, I was upset for Gio first and foremost, but then you start to think about what will happen with you. But having been through it before, I knew to stay away from the speculation and the frustrations that brings. This is a fantastic place to work, and I've been lucky that it's worked out for me.'

So, what does a working week in the life of a Rangers goalkeeper and their goalkeeping coach look like?

'You have two different weeks at Rangers,' admitted Stewart. 'There will be some weeks that are unique in the respect that there is no midweek game, but for the past few years, we've been playing European football which means three games a week.'

He added, 'If we play on the Saturday and have no midweek game then the players usually have the day off on a Sunday to recover. We then have a two-day training block. The first day will be gym work for the likes of Allan and Jon, but you also have the younger goalkeepers to support. And if any of the lads are injured, you are meeting with the physios and doctors to see how their rehab is going.

'The second day is then a working session. This is more physical and because there isn't a game close, you can work the goalies a wee bit harder. They'll then have another day off on the Wednesday before we have a couple of days leading into the game at the weekend. The first of those will be more physical work before we move on to the tactical side, focusing on what we think the opposition might do. There are a lot of set plays in Scottish Football, so we'll use these sessions to do some crossing work so the goalies can get their eye in. After that we'll look at once we recover the ball what are we going to do with it. And the day before the game will be a lighter session where we focus on handling, movement and reactionary stuff.'

There's also a competitive element to training as Stewart explains.

'The goalies have wee fun competitions throughout the season and that helps breed the winning mentality. It's not about motivation – the club, the badge, the fans, they all keep you motivated – but it gives them a competitive edge and a focus on being the best. It's also a good way of taking the pressure off them and letting them enjoy themselves.'

But Stewart isn't just interacting with the goalkeepers, there are other key protagonists too.

'We work closely with the analysts to get a package ready for the goalies before the game. They'll get hit with all the stats and pre-match analysis, and that is likely to raise questions, so at that point I'm reaffirming the message from the manager.'

Training can see the players forming disparate groups, although the common goal – creating a winning Rangers team – is the same.

'The goalies warm up on their own, but we'll integrate with the defenders for certain routines,' said Stewart. 'That all depends on what the boss wants. It might be playing out from the back, defending the space, or defending cross balls or set plays. We have a set-play committee which comprises the senior players that form the main structure of the team. Harry [Watling] and I will usually organise that. That gives us organisation and structure most of the time.'

In contrast, if Rangers have a European tie midweek, the landscape is different.

'In that scenario, it's all about recovery and being ready to play,' said Stewart. 'That's why it's important to have two or even three number one goalkeepers at the club. In season 2022/23 we could be playing on a Wednesday night then again on the Saturday lunchtime. At that point, you're just keeping the goalies ticking over. On some occasions, we might stay overnight after the game. That gives the lads the chance to sleep, then have a recovery breakfast before going to the gym or the pool to do some exercises. In that instance, you're not training as much physically, but mentally you're trying to get the boys relaxed and focused on the next game.'

He continued, 'If it was a home game then the Thursday will be determined by the goalkeeper. They'll come in in the afternoon, and they might want to do some handling, or alternatively work in the gym or in the pool to do some stretching. That's almost a "suck it and see moment" as it will have a lot to do with how they have slept for example. One of the hardest things we find after night games is that the players struggle to sleep, and you want the lads to be fresh. But while the first-team goalies are doing that, we'll still have to take the young lads out to keep their fitness levels up. And on the Friday, we are back into analysis and set plays again ahead of the game. The players would then get a day off on the Sunday.'

The current Rangers squad has depth in all departments, but the goalkeeping group is particularly strong. That is testament to the work that Stewart and his team of coaches have done and are still doing. But with recruitment of a goalkeeper on the agenda for the summer of 2023, what are the hierarchy looking for?

'They need to be able to show a calmness in the face of adversity,' said Stewart. 'If the team aren't playing well, if decisions are going against us, or they've made a mistake, the goalkeeper needs to stay calm, so they make the right decisions. And they need to be able to make that big save. Most of the goalkeepers that have played for Rangers have been able to do that. All of our goalkeepers have got different traits. Since I took over at first-team level, we've played a huge number of games and the expectation at this club is that we win them all, so we need to have belief and trust in all of them that they can make that big save. And when I have been working with the guys, we have had those moments, and they have produced much more than they haven't.'

He added, 'You only have to look at the saves that Allan has made at key moments. The penalty save against Maribor and the one at the back post away from home against Ufa when we were down to nine men come to mind. But Allan's been making saves like that for years even back when he was working with my dad and Billy [Thomson]. Jon has made some important blocks too, and one save away to Hamilton when he clawed the ball away was crucial. And the saves he made in Eindhoven against PSV gave us the platform to qualify for the group stages of the Champions League.'

Mentality and mindset are therefore key for a Rangers goalkeeper and nurturing that is one of the most important tasks that Stewart has, although he feels the goalies tend to bear the brunt of the criticism when things aren't going well.

'I don't know what it is, but it seems to be that if you're losing games, there must be a problem with the goalkeeper. I've been victim to that myself. Goalkeepers will make mistakes. That's one of the only promises we can give them; they will make mistakes. But from the first team down to the Academy, it's about how you deal with that when that happens. At this club we have to win, so if one of the lads does make a mistake that costs us victory, then they have to have the character to recover and, fortunately, we have that in the current group of goalkeepers at Ibrox.'

And one of the best at recovering from making a mistake is Allan McGregor, although Jon McLaughlin has responded well too.

'You don't have the career that Allan has had without making errors,' said Stewart. 'But he has had a level of trust from those around him throughout his career. He made good use of the loan system to go and learn his trade and that has set him up for what has been an unbelievable and fantastic career. Jon is similar too. Before he came here, he had played over 400 games, and he has earned the right to face the challenges that come with being a Rangers goalkeeper.'

Stewart concluded, 'We have an excellent group of young goalkeepers at Rangers, and they are now pushing the senior ones for a starting position in the first team. The reality is that the step up from playing in the Lowland League with the B team to playing in the Champions League is significant, but Robby McCrorie has done that. That shows the processes we have in place are working; it's now up to them and us to work together to make sure that the young lads stay here and are the Rangers goalkeepers of the future.'

Appendix – Stat Attack

League Football

Rangers Football Club was among the ten clubs that contested the inaugural Scottish Football League championship in season 1890/91. Since then a total of 80 goalkeepers have made at least one league appearance for Rangers. The top 20 appearance makers are listed below (GC = goals conceded, SO = shut outs):

	Goalkeeper	*App*	*GC*	*SO*	*Notes*
1	Peter McCloy	351	350	132	
2	Allan McGregor	346	258	160	
3	Tom Hamilton	243	227	91	
4	Jerry Dawson	241	272	74	Excludes league appearances during WWII
5	Willie Robb	227	162	102	
6=	George Niven	221	260	67	
6=	Herbert Lock	221	199	92	
8	Bobby Brown	211	214	74	
9=	Billy Ritchie	207	205	77	
9=	Stefan Klos	207	152	100	
11	Andy Goram	184	144	83	
12	Chris Woods	173	108	96	
13	John Hempsey	147	129	69	
14	Matthew Dickie	141	189	38	
15	Wes Foderingham	112	118	40	36 in the Scottish Championship
16	Stewart Kennedy	99	100	34	
17=	Nick Walker	75	76	31	
17=	Norrie Martin	75	73	25	
19	David Haddow	66	121	12	
20	Neil Alexander	62	52	25	36 in SFL3

In their history, Rangers have won 55 top-flight Scottish league titles. The goalkeepers who have tried to foil forwards in each of those campaigns are:

Season	*Goalkeeper(s)*	*App*	*GC*	*SO*	*Notes*
1890/91	David Hill	17	23	5	Includes one appearance in Championship play-off v Dumbarton
	A.B. McKenzie	2	2	0	Also played at outside-right in final league match v Third Lanark, scoring a hat-trick in a 4-1 win
1898/99	Matthew Dickie	18	18	7	
1899/1900	Matthew Dickie	17	26	3	
	William Howden	1	1	0	
1900/01	Matthew Dickie	20	25	4	
1901/02	Matthew Dickie	15	25	3	
	John McPherson	1	2	0	
	Noble McPherson	2	2	0	
1910/11	Herbert Lock	34	34	13	
1911/12	Herbert Lock	33	31	12	
	Thomas Farrington	1	3	0	
1912/13	Herbert Lock	6	6	3	
	Thomas Farrington	7	12	1	
	William Gibson	3	5	0	
	John Hempsey	17	17	7	
	R. G. Campbell	1	1	0	
1917/18	John Hempsey	25	15	15	
	Thomas Singleton	2	2	1	
	Herbert Lock	7	7	2	
1919/20	Herbert Lock	35	20	19	
	Willie Robb	7	5	2	
1920/21	Willie Robb	42	24	22	
1922/23	Willie Robb	38	29	15	
1923/24	Willie Robb	38	22	21	
1924/25	Willie Robb	38	26	17	
1926/27	Tom Hamilton	37	40	13	
	Willie Moyles	1	1	0	

1927/28	Tom Hamilton	33	27	12	
	Willie Moyles	2	3	0	
	Duncan Yuill	3	6	0	
1928/29	Tom Hamilton	38	32	15	
1929/30	Tom Hamilton	38	32	17	
1930/31	Tom Hamilton	37	28	15	
	Jerry Dawson	1	1	0	
1932/33	Jerry Dawson	20	29	4	
	Tom Hamilton	18	14	9	
1933/34	Jerry Dawson	30	28	10	
	George Jenkins	7	12	1	
	Tom Hamilton	1	1	0	
1934/35	Jerry Dawson	37	44	9	
	George Jenkins	1	2	0	
1936/37	Jerry Dawson	38	32	17	
1938/39	Jerry Dawson	33	50	6	
	George Jenkins	5	5	2	
1946/47	Bobby Brown	30	26	12	
1948/49	Bobby Brown	30	32	9	
1949/50	Bobby Brown	30	26	14	
1952/53	George Niven	30	39	8	
1955/56	George Niven	31	26	14	
	Bobby Brown	3	1	2	
1956/57	George Niven	34	48	10	
1958/59	George Niven	34	51	7	
1960/61	George Niven	22	24	7	
	Billy Ritchie	12	21	3	
1962/63	Billy Ritchie	33	27	12	
	Norrie Martin	1	1	0	
1963/64	Billy Ritchie	34	31	14	
1974/75	Stewart Kennedy	34	33	11	
1975/76	Peter McCloy	24	13	14	
	Stewart Kennedy	12	11	4	
1977/78	Peter McCloy	14	15	6	
	Stewart Kennedy	22	24	8	
1986/87	Chris Woods	42	23	25	

	Nicky Walker	2	0	2	
1988/89	Chris Woods	24	16	13	
	Nicky Walker	12	10	4	
1989/90	Chris Woods	32	15	18	
	Bonni Ginzburg	4	4	1	
1990/91	Chris Woods	36	23	21	
1991/92	Andy Goram	44	31	20	
1992/93	Andy Goram	34	22	17	
	Ally Maxwell	10	13	3	
1993/94	Ally Maxwell	32	31	1	One appearance as substitute v Dundee United, 05/04/94
	Colin Scott	6	5	2	One appearance as substitute v Raith Rovers, 02/10/93
	Andy Goram	8	5	3	
1994/95	Andy Goram	19	14	8	One appearance as substitute v Partick Thistle, 13/05/95
	Ally Maxwell	11	10	5	One appearance as substitute v Celtic, 07/05/95
	Billy Thomson	5	8	1	
	Colin Scott	4	3	1	One appearance as substitute v Partick Thistle, 07/01/95
1995/96	Andy Goram	30	20	17	
	Colin Scott	3	2	2	
	Billy Thomson	1	1	0	
	Theo Snelders	2	2	1	
1996/97	Andy Goram	25	21	11	
	Theo Snelders	4	5	1	
	Andy Dibble	7	7	4	
1998/99	Antti Niemi	7	11	2	
	Lionel Charbonnier	11	5	6	
	Stefan Klos	18	15	7	
1999/2000	Stefan Klos	24	17	12	
	Lionel Charbonnier	7	5	3	
	Thomas Myhre	3	3	1	
	Mark Brown	1	0	1	
	Antti Niemi	1	1	0	
2002/03	Stefan Klos	38	28	19	
2004/05	Stefan Klos	23	11	12	

	Allan McGregor	2	1	1	
	Ronald Waterreus	13	10	5	
2008/09	Allan McGregor	27	21	12	
	Neil Alexander	11	7	5	
2009/10	Allan McGregor	34	22	15	
	Neil Alexander	5	6	2	One appearance as substitute v Celtic, 04/05/10
2010/11	Allan McGregor	37	28	18	
	Neil Alexander	1	1	0	
2020/21	Allan McGregor	27	10	17	
	Jon McLaughlin	11	3	9	

Rangers in the Scottish Cup

In their Scottish Cup history, Rangers have called upon 50 goalkeepers. The data for those who have appeared the most is:

	Goalkeeper	*App*	*GC*	*SO*	*Notes*
1	Peter McCloy	55	48	22	
2	Tom Hamilton	38	27	19	
3	Billy Ritchie	37	32	15	
4	Matthew Dickie	34	30	14	
5	Bobby Brown	33	27	17	
6	George Niven	32	39	13	
7=	Jerry Dawson	30	25	12	
7=	Allan McGregor	31	26	15	Two appearances as substitute
9	Stefan Klos	29	15	19	
10	Andy Goram	26	18	11	
11	Willie Robb	24	20	11	
12	George Gillespie	19	25	10	
13	Willie Chalmers	18	27	5	
14	Herbert Lock	17	15	9	
15	David Haddow	16	17	7	

The goalkeepers who have played in the successful finals are:

Season	*Goalkeeper*
1893/94	David Haddow
1896/97	Matthew Dickie
1897/98	Matthew Dickie
1902/03	Matthew Dickie
1927/28	Tom Hamilton
1929/30	Tom Hamilton
1931/32	Tom Hamilton
1933/34	Tom Hamilton
1934/35	Jerry Dawson
1935/36	Jerry Dawson
1947/48	Bobby Brown
1948/49	Bobby Brown
1949/50	Bobby Brown
1952/53	George Niven
1959/60	George Niven
1961/62	Billy Ritchie
1962/63	Billy Ritchie
1963/64	Billy Ritchie
1965/66	Billy Ritchie
1972/73	Peter McCloy
1975/76	Peter McCloy
1977/78	Peter McCloy
1978/79	Peter McCloy
1980/81	Jim Stewart
1991/92	Andy Goram
1992/93	Andy Goram
1995/96	Andy Goram
1998/99	Stefan Klos
1999/00	Stefan Klos
2001/02	Stefan Klos
2002/03	Stefan Klos
2007/08	Neil Alexander
2008/09	Neil Alexander
2021/22	Jon McLaughlin/Allan McGregor

Rangers in the Scottish League Cup

Rangers have won the League Cup on 27 occasions, and in their League Cup history, 35 different goalkeepers have been called upon.

The top ten in terms of appearances made are:

	Goalkeeper	*Appearances*	*GC*	*SO*
1	Peter McCloy	86	61	47
2	Billy Ritchie	66	71	21
3	George Niven	59	73	22
4	Bobby Brown	52	54	19
5=	Chris Woods	21	16	8
5=	Jim Stewart	21	18	6
7=	Andy Goram	19	17	8
7=	Allan McGregor	19	19	8
7=	Stewart Kennedy	19	28	4
10=	Neil Alexander	14	13	5
10=	Norrie Martin	14	15	5
10=	Stefan Klos	14	14	5

The goalkeepers who have played in the successful finals are:

Season	*Goalkeeper*
1946/47	Bobby Brown
1948/49	Bobby Brown
1960/61	George Niven
1961/62	Billy Ritchie
1963/64	Billy Ritchie
1964/65	Billy Ritchie
1970/71	Peter McCloy
1975/76	Stewart Kennedy
1977/78	Stewart Kennedy
1978/79	Peter McCloy
1981/82	Jim Stewart
1983/84	Peter McCloy
1984/85	Peter McCloy
1986/87	Chris Woods
1987/88	Nicky Walker

1988/89	Chris Woods
1990/91	Chris Woods
1992/93	Andy Goram
1993/94	Alistair Maxwell
1996/97	Andy Goram
1998/99	Antti Niemi
2001/02	Stefan Klos
2002/03	Stefan Klos
2004/05	Ronald Wattereus
2007/08	Allan McGregor
2009/10	Neil Alexander
2010/11	Neil Alexander

Rangers in Europe

In their various continental sojourns over the years, Rangers have chosen 27 different goalkeepers. Their respective records are:

	Goalkeeper	*Apps*	*GC*	*SO*	*Notes*
1	Allan McGregor	109	124	41	
2	Stefan Klos	47	44	18	One substitute appearance v Hapoel Tel Aviv, 22/02/07
3	Peter McCloy	43	49	14	
4	Andy Goram	31	40	6	
5	Billy Ritchie	30	53	7	
6	Chris Woods	21	22	7	
7=	George Niven	15	31	3	
7=	Norrie Martin	15	10	7	
9	Ronald Waterreus	10	11	2	
10	Lionel Charbonnier	9	9	2	
11	Antti Niemi	8	8	4	One substitute appearance v Bayer Leverkusen, 05/11/99
12	Jon McLaughlin	7	9	3	
13=	Erik Sorensen	6	7	2	
13=	Gerry Neef	6	8	2	

13=	Jim Stewart	6	7	3	
16	Neil Alexander	5	3	3	
17=	Nicky Walker	3	5	1	
17=	Stewart Kennedy	3	7	0	
17=	Theo Snelders	3	7	0	
17=	Wes Foderingham	3	2	1	
21=	Ally Maxwell	2	4	0	
21=	Jesper Christiansen	2	4	0	
21=	Thomas Myhre	2	2	1	
24=	Bonni Ginzburg	1	0	1	
24=	Lionel Letizi	1	2	0	
24=	Billy Thomson	1	3	0	Appearance as substitute v Juventus, 01/05/95
24=	Robby McCrorie	1	0	1	

Of the above goalkeepers, only five – Billy Ritchie (European Cup Winners' Cup 1961), Norrie Martin (European Cup Winners' Cup 1967), Peter McCloy (European Cup Winners' Cup 1972), Neil Alexander (UEFA Cup 2008), and Allan McGregor (Europa League 2022) – have played for the club in a major European final.

Rangers in the Glasgow Merchants' Charity Cup

Including matches played during World War II, Rangers played 172 Charity Cup ties, calling upon 24 different goalkeepers. Their data is listed below:

	Goalkeeper	*Apps*	*GC*	*SO*	*Notes*
1	Jerry Dawson	23	21	9	Includes ties played during WWII
2	Tom Hamilton	19	22	3	
3	Bobby Brown	15	12	7	
4	George Niven	14	11	6	
5=	Matthew Dickie	12	10	3	
5=	Willie Robb	12	7	8	
7	George Gillespie	11	21	1	
8	Herbert Lock	10	9	3	
9=	David Haddow	8	21	1	
9=	Willie Chalmers	8	12	0	
11=	Harry Rennie	6	10	0	
11=	John Hempsey	6	12	1	
11=	George Jenkins	6	3	3	includes ties played during WWII
14=	Jimmy Nicholl	3	11	0	
14=	Thomas Sinclair	3	10	0	
14=	Sandy Newbigging	3	0	3	
14=	Billy Ritchie	3	6	0	
18=	Thomas Farrington	2	2	1	
18=	James Watt	2	6	0	
18=	John G. Watson	2	2	1	
21=	J. Warner	1	1	0	
21=	David Guthrie Reid	1	2	0	
21=	James Yuill	1	6	0	
21=	Willie Moyles	1	6	0	

Rangers would go on to lift the trophy on 32 occasions. The winning goalkeepers in each of those successes were:

Season	*Goalkeeper*
1878/79	George Gillespie
1896/97	Matthew Dickie
1899/1900	Matthew Dickie
1903/04	John G. Watson
1905/06	Tom Sinclair
1906/07	Sandy Newbigging
1908/09	Harry Rennie
1910/11	Herbert Lock
1918/19	Herbert Lock
1921/22	Willie Robb
1922/23	Willie Robb
1924/25	Tom Hamilton
1927/28	Tom Hamilton
1928/29	Tom Hamilton
1929/30	Tom Hamilton
1930/31	Tom Hamilton
1931/32	Tom Hamilton
1932/33	Jerry Dawson
1933/34	Jerry Dawson
1938/39	George Jenkins
1939/40	Jerry Dawson
1940/41	Jerry Dawson
1941/42	Jerry Dawson
1943/44	George Jenkins
1944/45	George Jenkins
1945/46	Bobby Brown
1946/47	Bobby Brown
1947/48	Bobby Brown
1950/51	Bobby Brown
1954/55	George Niven
1956/57	George Niven
1959/60	George Niven

Rangers in the Glasgow Cup

Up until 1988 when the competition became a reserve/youth tournament, Rangers played in 264 Glasgow Cup ties, using 29 different goalkeepers. The top ten in terms of appearances made are:

	Goalkeeper	*Appearances*	*GC*	*SO*	*Notes*
1	Jerry Dawson	33	32	11	Includes ties played during World War II
2	Matthew Dickie	27	28	8	
3	George Niven	26	30	9	
4	Herbert Lock	20	18	7	
5	Willie Robb	19	14	9	
6	Tom Hamilton	16	14	7	
7=	Bobby Brown	14	24	1	
7=	Jimmy Nicholl	14	20	4	
9	David Haddow	13	18	4	
10	Peter McCloy	11	8	6	

Rangers' Glasgow Cup-winning goalkeepers were:

Season	*Goalkeeper*
1892/93	David Haddow
1893/94	David Haddow
1896/97	Matthew Dickie
1897/98	Matthew Dickie
1899/1900	Matthew Dickie
1900/01	Matthew Dickie
1901/02	Matthew Dickie
1910/11	Herbert Lock
1911/12	Herbert Lock
1912/13	John Hempsey
1913/14	Herbert Lock
1917/18	John Hempsey
1918/19	John Hempsey
1921/22	Willie Robb
1922/23	Willie Robb
1923/24	Willie Robb

1924/25	Willie Robb
1929/30	Tom Hamilton
1931/32	Jerry Dawson
1932/33	Tom Hamilton
1933/34	Jerry Dawson
1935/36	Jerry Dawson
1936/37	Jerry Dawson
1937/38	Jerry Dawson
1939/40	Jerry Dawson
1941/42	Jerry Dawson
1942/43	George Jenkins
1943/44	George Jenkins
1944/45	George Jenkins
1947/48	Bobby Brown
1949/50	Bobby Brown
1953/54	George Niven
1956/57	George Niven
1957/58	Billy Ritchie
1959/60	George Niven
1968/69	Gerry Neef
1970/71	Peter McCloy
1974/75	Peter McCloy
1975/76	Peter McCloy
1978/79	Stewart Kennedy
1982/83	Peter McCloy
1984/85	Andy Bruce
1985/86	Nicky Walker
1986/87	Nicky Walker

The Glasgow Cup reverted to an U19 tournament in 1990 before the age level was dropped to U17 in 2007. It is now contested for by the B teams of Rangers and Celtic and the senior sides of Clyde, Queen's Park and Partick Thistle.

Rangers in World War II

Often excluded from 'official' records, the appearances made by Rangers goalkeepers between the start of hostilities in 1939 and the cessation in 1945 are:

		Scottish Regional League Western Division			Scottish Emergency War Cup		
		Apps	*Goals Conceded*	*Shutouts*	*Apps*	*Goals Conceded*	*Shutouts*
1939/40	Jerry Dawson	26	29	8	7	7	2
	George Jenkins	5	7	1	0	0	0

		Southern League			Southern League Cup		
		Apps	*Goals Conceded*	*Shutouts*	*Apps*	*Goals Conceded*	*Shutouts*
1940/41	Jerry Dawson	25	30	9	9	11	2
	George Jenkins	5	3	2	0	0	0
1941/42	Jerry Dawson	22	26	10	8	5	4
	George Jenkins	7	7	3	0	0	0
	Scot Symon	1	2	0	0	0	0
1942/43	Jerry Dawson	28	21	11	8	2	6
	George Jenkins	1	1	0	0	0	0
	Bertram Bell	1	1	0	0	0	0
1943/44	Jerry Dawson	18	16	7	8	7	4
	George Jenkins	12	11	4	0	0	0
1944/45	George Jenkins	29	26	13	8	6	3
	Jerry Dawson	1	1	0	0	0	0
1945/46	George Jenkins	3	7	0	0	0	0
	Jerry Dawson	9	10	3	0	0	0
	John Shaw	18	24	4	9	8	4

Rangers also took part in the Summer Cup and the Victory Cup. In the former, they lost to Hibernian in the final in season 1940/41, defeated the men from Easter Road on a toss of a coin the following season, then lost to St Mirren in the final in season 1942/43, while in the latter, a 3-1 win over Hibernian at Hampden secured the trophy.

Goalkeepers who appeared in those competitions were:

		Summer Cup		
		Appearances	*Goals Conceded*	*Shutouts*
1940/41	Jerry Dawson	6	14	0
1941/42	Jerry Dawson	6	6	2
1942/43	Jerry Dawson	6	4	2

		Victory Cup		
		Appearances	*Goals Conceded*	*Shutouts*
1945/46	John Shaw	2	2	0
	Bobby Brown	6	2	4